A Handbook of
Rare and Endemic Plants of New Mexico

A HANDBOOK OF

Rare and Endemic Plants of New Mexico

The New Mexico Native Plant
Protection Advisory Committee

University of New Mexico Press / *Albuquerque*

Library of Congress Cataloging in Publication Data
A handbook of rare and endemic plants of New Mexico.
    Includes bibliographical references and index.
    1. Rare plants—New Mexico.   2. Botany—New Mexico.   I. New
Mexico Native Plant Protection Advisory Committee.   II. Title:
Endemic plants of New Mexico.
QK86.U6H36   1983   582.09789   83-16865
ISBN 0-8263-0722-1
ISBN 0-8263-0723-X (pbk.)

Library of Congress Catalog Card Number 83-16865.
First Edition

CONTENTS

Acknowledgments   xi

Preface   xiii

APIACEAE

   Aletes filifolius 2   Aletes sessiliflorus 4   Pseudocymopterus
longiradiatus 6   Pteryxia davidsonii 8

ASTERACEAE

   Aster horridus 10   Aster neomexicanus 12   Brickellia
chenopodina 14   Chaetopappa elegans 16   Chaetopappa
hersheyi 18   Chrysothamnus spathulatus 20   Cirsium
gilense 22   Cirsium inornatum 24   Cirsium vinaceum 26
Erigeron hessii 28   Erigeron rhizomatus 30   Erigeron rybius 32
Erigeron scopulinus 34   Erigeron subglaber 36   Haplopappus
microcephalus 38   Helianthus paradoxus 40   Helianthus
praetermissus 42   Hymenoxys olivacea 44   Hymenoxys
vaseyi 46   Lepidospartum burgessii 48   Machaeranthera
amplifolia 50   Perityle cernua 52   Perityle quinqueflora 54
Perityle staurophylla 56   Senecio cardamine 58   Senecio
quaerens 60   Senecio sacramentanus 62   Tetradymia filifolia
64

BORAGINACEAE

   Cryptantha paysonii 66   Mertensia viridis var. caelestina 68

Contents

BRASSICACEAE

Draba mogollonica 70   Lesquerella aurea 72   Lesquerella gooddingii 74   Sibara grisea 76

CACTACEAE

Cereus greggii 78   Coryphantha duncanii 80   Coryphantha organensis 82   Coryphantha scheeri 84   Coryphantha sneedii var. leei 86   Coryphantha sneedii var. sneedii 88   Echinocerus fendleri var. kuenzleri 90   Escobaria orcuttii var. koenigii 92   Escobaria orcuttii var. macraxina 94   Escobaria sandbergii 96   Escobaria villardii 98   Ferocactus wislizenii 100   Mammillaria wrightii var. wilcoxii 102   Mammillaria wrightii var. wrightii 104   Mammillaria viridiflora 106   Opuntia arenaria 108   Opuntia clavata 110   Opuntia viridiflora 112   Pediocactus knowltonii 114   Sclerocactus mesae-verdae 116   Sclerocactus whipplei var. heilii, var. reevesii 118   Toumeya papyracantha 120

CAPPARIDACEAE

Cleome multicaulis 122

CARYOPHYLLACEAE

Silene plankii 124   Silene wrightii 126

CHENOPODIACEAE

Atriplex griffithsii 128

COMMELINACEAE

Tradescantia wrightii 130

CROSSOSOMATACEAE

Apacheria chiricahuensis 132

CUCURBITACEAE

Sicyos glaber 134

EUPHORBIACEAE

Euphorbia strictior 136

FABACEAE

Astragalus accumbens 138   Astragalus altus 140   Astragalus castetteri 142   Astragalus cyaneus 144   Astragalus feensis 146 Astragalus gypsodes 148   Astragalus humillimus 150 Astragalus kentrophyta var. neomexicanus 152   Astragalus knightii 154   Astragalus micromerius 156   Astragalus mollissimus var. mathewsii 158   Astragalus monumentalis var. cottamii 160   Astragalus monumentalis var. monumentalis 162 Astragalus naturitensis 164   Astragalus neomexicanus 166 Astragalus oocalycis 168   Astragalus puniceus var. gertrudis 170   Astragalus siliceus 172   Astragalus wittmanii 174 Dalea scariosa 176   Lupinus sierrae-blancae 178   Sophora gypsophila var. guadalupensis 180   Trifolium longipes var. neurophyllum 182

HYDROPHYLLACEAE

Nama xylopodum 184

LAMIACEAE

Agastache cana 186   Agastache mearnsii 188   Hedeoma apiculatum 190   Hedeoma pulcherrimum 192   Hedeoma todsenii 194   Salvia summa 196

LILIACEAE

Allium gooddingii 198

LOASACEAE

Mentzelia perennis 200

MALVACEAE

Iliamna grandiflora 202   Sphaeralcea procera 204   Sphaeralcea wrightii 206

Contents

MARTYNIACEAE

Proboscidea sabulosa 208

NYCTAGINACEAE

Abronia bigelovii 210

ONAGRACEAE

Oenothera organensis 212

PAPAVERACEAE

Argemone pleiacantha ssp. pinnatisecta 214

POACEAE

Stipa curvifolia 216

POLEMONIACEAE

Gilia formosa 218   Ipomopsis pinnatifida 220   Phlox
caryophylla 222

POLYGALACEAE

Polygala rimulicola var. mescalerorum 224   Polygala
rimulicola var. rimulicola 226

POLYGONACEAE

Eriogonum densum 228   Eriogonum gypsophilum 230
Eriogonum jamesii var. wootonii 232   Rumex tomentellus 234

PORTULACACEAE

Talinum humile 236   Talinum longipes 238

RANUNCULACEAE

Aquilegia chaplinei 240   Delphinium alpestre 242

ROSACEAE

Crataegus wootoniana 244   Potentilla sierrae-blancae 246
Vauquelinia pauciflora 248

SAXIFRAGACEAE

Heuchera pulchella 250   Heuchera wootonii 252

SCROPHULARIACEAE

Besseya oblongifolia 254   Castilleja organorum 256   Castilleja
wootonii 258   Penstemon alamosensis 260   Penstemon
cardinalis ssp. cardinalis 262   Penstemon cardinalis ssp. regalis
264   Penstemon dasyphyllus 266   Penstemon neomexicanus
268   Scrophularia laevis 270   Scrophularia macrantha 272

VALERIANACEAE

Valeriana texana 274

Glossary   277

Abbreviations of the Authors' Names   283

ACKNOWLEDGMENTS

Authors: Reggie Fletcher, Bill Isaacs, Paul Knight, William Martin, David Sabo, Richard Spellenberg, Thomas Todsen

Editors: Reggie Fletcher, Bill Isaacs, Paul Knight, William Martin, Richard Spellenberg, Gail Tierney

Artists: Barbara Angell, James Cogswell, Dan Godfrey, Paul Knight, Carl Victor Stein, Richard Spellenberg, Niki Threlkeld, Frank Tierney, Wendy Haggren-Philpot

Photo Credits: Reggie Fletcher, Paul Knight

Contributors: Janie Chavez, William Dick-Peddie, Terry Fox, Carol Justice, Hal Mackay, Greg Marley, Prince Pierce, Gail Tierney, Warren Wagner, Dale Zimmerman

Financial Support: James Meem, New Mexico State University, New Mexico Natural Resources Department, Plants of the Southwest, Public Service Company of New Mexico, U.S.D.A. Forest Service, U.S.D.A. Soil Conservation Service, U.S.D.I. Bureau of Land Management, U.S.D.I. Bureau of Reclamation, U.S.D.I. Fish and Wildlife Service

We would like to thank Gail Tierney and Terry Fox for their countless hours on the early preparation of the manuscript; Los Alamos National Laboratory for assistance in the preparation of the early manuscript; Dr. Hal Mackay for his comments on and editing of portions of the early manuscript; the periodicals: *Madrõno, Brittonia, Bulletin of the Torrey Botanical Club,* and *Memoirs of the New York Botanical Garden* as well as *U.S. Fish and Wildlife,* all of which allowed us to reproduce drawings from their publications. Finally, we thank all of the members and participants of the New

Acknowledgments

Mexico Plant Protection Advisory committee who contributed their time, efforts, and ideas to the preparation of this book, and the past secretary of Natural Resources, William Huey, and his successor, Dr. Shirley Witt, for their support of this project.

PREFACE

The New Mexico Native Plant Protection Advisory Committee is an *ad hoc* group of professionals in the field of botany, representing the academic community, land managers, and private industry. The committee has served informally at the discretion of the governor, under the direction of the secretary of Natural Resources of New Mexico since 1977. The New Mexico Natural Heritage Program serves as secretary for the committee.

Although the committee has provided the U.S. Fish and Wildlife Service and the New Mexico Natural Heritage Program with information and advice regarding the status of our rarer plant species, this is the first major work produced as a committee effort.

In compiling data for this book, the committee has attempted to provide a single source of information on rare and endemic plants useful both to land managers and to the general public. Plants covered either are principally found in New Mexico or require special management attention. All plants nominated for protection under the Endangered Species Act are included, regardless of their relative abundance.

The Smithsonian report to Congress on endangered and threatened plant species of the United States (1975) was the impetus for gathering some of the material in this book. In the four years since our efforts began on this project, however, information on most of the species included has increased severalfold. Not only have known distributions been altered, but numerous additions and deletions have been made to the list of species included.

New Mexico is still not well explored botanically, and undescribed species will apparently continue to be discovered in the foreseeable future so that modifications of the handbook will be needed.

In a treatment of this type, one can expect inadvertent omissions. We have been as thorough as our expertise and time have allowed. If we have left out taxa that merit inclusion, the committee encourages submission of such candidates for inclusion in a later edition. In its 1974 report to Congress, the Smithsonian Institution recommended that

> lists and illustrations of endangered plants . . . be given wide exposure and publicity, and copies . . . be made available to appropriate organizations and to the public at large. . . . The lists should be of value to land use planners and to all agencies involved in preparing environmental impact statements in conformance with the National Environmental Policy Act of 1969. An awareness of the endangered and threatened species of plants should be urged upon all people involved in the exploitation, development, management, and preservation of the land. A major value of the lists should be to assist in the selection of areas for preservation and in the designation of natural areas to be protected.

We hope that this handbook fulfills the Smithsonian's recommendations and that it will stimulate continued research and exploration on New Mexico's diverse flora. We hope also that this work will enhance the chances for survival of our rare plant species both through general public awareness and proper attention by land management.

Since so much of New Mexico has a complex ownership pattern, special attention has been paid to identifying the principal management agencies for lands that contain rare plants.

The data on each species in this book are presented in a brief text, under a series of topic headings. These include: Family Name, Scientific Name, Common Name, Classification, Federal Action, Common Synonyms, Description, Known Distribution, Habitat, Ownership, Threats to Taxon, Similar Species, Remarks, and Important Literature. Explanations of each of these topic headings follow.

Family Names in this text all end in "aceae." By using this scheme, we have chosen the more uniform treatment of the names that replaces many of the original names which end in "ae." For example, the older name for the bean family is *Leguminosae,* while we have utilized *Fabaceae.* Where an older ending has been replaced by "aceae," the older name will appear in parentheses after the one utilized in the text.

The *Scientific Name* as used here generally follows the current accepted taxonomic treatment as presented in J. T. Kartesz and R. Kartesz, *A Synonymized Checklist of the Vascular Flora of the United States, Canada, and Greenland* (1980).

The *Common Name* appearing in the text is the most widely used colloquial name. In many cases, especially among the rarer plants, no common name exists. In this situation, the committee created a common name to reflect some conspicuous feature of the plant.

The category of *Classification* divorces itself from any federal action and attempts to present the biological status of the plant based on current knowledge. Three possible headings are utilized within this category: Biologically endangered, Biologically threatened, and State priority 1. For biologically endangered plants, the taxon is restricted to one or only a few sites, or is of very restricted distribution and is seriously declining and in danger of rapid extinction throughout its range. For biologically threatened plants, the taxon is of restricted distribution or has the potential for relatively rapid extinction throughout all of its range. For state priority 1, the taxon may be common in New Mexico but wholly endemic to the state, or of restricted distribution in New Mexico, commercially exploited, and usually being eradicated in much of its historic range. Or the taxon may be widely distributed but of local distribution in New Mexico and subject to exploitation or adverse land practices.

Federal Action describes the status of the taxon as listed in the *Federal Register.* This includes federally endangered, federally threatened, or federal candidate species. If the taxon has not been recommended for federal protection, the word *none* will appear.

Common Synonyms lists the scientific names synonymous with the accepted name.

Description attempts to present a layman's version of a technical plant description. Technical terms not given in the glossary are replaced by their corresponding nontechnical ones. Each description follows a specific arrangement, starting with the general growth form of the plant, and proceeds through the stem, the leaves, the flowers, the fruit, and finally the flowering time.

The *Known Distribution* section is an alphabetized listing of the counties in New Mexico where the species is known to occur. Species extending across political boundaries into adjacent states or Mexico are so indicated.

The *Habitat* category provides a general description of the essential habitat requirements as presently known. In some cases, these descriptions are brief, owing to the limited information available.

The designation of *Ownership* is one of convenience, for much of New Mexico is public domain and managed by federal or state agencies. Since so much of New Mexico possesses a complex ownership pattern, special attention has been given to identifying the managing agency or entity. For example, the United States Department of Interior, Bureau of Land Management; the United States Department of Agriculture, Forest Service; and the United States Department of Interior, Fish and Wildlife Service are all federal agencies charged with the management of public lands in New Mexico. Indian lands are also cited under ownership. These lands are, in fact, held in trust by the federal government for the various tribes. State of New Mexico lands are public domain administered by the State Land Office of New Mexico. The majority of these lands are leased to private users to generate revenues for the State of New Mexico. Other important state-owned lands include Highway Department rights-of-way, state parks, Game and Fish Department lands, and so on.

The designation *Private lands* refers to lands, owned by individuals or corporations, that fall outside of the jurisdiction of federal or state agencies.

The *Threats to Taxon* category designates known or existing threats. Hypothetical threats have not been acknowledged in this work.

The category *Similar Species* presents characteristics to differentiate other plants similar in appearance to those rare or endemic species covered here. Only similar species sharing the range of a rare or endemic plant are mentioned. When appropriate, distinguishing features are listed separating all close relatives from the described taxon.

The category of *Remarks* attempts to provide the important or unusual aspects of the species. In some instances, pertinent taxonomic or management information is provided under this heading.

Important Literature does not attempt to provide a full bibliography of the species. It does provide the citations most significant for an understanding of the species.

A Handbook of
Rare and Endemic Plants of New Mexico

Family: APIACEAE (Umbelliferae)
Scientific Name: *Aletes filifolius* Math., Const. & Theobald
Common Name: Threadleaf false carrot
Classification: State priority 1
Federal Action: Federal Register, 15 December 1980, removed from consideration for federal protection
Common Synonyms: None

Description: Densely tufted perennial rising from a woody root crown with a carrotlike or celerylike odor, the crown possessing a basal cluster of both old leaf sheaths and current year leaves; stems 20–40 cm (8–16 in.) tall, leafless or with one or two leaves; leaves stalked and parted into three major divisions, which, in turn, further divide into slender, very narrow segments mostly 1–2 mm (less than 0.12 in.) wide, and 5–60 mm (0.2–2.4 in.) long; flower cluster umbellate, slightly exceeding the leaves, with filamentous or lance-shaped bracts at the base of the umbel; yellow, very small flowers, each on individual stalks about 2–5 mm (0.1–0.2 in.) long; fruits oblong, round in cross section, 3–8 mm (0.1–0.3 in.) long, the ribs prominent and forming corky wings. Flowers from May to August.
Known Distribution: Catron, Doña Ana, Eddy, Grant, Hidalgo, Lincoln, Otero, Socorro, and Torrance counties, New Mexico, and adjacent Texas
Habitat: Canyons and open slopes at the pinyon-juniper level; 1,678–2,227 m (5,500–7,500 ft.)
Ownership: Bureau of Land Management, Forest Service, National Park Service, and private
Threats to Taxon: None known
Similar Species: No species within its range are similar.
Remarks: This *Aletes* is very local in south-central New Mexico. The eastern collection of this species may represent a distinct taxon.
Additional collection of this species would be useful in allowing us to understand its range and populational variation.

Important Literature:
Theobold, W. L., C. C. Tseng, and M. E. Mathias. A revision of *Aletes* and *Neoparrya* (Umbelliferae). Brittonia 16:296–315; 1963.

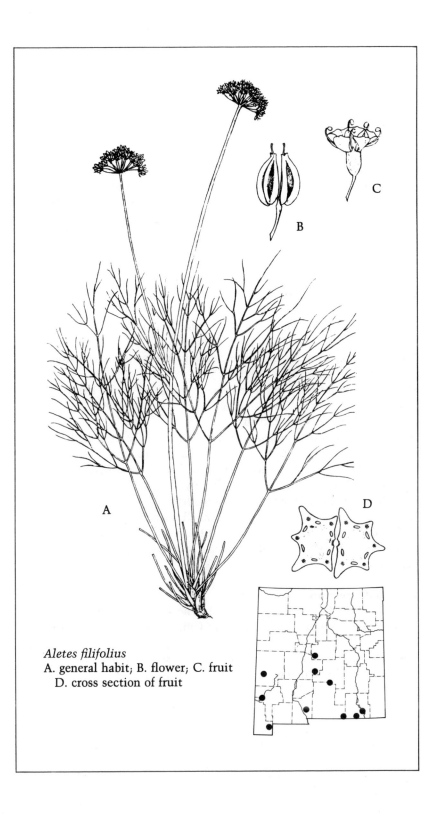

Aletes filifolius
A. general habit; B. flower; C. fruit
   D. cross section of fruit

Family: APIACEAE (Umbelliferae)
Scientific Name: *Aletes sessiliflorus* Theobald & Tseng
Common Name: Sessile-flowered false carrot
Classification: State priority 1
Federal Action: None
Common Synonyms: None

Description: Densely tufted perennial, mostly 10–20 cm (4–8 in.) tall; leaves bright green, mostly 3–10 cm (1.5–4.0 in.) long, pinnately divided into 5–9 narrow segments that sometimes have three lobes; flower clusters densely umbellate, usually among or rarely slightly exceeding the leaves, mostly without bracts at the base of the branches, the branches about 7 cm (3 in.) long; flowers tiny, pale yellow, on slender stalks, each with slender bractlets at the base; fruits oblong, nearly round in cross section, 2–4 mm (0.1–0.2 in.) long, the wings not prominent. Flowers from May to June.
Known Distribution: McKinley, Rio Arriba, Sandoval, and Taos counties, New Mexico
Habitat: Rocky canyons and slopes, usually in basaltic or sandstone areas; 2,000–2,500 m (6,500–8,100 ft.)
Ownership: Bureau of Land Management, Jicarilla Apache Reservation, private
Threats to Taxon: None known
Similar Species: *Aletes macdougalii* is similar but bears pedicillate flowers. Also species of *Lomatium* and *Cymopterus* that grow among pinyon and juniper in this region might at first be confused with *A. sessiliflorus*. They may be distinguished by their highly divided grayish green leaves and prominent wings on the fruit.
Remarks: This taxon often occurs in small, local populations that are susceptible to destruction. However, it has a wide range and, at present, does not appear to be affected significantly by grazing or human activities.

Important Literature:

Mathias, M. E., L. Constance, and W. L. Theobald. Two new species of *Umbelliferae* from the southwestern United States. Madroño 20:214–19; 1969.

Theobald, S. L., C. C. Tseng, and M. E. Mathias. A revision of *Aletes* and *Neoparrya* (Umbelliferae). Brittonia 16:296–315; 1963.

4

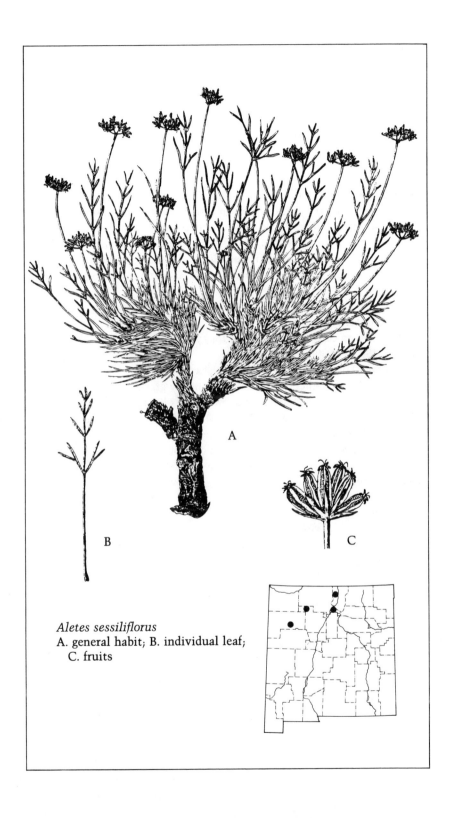

Aletes sessiliflorus
A. general habit; B. individual leaf;
C. fruits

Family: APIACEAE (Umbelliferae)
Scientific Name: *Pseudocymopterus longiradiatus* Math., Const., & Theobald
Common Name: Desert parsley
Classification: State priority 1
Federal Action: None
Common Synonyms: None

Description: Densely tufted perennial; stems to 90 cm (36 in.) tall; leaves compound, the leaflets divided into linear-oblong to obovate divisions; flower cluster loose, the secondary clusters subtended by slender bracts often 8–11 mm (0.3–0.45 in.) long, the primary branches 18–55 mm (0.7–2.2 in.) long; fruits oblong, glabrous, flattened, 4–6 mm (0.15–0.25 in.) long, the lateral ribs winged. Flowers from April to August.
Known Distribution: Eddy and Otero counties, New Mexico, and adjacent Texas
Habitat: Damp canyon, in sandy or rocky ground, usually in shade; 1,830–2,288 m (6,000–7,500 ft.)
Ownership: Forest Service, National Park Service
Threats to Taxon: Affected adversely by heavy grazing pressure
Similar Species: *Pseudocymopterus montanus* (Gray) Coulter and Rose which has primary branches only 10–20 mm (0.4–0.8 in.) long
Remarks: In most areas, it appears to be in restricted or protected locations beneath thorn scrub, where it cannot be readily taken. Guadalupe Mountains and Carlsbad Caverns National Park provide adequate protection.

Important Literature:
Theobald, C., C. Tseng, and M. Mathias. Two new species of *Umbelliferae* from the southwestern United States. Madroño 20:214–19; 1969.

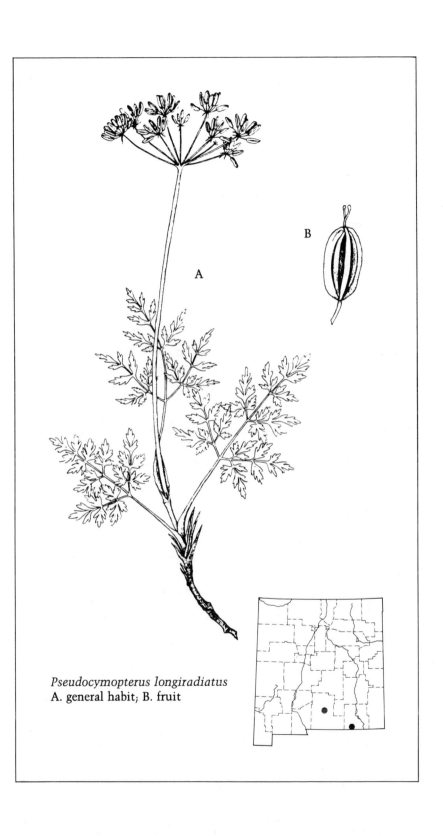

B

A

Pseudocymopterus longiradiatus
A. general habit; B. fruit

Family: APIACEAE (Umbelliferae)
Scientific Name: *Pteryxia davidsonii* (Coult. & Rose) Math. & Const.
Common Name: Davidson's cliff carrot
Classification: State priority 1
Federal Action: None
Common Synonyms: *Aletes davidsonii* Coult. & Rose
Pseudocymopterus filicinus Woot. & Standl.
Pseudocymopterus davidsonii (Coult. & Rose) Mathias

Description: Perennial; stems branching above, about 15–40 cm (6–14 in.) high, faintly scabrous hairy; leaves oblong to somewhat oblong-oval in outline, the blade 1.5–14 cm (0.6–5.6 in.) long and 1–9 cm (0.4–3.6 in.) broad, tripinnate, the ultimate divisions linear, acute at the tip, to 30 mm (1.2 in.) long and 1–3 mm (0.04–0.12 in.) wide, leaf stalks to 7 cm (2.5 in.) long; several stem leaves; flower clusters umbellate, on stalks 4–14 cm (1.6–5.6 in.) long, each umbel slightly hairy at the base; primary flower bracts (involucre) partially enclosing the stems, the smaller, secondary bracts filamentous, entire, 2–7 mm (to 0.3 in) long; rays of flower cluster 5–9, spreading; flowers yellow or purple, on stalks (pedicels) 1–5 mm to (0.2 in.) long; fruits oblong, 3–4 mm (0.12–0.16 in.) long, 1–2 mm to (0.1 in.) wide, smooth at maturity with short wings. Flowers in August.
Known Distribution: Catron, Grant, and Socorro counties, New Mexico, and adjacent Arizona
Habitat: Moist, rocky places; 1,983–2,440 m (6,500–8,000 ft.)
Ownership: Forest Service
Threats to Taxon: None known
Similar Species: This species is poorly understood and requires further field study. It may be rare or merely mistaken in the field for *Pseudocymopterus montanus*. The distinctions between *Pteryxia* and *Pseudocymopterus* are slight; *Pteryxia* has narrowly winged fruits where *Pseudocymopterus* has broader ones. They may be considered congeneric.
Remarks: The rocky, inaccessible habitat of this species excludes it from most threats.

Important Literature:
Coulter, J. M., and J. N. Rose. Monograph of the North American *Umbelliferae*. Contr. U.S. Nat. Herb. 7:1–256; 1900.
Mathias, M. L. Studies in the *Umbelliferae* III: A monograph of *Cymopterus* including a critical study of related genera. Ann. Missouri Bot. Gard. 17:213–467; 1930.
Mathias, M. L., and L. Constance. New combinations and new names in the *Umbelliferae* II. Bull. Torr. Bot. Club 69:244–49; 1942.

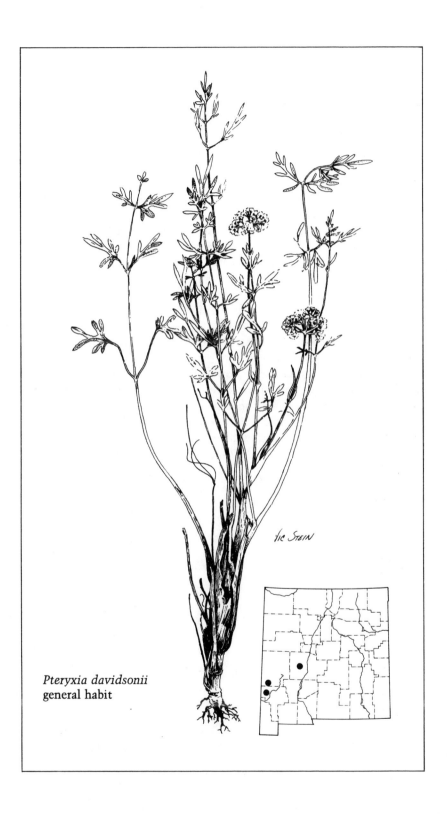

Pteryxia davidsonii
general habit

Family: ASTERACEAE (Compositae)
Scientific Name: *Aster horridus* (Woot. & Standl.) Blake
Common Name: Spiny aster
Classification: State priority 1
Federal Action: None
Common Synonyms: *Herrickia horrida* Woot. & Standl.

Description: Perennial to about 50 cm (20 in.) tall, glandular; leaves rigid, thick, spiny toothed, oblong to oblong-ovate, to 45 mm (1.8 in.) long, without petioles; flower heads about 10 mm (0.4 in.) high, outer involucral bracts leaflike, inner bracts spine tipped to merely sharp pointed; rays purple; achenes hairless, topped with numerous stiff bristles. Flowers from July to October.
Known Distribution: Colfax, Harding, and Mora counties, New Mexico, and adjacent Colorado
Habitat: Rocky hillsides and steep, narrow canyon bottoms; 1,670–2,700 m (5,500–9,000 ft.)
Ownership: Forest Service, private, State of New Mexico
Threats to Taxon: None known
Similar Species: No other purple-flowered members of the composite family in New Mexico have thick, oblong, stiff spiny-toothed leaves.
Remarks: Most of the known populations of this species are found in the rugged canyons of the Canadian River drainage. Habitat maintenance is provided through management by the Cibola National Forest.

Important Literature:
Blake, S. F. Jour. Washington Acad. Sci. 27:379; 1937.

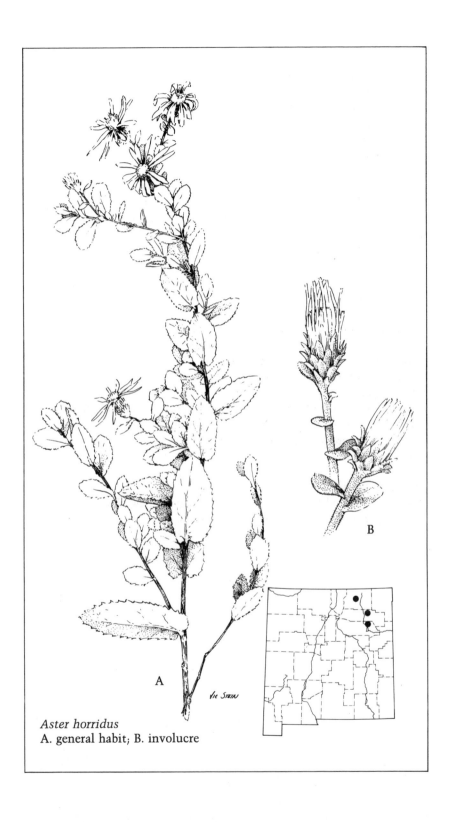

Aster horridus
A. general habit; B. involucre

Family: ASTERACEAE (Compositae)
Scientific Name: *Aster neomexicanus* Woot. & Standl.
Common Name: New Mexico aster
Classification: State priority 1
Federal Action: None
Common Synonyms: None

Description: Perennial, with highly branched smooth, green stems to 1 m (39 in.) tall; leaves fleshy, green, few, narrowly linear to narrowly lance shaped, up to 8 cm (3.25 in.) long, acute at the tip; flower heads solitary at the ends of the branches, the heads 6–8 mm (0.25–0.3 in.) high, the stalks beneath the heads with numerous tiny lance-shaped leaves; involucral bracts subtending the heads in several series, green with transparent or translucent margins; ray flowers purple, 3–4 mm (1.2–1.6 in.) long; fruits a nearly smooth achene. Flowers in August and September.
Known Distribution: Chaves County, New Mexico
Habitat: Damp ground; 1,068–1,678 m (3,500–5,500 ft.)
Ownership: Bureau of Land Management, private
Threats to Taxon: None known
Similar Species: Many species of *Aster* are outwardly similar; this species is distinguished by the complete absence of glandular hairs, the glabrous bracts and stems, and the thick, fleshy glabrous leaves.
Remarks: Apparently, this species is very local, poorly understood, and in need of field study.

Important Literature:
Wooton, E. O., and P. C. Standley. Descriptions of new plants preliminary to a report upon the flora of New Mexico. Contr. U.S. Nat. Herb. 16:109–96; 1913.

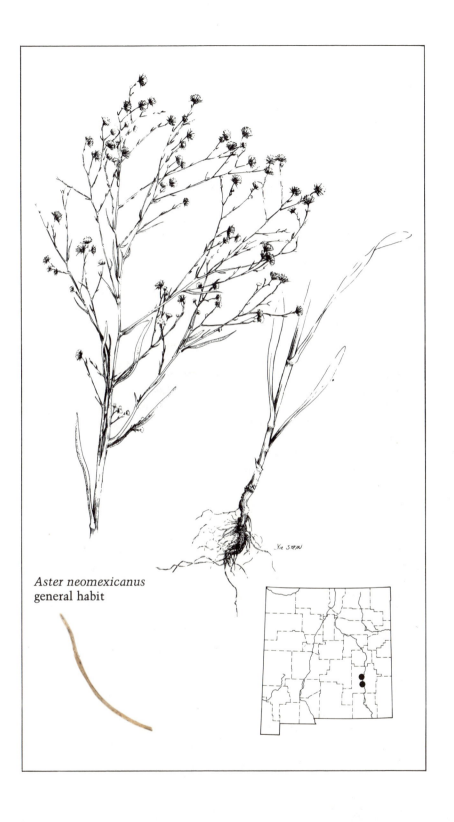

Aster neomexicanus
general habit

Yic STEIN

Family: ASTERACEAE (Compositae)
Scientific Name: *Brickellia chenopodina* (Greene) Robins.
Common Name: Gila bricklebush
Classification: State priority 1
Federal Action: None
Common Synonyms: *Coleosanthus chenopodinus* Greene

Description: Much-branched shrub with loose, scaly bark; leaves alternate, ovate or lanceolate, mostly 25–60 mm (1.0 to 2.3 in.) long, 12–25 mm (0.5–1.0 in.) wide, irregularly serrate, acute at the tip, rounded or broadly tapered at the base, petiolate; flower heads with pinkish tinge, about 28 flowered, 12 mm (0.5 in.) high, on stalks 2–4 mm (0.1–0.25 in.) long, in open, glandular panicles; involucral bracts of the heads (phyllaries) lanceolate to linear, glandular-viscid, conspicuously nerved; fruits achenes, about 3 mm (0.1 in.) long, with ten nerves; pappus of minutely barbed capillary bristles. Flowers from June to September.
Known Distribution: Grant County, New Mexico
Habitat: In alluvial soil along the Gila River, at about 1,375 m (4,500 ft.)
Ownership: Bureau of Land Management, private
Threats to Taxon: Grazing and stream flooding as well as development in this area are the principal concerns. Also, the Connor Dam proposal could flood the only known location of this plant.
Similar Species: *Brickellia floribunda* is similar to *B. chenopodina*; it differs by its longer stalks beneath the flower heads (up to 1 cm long), and its truncate or heart-shapes leaf bases.
Remarks: *B. chenopodina* may be simply a shade form *B. floribunda* growing in rich soil.

Important Literature:
Robinson, B. A monograph of the genus *Brickellia*. Mem. Gray Herb. 1:1–155; 1917.
Wooton, E. O., and P. C. Standley. Descriptions of new plants preliminary to a report upon the flora of New Mexico. Contr. U.S. Nat. Herb. 16:109–96; 1913.

A

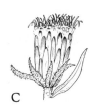

B

Brickellia chenopodina
A. general habit; B. disk flower;
   C. involucre

C

Family: ASTERACEAE (Compositae)
Scientific Name: *Chaetopappa elegans* Soreng & Spellenberg (in ed.)
Common Name: Sierra Blanca cliff daisy
Classification: Biologically endangered
Federal Action: None
Common Synonyms: None

Description: Plants densely tufted, the stems generally less than 2.5 cm (1 in.) long, but sometimes up to 10 cm (4 in.) long; leaves spatula shaped, often wider above the middle, the upper leaves much smaller than the lower, 6–18 mm (0.26–0.75 in.) long, up to 3 mm (0.1 in.) wide, the margins with short, stiff hairs; flower heads single at the end of the stem, the involucral bracts overlapping, not all the same length, the 10–24 rays 5–9 mm (about 0.25 in.) long, pale pink-lavender to nearly white; achenes densely silky-hairy, the bristles at the top 14–19 in number, about equal in length to the tube of the disk corolla, with an additional outer ring of very short bristles or scales. Flowers in May and June.
Known Distribution: Lincoln County, New Mexico
Habitat: On diorite rock in openings of mixed conifer woods, at about 2,170 m (8,000 ft.)
Ownership: Forest Service
Threats to Taxon: None known
Similar Species: *Chaetopappa hersheyi,* from limestone cliffs in the Guadalupe Mountains, is the most similar species to this taxon and is probably the most closely related. Its rays rarely exceed 5 mm (0.25 in.) in length, and its achenes have only about five bristles at the top. It also resembles tufted species in the genus *Erigeron,* but those generally have more rays, bracts of the head all about the same length, and achenes with two prominent ribs.
Remarks: This species, known from a single canyon, is fairly common in its limited habitat on the east side of Sierra Blanca.

Important Literature:
Soreng, R., and R. Spellenberg. An unusual new *Chaetopappa* (Asteraceae: Astereae) from New Mexico. Sys. Bot.; 1984.

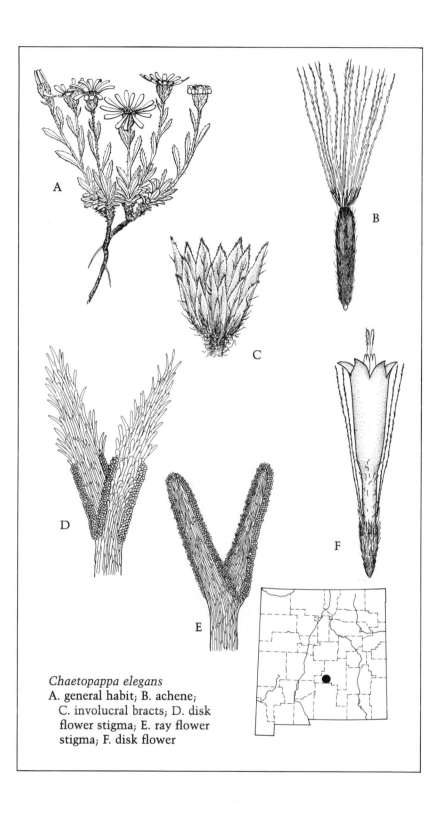

Chaetopappa elegans
A. general habit; B. achene;
C. involucral bracts; D. disk
flower stigma; E. ray flower
stigma; F. disk flower

Family: ASTERACEAE (Compositae)
Scientific Name: *Chaetopappa hersheyi* Blake
Common Name: Hershey's cliff daisy
Classification: Biologically threatened
Federal Action: Federal Register, 15 December 1980, candidate for federal protection
Common Synonyms: None

Description: Matted perennial from woody rootstocks; stems to 5 cm (2 in.) tall, simple ascending, sparsely and finely hairy, terminated by a solitary flower head or by a tuft of small leaves; basal leaves clustered, spatulalike or lance shaped, translucent and spiny at the tip, 1.5–6 mm (0.06–0.25 in.) long, to 1 mm (0.04 in.) wide; stem leaves 4–7, threadlike or narrowly lance shaped, 3.0–7.5 mm (0.12–0.3 in.) long, to 1 mm (0.04 in.) wide, acute with a translucent spiny tip, and a sparsely and stiffly hairy or smooth surface; involucre 4–6 mm (0.16–0.2 in.) high, the involucral bracts in about four series, lance shaped, slenderly spine-tipped, with sparse fine hairs in the midsection, the margins finely whitish hairy; ray flowers 6–10, the rays bluish at first, fading to white, about 5 mm long (0.2 in.); five or six disk flowers; achene pappus of five awns and five shorter scales. Flowers in May.
Known Distribution: Eddy County, New Mexico, and adjacent Texas
Habitat: Rare on limestone cliffs and ledges, at about 1,525 m (5,000 ft.)
Ownership: Forest Service, National Park Service
Threats to Taxon: None known
Similar Species: See comments under *Chaetopappa elegans.*
Remarks: This species is endemic to the Guadalupe Mountains; it is common along some of the trails and therefore is susceptible to collectors.

Important Literature:
Blake, S. F. A new *Chaetopappa* from the Guadalupe Mountains of New Mexico and Texas. Proc. Biol. Soc. Washington 59:47–48; 1946.
Correll, D. S., and M. C. Johnston. Manual of the Vascular Plants of Texas. Renner, Tex.: Texas Research Foundation; 1970.
Shinners, L. H. Revision of the genus *Chaetopappa* DC. Wrightia 1:63–81; 1946.

Chaetopappa hersheyi

Family: ASTERACEAE (Compositae)
Scientific Name: *Chrysothamnus spathulatus* L. C. Anderson
Common Name: Spoonleaf rabbitbrush
Classification: State priority 1
Federal Action: None
Common Synonyms: *Chrysothamnus viscidiflorus* (Hook.) Nutt. ssp. *ludens* Shinners

Description: Shrub, to about 1 m (39 in.) tall, the younger branches hairy; leaves narrow, widest above the middle, 2.5–5.0 cm (1–2 in.) long, 1–3 mm (to 0.12 in.) wide; flowering heads 5–6 mm (0.2–0.25 in.) high, yellow, ray flowers rare; achenes sparsely hairy, nearly hairless at maturity. Flowers in August and September.
Known Distribution: Eddy, Otero, Sierra, and Socorro counties, New Mexico, and in the Guadalupe Mountains of adjacent Texas
Habitat: Usually found in the pinyon-juniper zone and in lower foothills more typical of creosote bush; 1,340 to 2,135 m (4,400–7,000 ft.)
Ownership: Bureau of Land Management, Forest Service, private, State of New Mexico
Threats to Taxon: None known
Similar Species: *Chrysothamnus spathulatus* is closely related to *Chrysothamnus viscidiflorus.* The former may be distinguished by its narrow stem leaves, which are widest above the middle, and its spoon-shaped cotyledon leaves.
Remarks: *Chrysothamnus spathulatus* occurs in areas that are little explored botanically, and is probably more common than collections indicate.

Important Literature:
Anderson, L. C. Taxonomic notes on the *Chrysothamnus viscidiflorus* complex (Asteraceae, Compositae). Madroño 17:222–27; 1964.

20

Chrysothamnus spathulatus
A. general habit; B. involucral bracts;
  C. achene with pappus;
  D. single involucre bract;
  E. stigma of disk flower

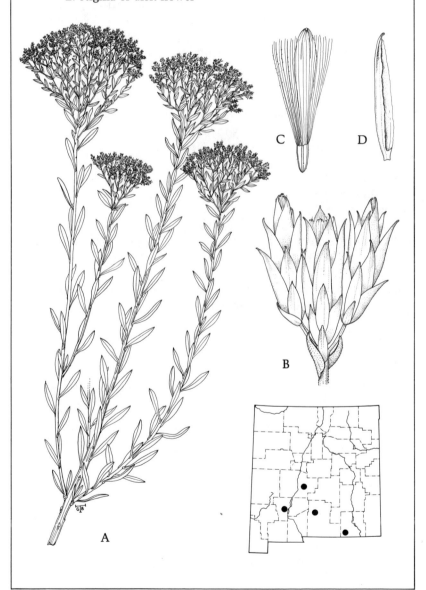

Family: ASTERACEAE (Compositae)
Scientific Name: *Cirsium gilense* Woot. & Standl.
Common Name: Gila thistle
Classification: State priority 1
Federal Action: None
Common Synonyms: None

Description: Biennial, up to 2 m (6.5 ft.) tall; stems sparingly branched, hairy; leaves about 40 cm (16 in.) long, pointed at the tip, lobed, the lobes toothed, teeth tipped with slender spines, upper surface of the leaves hairy, lower surface without hairs; the base of the stem leaves partly surrounding the stem; flower heads greenish yellow, usually solitary at the ends of the branches, about 3 cm (1.2 in.) broad, and nearly as high; outer bracts of the flower head with cobwebby hairs and numerous small, spiny teeth of even length along the margins, much like that of a comb. Flowers from July to September.
Known Distribution: Catron County, New Mexico
Habitat: Damp ground in meadows or near streams; 2,135–2,440 m (7,000–8,000 ft.)
Ownership: Forest Service
Threats to Taxon: None known
Similar Species: *Cirsium gilense* can be differentiated from the other yellow-flowered thistles in New Mexico by flowering heads that are at least 3 cm (1.2 in.) high and are solitary at the ends of branches. The bracts of the heads have broad green trips.
Remarks: The relative abundance and distribution of this endemic are not well understood. It appears to increase with disturbance.

Important Literature:
Wooton, E. O., and P. C. Standley. New Plants from New Mexico. Contr. U.S. Nat. Herb. 16:109–96; 1913.
Wooton, E. O., and P. C. Standley. Flora of New Mexico. Contr. U.S. Nat. Herb. 19:1–793; 1915.

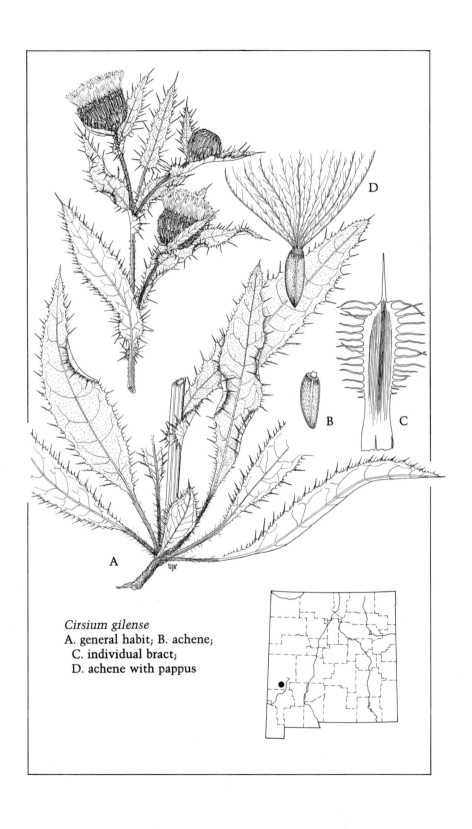

Cirsium gilense
A. general habit; B. achene;
C. individual bract;
D. achene with pappus

Family: ASTERACEAE (Compositae)
Scientific Name: *Cirsium inornatum* Woot. & Standl.
Common Name: Plain thistle
Classification: State priority 1
Federal Action: None
Common Synonyms: *Carduus inornatus* Woot. & Standl.

Description: Biennial; stems to 1 m (39 in.) tall, simple (unbranched) below the middle, with few ascending branches above, densely cobwebby and finely hairy at first, becoming sparsely hairy to nearly naked as it ages; leaves lance shaped to nearly filamentous in outline, to 20 cm (8 in.) long, glabrous on both surfaces except the midveins often sparsely long hairy; upper leaves lance shaped or oblong, clasping, with rounded earlike lobes at the base, spiny on the margins; flowers yellowish to greenish yellow, the heads in clusters of three at the ends of the branches, or occasionally solitary, up to 2 cm (0.8 in.) wide, subtended by reduced spiny leaves; involucral bracts in several series, outer bracts lance shaped, spine tipped, smooth, or faintly cobwebby, margins with yellowish spines. Flowers from July to September.
Known Distribution: Cibola, Lincoln, Otero, Rio Arriba, and Taos counties, New Mexico
Habitat: Mountain slopes over 2,288 m (7,500 ft.)
Ownership: Forest Service
Threats to Taxon: None known
Similar Species: *Cirsium parryi*, which has conspicuously cobwebby, hairy involucral bracts
Remarks: This is a local species of peculiar distribution. It is closely related to *C. parryi* and might be considered a subspecies of it.

Important Literature:
Wooton, E. O., and P. C. Standley. Flora of New Mexico. Contr. U.S. Nat. Herb. 19:1–793, 1915.

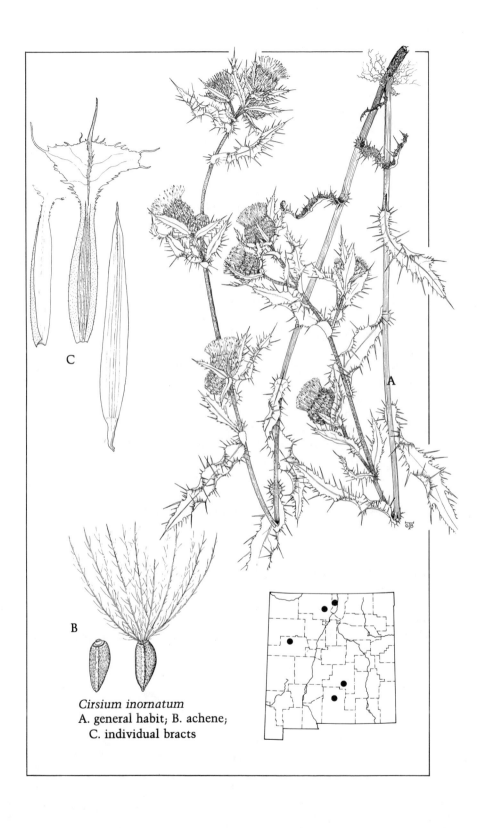

Cirsium inornatum
A. general habit; B. achene;
C. individual bracts

Family: ASTERACEAE (Compositae)
Scientific Name: *Cirsium vinaceum* (Woot. & Standl.) Woot. & Standl.
Common Name: Mescalero thistle
Classification: Biologically endangered
Federal Action: Federal Register, 15 December 1980, candidate for federal protection
Common Synonyms: *Carduus vinaceus* Woot. & Standl.

Description: Stout biennial, 90–180 cm (3–6 ft.) tall, with many ascending branches; stems brown-purple; basal leaves green, not hairy, 30–50 cm (12–20 in.) long, up to 20 cm (8 in.) wide, elliptic in outline, divided nearly to the midrib, ragged edged, the edges with slender yellowish spines; flower heads numerous at the ends of the branches, naked, bell shaped; involucral bracts of several ranks, deep red-purple; narrowly lance shaped, bent back at about the middle, the tips spreading; flower head 5 cm (2 in.) in diameter and almost as high; individual flowers rose-purple. Flowers from July to September.
Known Distribution: Otero County, New Mexico
Habitat: Limestone seep areas and wet canyon bottoms; above 2,440 m (8,000 ft.)
Ownership: Forest Service, private, Mescalero Apache Indian Reservation
Threats to Taxon: Cattle gradually extirpate it. Increased use of ground water is drying up the spring and seep areas in which this taxon grows. (Because of such development, it is no longer found at the type locality.) Also, the weedy musk thistle (*Carduus nutans*) and teasle (*Dipsicus silvestrus*) are invading some populations of the Mescalero thistle and crowding this species out.
Similar Species: *Carduus* is superficially similar but has hairlike bristles at the top of the achene. In *Cirsium*, the bristles are feathery. The other *Cirsium* species in the area have cream-colored flowers or greenish, hairy bracts.
Remarks: Cattle have recently been excluded from some of the population sites.

Important Literature:
Wooton, E. O., and P. C. Standley. Description of new plants, etc., Contr. U.S. Nat. Herb. 16:109–96; 1913.
Wooton, E. O., and P. C. Standley. Flora of New Mexico. Contr. U.S. Nat. Herb. 19:1–793; 1915.

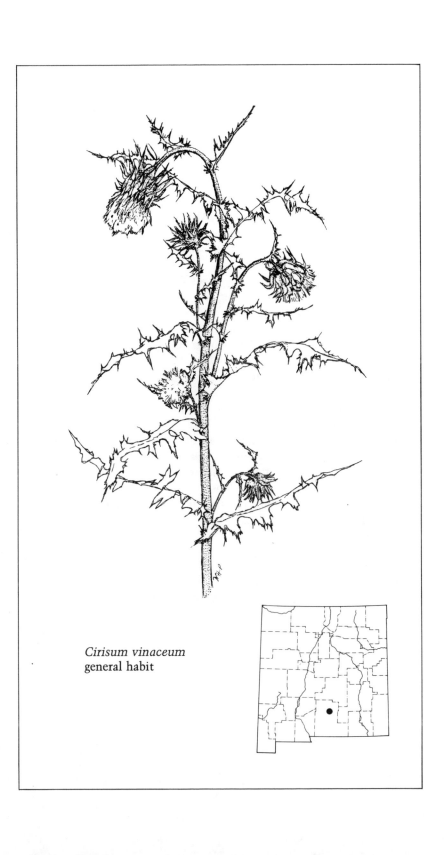

Cirisum vinaceum
general habit

Family: ASTERACEAE (Compositae)
Scientific Name: *Erigeron hessii* Nesom
Common Name: Hess's fleabane
Classification: Biologically threatened
Federal Action: Federal Register, 15 December 1980, candidate for federal protection
Common Synonyms: None

Description: Densely tufted, sparsely hairy perennial herb 5–16 cm (2–6.5 in.) high, the short branches thicker near the tips, with old leaf bases attached; basal leaves lance shaped, broader above the middle, to 7 cm (2.75 in.) long and 7 mm (0.25 in.) wide, the blades about one-half the length of the leaf, tapering gradually to a flattened petiole; 5–11 leaves on the stem, without petioles, becoming progressively much smaller upwards; flower heads solitary at the ends of stems, involucral bracts finely glandular, the ray flowers 44–75 in number, white; achenes hairy, with 13–18 bristles at the summit. Flowers in August.
Known Distribution: Catron County, New Mexico
Habitat: Crevices of exposed rock, at about 3,300 m (10,000 ft.) in the Mogollon Mountains
Ownership: Forest Service
Threats to Taxon: None known
Similar Species: *Erigeron kuscheii*, from the Chiricahua Mountains of southeast Arizona, is the most similar, differing in its less compact habit. Other species in the region are either more hairy, matted, and have a strong central axis, or are taller or looser in stature.
Remarks: This plant is presently known from only a few trails in the Gila Wilderness.

Important Literature:
Nesom, G. L. *Erigeron hessii* sp. nov. and *Erigeron kuscheii* Eastwood (*Compositae*), two closely related narrow endemics from the southwestern United States. Brittonia 30:440–46; 1978.

28

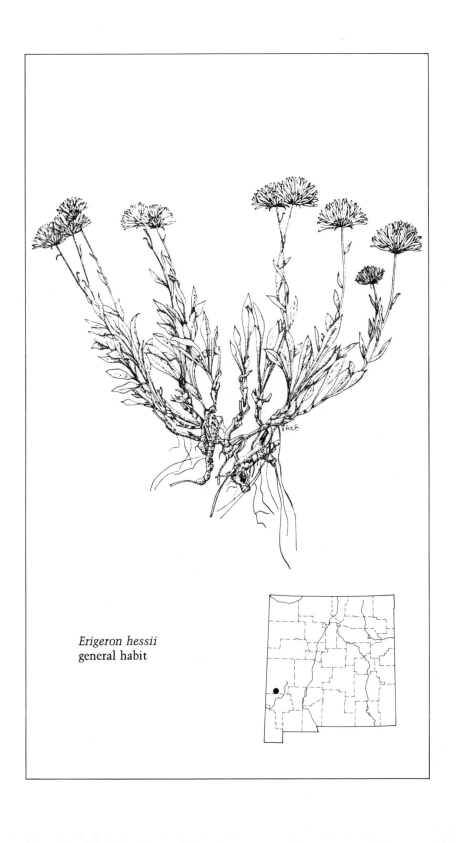

Erigeron hessii
general habit

Family: ASTERACEAE (Compositae)
Scientific Name: *Erigeron rhizomatus* Cronq.
Common Name: Zuni fleabane
Classification: Biologically endangered
Federal Action: Federal Register, 15 December 1980, candidate for federal protection
Common Synonyms: None

Description: Perennial with creeping rhizomes; stems 25–45 cm (10–18 in.) tall, sparsely leafy, growing in clumps to about 30 cm (1 ft.) in diameter; leaves narrow, about 1 cm (0.5 in.) long with only a few sparse, stiff hairs; flower heads 13–16 mm (0.5–0.6 in.) wide; ray flower white or tinged with blue-violet, 6–7 mm (0.25 in.) long with 25–35 fragile bristles at the summit; the body of the achene hairless or slightly hairy. Flowers in May and June.
Known Distribution: Catron and McKinley counties, New Mexico
Habitat: Steep, highly erodable sandstone slopes and clay banks in the Zuni and Datil mountains, usually in close association with Chinle shale outcrops; 2,200–2,400 m (7,300–8,000 ft.)
Ownership: Bureau of Land Management, Forest Service
Threats to Taxon: This narrow endemic is threatened by uranium mining and exploration.
Similar Species: This species is very distinct. The nearly hairless achenes with 5–6 nerves, the rhizomatous habit, and the few hairs on the stem and leaves provide easy recognition.
Remarks: This is a primary successional plant with narrow habitat requirements, and apparently is intolerant of competition.

Important Literature:
Cronquist, A. A revision of the North American species of *Erigeron* north of Mexico. Brittonia 6:121–300; 1974.

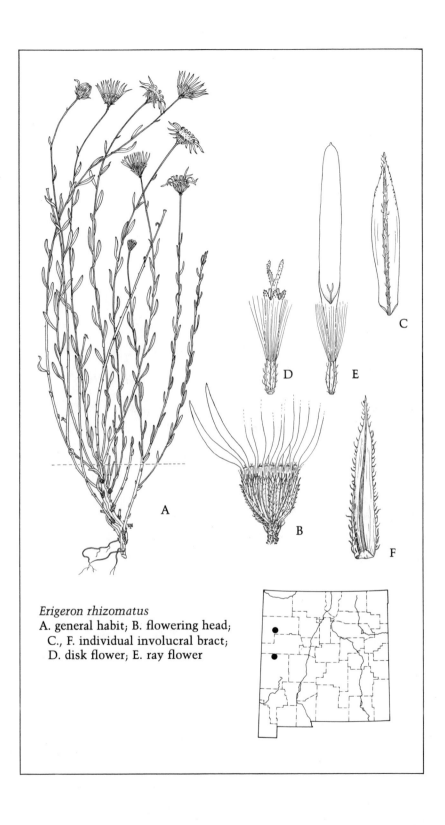

Erigeron rhizomatus
A. general habit; B. flowering head;
C., F. individual involucral bract;
D. disk flower; E. ray flower

Family: ASTERACEAE (Compositae)
Scientific Name: *Erigeron rybius* Nesom
Common Name: Sacramento Mountain fleabane
Classification: State priority 1
Federal Action: None
Common Synonyms: None

Description: Perennial herb arising from woody rhizomes, with erect stems to 35 cm (14 in.) tall; basal leaves 1.8–13.5 cm (0.7–5.4 in.) long, 6–27 mm (0.25–1.0 in.) wide, lance shaped, with 3–8 pairs of shallow teeth, 9–14 stem leaves, equally distributed and somewhat reduced in size upward; 1–6 heads per stem on stalks 1–3 cm (0.4–1.2 in.) long; involucral bracts in three equal series, reflexed to spreading at maturity; ray flowers 45–100, white, frequently drying lilac, 11–20 mm (0.45–0.8 in.) long; achenes, 1.8–2.1 mm (0.7–0.8 in.) long, with 20–30 slender bristles at the apex. Flowers from July to September.
Known Distribution: Lincoln and Otero counties, New Mexico
Habitat: Damp meadows and open ridges in mixed conifer forest; 2,100–2,800 m (7,500–10,000 ft.)
Ownership: Forest Service, Mescalero Indian Reservation, State of New Mexico
Similar Species: The closest species is *Erigeron rusbyi*, which arises from a thickened woody taproot rather than from slender horizontal rhizomes.
Remarks: *Erigeron rybius* was only recently distinguished from *E. rusbyi*, which lacks rhizomes and has a taproot. *Erigeron rybius* is a narrow endemic, restricted to the meadows of the Sacramento Mountains.

Important Literature:
Nesom, G. L. Systematics of the *Erigeron rusbyi* group (*Asteraceae*) and delimitation of sect. *Peregrinus*. Sys. Bot. 7(4):457–70; 1982.

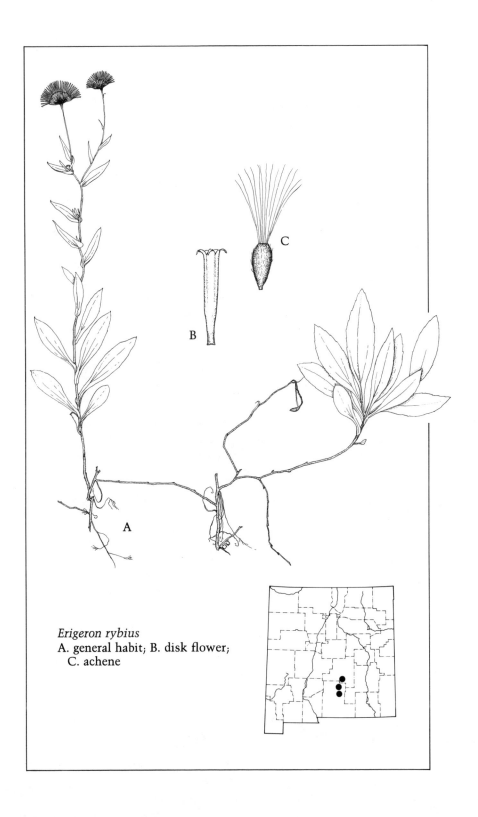

Erigeron rybius
A. general habit; B. disk flower;
   C. achene

Family: ASTERACEAE (Compositae)
Scientific Name: *Erigeron scopulinus* Nesom and Roth
Common Name: Rock fleabane
Classification: State priority 1
Federal Action: None
Common Synonyms: None

Description: Perennial, mat-forming herb with fibrous root system of slender rhizomes up to 15 cm (6 in.) long with clusters of leaves at the tips of the rhizomes; leaves 5–12 mm (0.2–0.5 in.) long, 1.0–3.5 mm (0.04–0.1 in.) wide, spatulate, or egg shaped, broadest above the middle, tapering toward the petiole, the margins entire; flowering heads solitary, 6–33 mm (0.25–1.25 in.) long; involucral bracts overlapping, lance shaped, narrowly pointed at the tip, 4.0–4.5 mm (0.2–0.25 in.) long, overlapping in 3–4 series; 15–20 ray flowers, 5.5–9.0 mm (0.25–0.5 in.) long, white but drying light violet. Flowers in May and June.
Known Distribution: Catron, Sierra, and Socorro, counties, New Mexico
Habitat: Crevices in cliff faces of rhyolitic rock; 1,800–2,800 m (6,000–9,000 ft.)
Ownership: Forest Service
Threats to Taxon: Mineral exploration in a few cases could disturb populations of this plant.
Similar Species: The low-matted habit and cliff habitat distinguishes this species from all other species of *Erigeron* in New Mexico.
Remarks: This fleabane remained undiscovered until the last decade. It serves as testimony to the incomplete botanical exploration of New Mexico.

Important Literature:
Nesom, G. L., and V. D. Roth, *Erigeron scopulinus* (Compositae) an endemic from the southwestern United States. Jour. Arizona-Nevada Acad. Sci. 16:39–42; 1982.

Erigeron scopulinus
A. fruiting head; B. achene; C. ray flower; D. flowering head;
  E. general habit

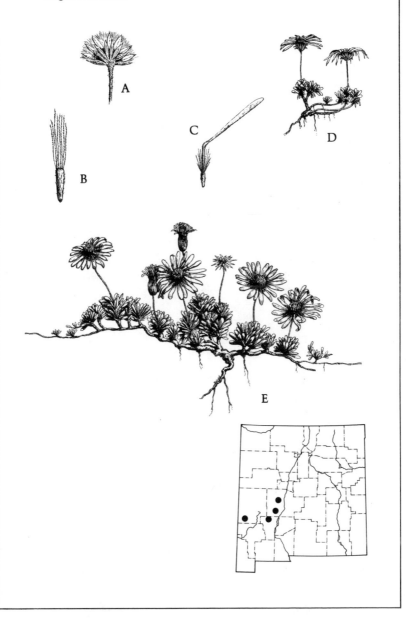

Family: ASTERACEAE (Compositae)
Scientific Name: *Erigeron subglaber* Cronq.
Common Name: Pecos fleabane
Classification: Biologically endangered
Federal Action: None
Common Synonyms: None

Description: Low perennial, with nearly hairless stems, mostly 3–7 cm
(1.2–2.8 in.) tall; leaves to 6 cm (2.4 in.) long and 6 mm (0.24 in.) wide,
the basal leaves broader above the middle, the upper leaves narrower than
the basal, often linear; flower heads solitary on each stem, involucral
bracts smooth and often purplish at the tip; 25–35 ray flowers, purplish
or bluish. Flowers in August and probably September.
Known Distribution: San Miguel County, New Mexico
Habitat: Montane ridges; 3,050–3,350 m (10,000–11,000 ft.)
Ownership: Forest Service
Threats to Taxon: None known
Similar Species: *Erigeron leiomerus* Gray differs in having glandular
bracts beneath the head, and in the generally broader leaves.
Remarks: Field collections of this taxon are needed. Its status and
affinities are being reviewed.

Important Literature:
Cronquist, A. A revision of North American species of *Erigeron* north of
    Mexico. Brittonia 6:121–300; 1974.

36

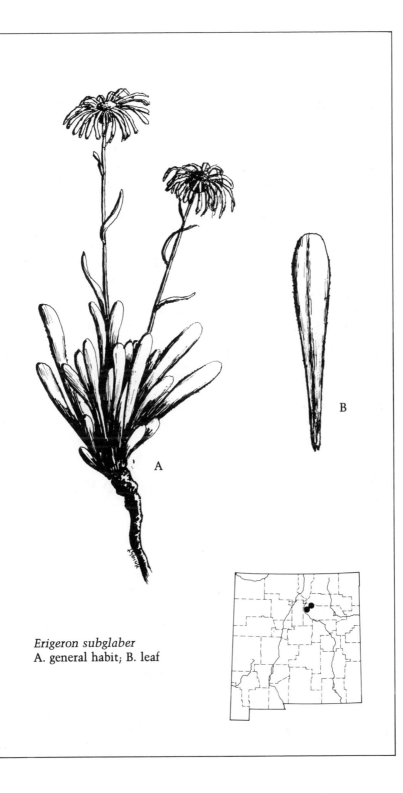

Erigeron subglaber
A. general habit; B. leaf

Family: ASTERACEAE (Compositae)
Scientific Name: *Haplopappus microcephalus* Cronq.
Common Name: Small-headed goldenweed
Classification: Biologically endangered
Federal Action: None
Common Synonyms: None

Description: Mat-forming perennial with spreading stems to about 5 cm
(2 in.) long; leaves numerous, broader above the middle, tapering to the
base, 2–4 cm (0.8–1.5 in.) long to 3.5 mm (0.1 in.) wide, usually without
teeth or sometimes with an occasional minute tooth; flower heads, 6–8
mm (0.25 in.) high, several to many in a rather flat-topped cluster, the
outer flowers of each head with inconspicuous yellow rays about 3 mm
(0.12 in.) long; involucral bracts firm, translucent, in several series, the
outermost bracts gradually tapering to a point. Flowers in June and July.
Known Distribution: Taos County, New Mexico
Habitat: Crevices on granite rocks, usually in ponderosa pine forests;
2,450–2,600 (8,000–8,500 ft.)
Ownership: Forest Service
Threats to Taxon: None known
Similar Species: No species of *Asteraceae* in the region combines the
matted habit with the clustered heads.
Remarks: This species is known only from one collection in New
Mexico; additional surveys of the Sangre de Cristo Mountains might
uncover new populations.

Important Literature:
Cronquist, A. A new *Haplopappus* from New Mexico. Madroño 11:186–
    87; 1951.

Happlopappus microcephalus
general habit

Family: ASTERACEAE (Compositae)
Scientific Name: *Helianthus paradoxus* Heiser
Common Name: Pecos sunflower
Classification: Biologically endangered
Federal Action: Federal Register, 15 December 1980, candidate for federal protection
Common Synonyms: None

Description: Annual; stems 1–2 m (40–80 in.) tall, short branched above; leaves three veined, lanceolate, tapering to a short stalk, mostly without teeth on the margins but lower leaves sometimes remotely toothed; flower heads, including ray flowers 3–5 cm (1.2–2.0 in.) across, the subtending ring of bracts 15–20, narrow acuminate; 12–20 ray flowers, yellow; achenes hairless or nearly so, with two short scales at the summit, these readily dropping off. Flowers from July to October.
Known Distribution: Cibola and Chaves counties, New Mexico, and western Texas
Habitat: Marshes and moist open areas; 1,250–1,800 m (4,000–6,000 ft.)
Ownership: Laguna Indian Pueblo, private
Threats to Taxon: Development of natural water sources and the alteration of habitat by the introduction and spread of salt cedar
Similar Species: Other small annual sunflowers may be mistaken for this, but they either have broader leaves, toothed leaves, or ciliate bracts around the head.
Remarks: This little-known sunflower has not been seen at the Laguna Indian Reservation for over a century and is probably extinct there. It has recently been discovered near Roswell.

Important Literature:
Heiser, C. B., Jr. The North American Sunflowers (*Helianthus*) Mem. Torr. Bot. Club 22:1–218, 1969.
Siler, G. J., luka cuk, and Charlie E. Rogers. New and interesting distribution records for *Helianthus paradoxus*. Southw. Nat. 26(4):431; 1981.

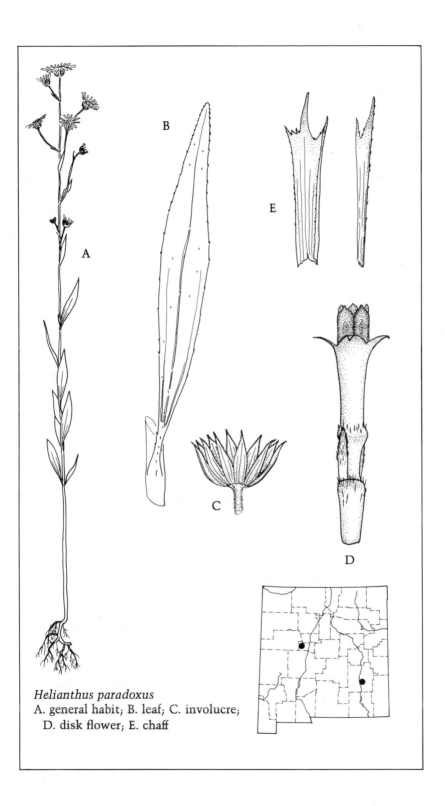

Helianthus paradoxus
A. general habit; B. leaf; C. involucre;
 D. disk flower; E. chaff

Family: ASTERACEAE (Compositae)
Scientific Name: *Helianthus praetermissus* E. E. Wats.
Common Name: Lost sunflower
Classification: Extinct?
Federal Action: Federal Register, 15 December 1980, removed from consideration for federal protection

Description: Possibly annual (root unknown); stems very slender, nearly 1 m (40 in.) tall, sparingly rough-hairy; leaves opposite below midstem, alternate above, narrowly lance shaped, to 6 cm (2.5 in.) long, tapering to the base, the margins entire, three veined but only the midvein prominent, the lateral veins very faint; head solitary, about 3 cm (1.25 in.) wide, including the rays, about 12 involucral bracts, lance shaped, minutely rough-hairy and finely tapered at the tip, about 13 rays, yellow, about 1 cm (0.4 in.) long; achenes hairy at the tip and with two readily falling scales at the summit. Probably flowers July to October.
Known Distribution: Possibly from near Laguna, Valencia County, near head of "Rio Laguna" (now Rio San Jose, see remarks)
Habitat: Moist ground, at about 1,830 m (6,000 ft.)
Ownership: If location is correct, Laguna Indian Reservation, private
Threats to Taxon: If extant, development and use of water sources could threaten it. However, a century of water use in the area, and the introduction and spread of salt cedar probably have made the original habitat completely unsuitable.
Similar Species: *Helianthus paradoxus*, which differs in having the lateral veins on the leaves more prominent, a branched top, and fewer hairs on the top of the seed
Remarks: There is considerable question as to whether this species was collected in New Mexico. It may have been collected in eastern Arizona.

Important Literature:
Watson, E. E. Contribution to a monograph of the genus *Helianthus*.
  Papers Mich. Acad. Sci., Arts, Letters 9:305–475, plus 38 plates; 1929.

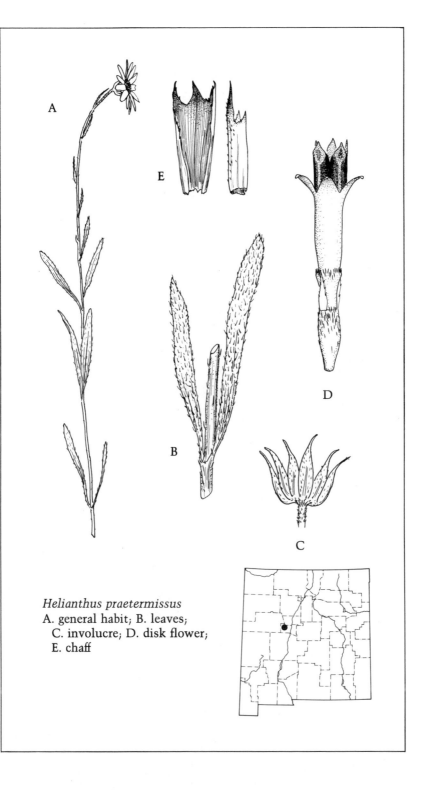

Helianthus praetermissus
A. general habit; B. leaves;
 C. involucre; D. disk flower;
 E. chaff

Family: ASTERACEAE (Compositae)
Scientific Name: *Hymenoxys olivacea* Cockll.
Common Name: Olivaceous bitterweed
Classification: State priority 1
Federal Action: None
Common Synonyms: None

Description: Perennial herb; usually glabrous or nearly so throughout; leaves grasslike, 6–10 cm (2.4–4.0 in.) long, those of the stem linear, strongly resin dotted, dark olive green, the upper ones sometimes with linear lateral lobes; several flower heads, on long stalks, the disk 8–10 mm (0.3–0.4 in.) wide, involucral bracts glabrous, the outer ones united to beyond the middle and keeled, the inner bracts fringed; ray flowers pale orange; achenes reddish brown, hairy, with reddish brown scales at the summit, these lobed on each side, broad at the base and tapering to a slender bristle tip. Flowers from July to September.
Known Distribution: Catron, Grant, and Sierra counties, New Mexico
Habitat: Hillsides and valleys in pinyon-juniper woodland; 1,900–2,200 m (6,200–7,200 ft.)
Ownership: Private
Threats to Taxon: None known
Similar Species: *Hymenoxys richardsonii*, differs in that the lower leaves are divided into linear segments.
Remarks: This plant needs to be evaluated taxonomically as it has been synonymized recently with *H. richardsonii*.

Important Literature:
Cockerell, T. D. A. The North American species of *Hymenoxys*. Bull. Torr. Bot. Club 31:461–509; 1904.

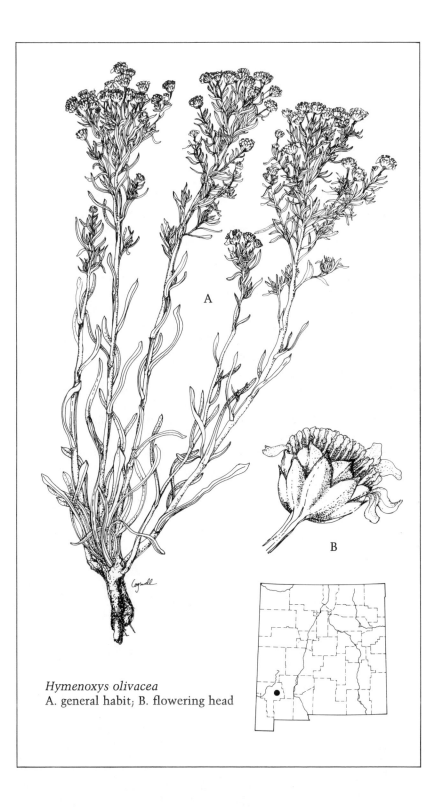

Hymenoxys olivacea
A. general habit; B. flowering head

Family: ASTERACEAE (Compositae)
Scientific Name: *Hymenoxys vaseyi* (Gray) Cockll.
Common Name: Vasey's bitterweed
Classification: State priority 1
Federal Action: None
Common Synonyms: *Actinellia vaseyi* Gray, *Picradenia vaseyi* (Gray) Greene

Description: Perennial; stems to about 30 cm (12 in.) tall, branching above, nearly glabrous; leaves once or twice three-parted into narrowly linear lobes; flower heads numerous, in broad clusters; involucres narrowly bell shaped, about 8 mm (0.3 in.) high, the outer bracts united to form a cup, the inner ones broadly oval, rounded with an abrupt point at the tip; disk flowers with corollas finely hairy at the base; achenes oblong or lance shaped, with blunt scales at the summit about half as long as the disk corollas. Flowers from September to November.
Known Distribution: Doña Ana and Socorro counties, New Mexico
Habitat: Dry hills; 1,400–2,000 m (4,500–6,500 ft.)
Ownership: Bureau of Land Management, private
Threats to Taxon: None known
Similar Species: Two species of *Hymenoxys* have divided leaves similar to this: *H. odorata*, which is an annual, and *H. richardsonii*, which is a perennial, but they have scales that gradually narrow to a fine point on the summit of the achenes.
Remarks: This is a poorly understood species in need of critical study.

Important Literature:
Cockerell, T. D. A. The North American Species of *Hymenoxys*. Bull. Torr. Bot. Club 31:461–509; 1904.
Wooton, E. O., and P. C. Standley. Flora of New Mexico. Contr. U.S. Nat. Herb. 19:1–793; 1915.

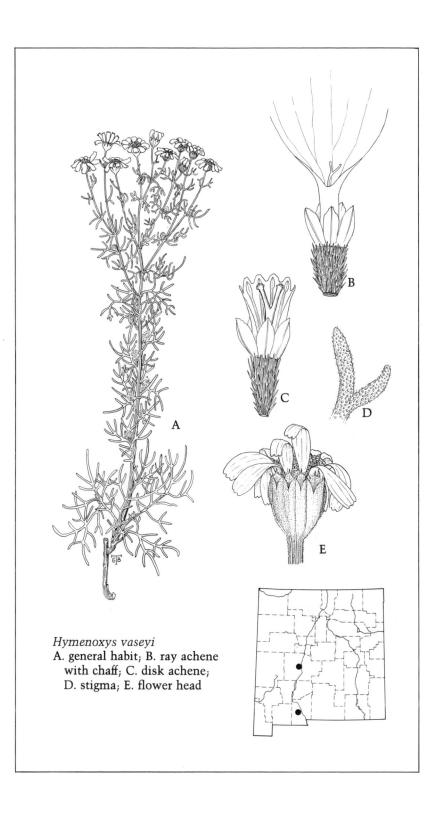

Hymenoxys vaseyi
A. general habit; B. ray achene
with chaff; C. disk achene;
D. stigma; E. flower head

Family: ASTERACEAE (Compositae)
Scientific Name: *Lepidospartum burgessii* Turner
Common Name: Gypsum scalebroom
Classification: Biologically threatened
Federal Action: Federal Register, 15 December 1980, candidate for federal protection
Common Synonyms: None

Description: Silvery white shrub up to 70 cm (28 in.) tall, the stems many times branched and covered with silvery, matted, feltlike hairs out of which protrude numerous small oil blisters; leaves needlelike, alternate, 5–12 mm (0.25–0.5 in.) long; 1–4 heads, terminal or axillary near the ends of broomlike branches, each head about 1 cm (0.4 in.) long, narrow, with about 10 bracts, but the lower six or seven reduced, the upper three long, about equal in length, blunt or rounded at the tip and conspicuously thickened along the center; flowers only three per head, all of the tube type, yellow; achenes densely covered with white, bristly hairs and topped by a pappus of numerous slender bristles. Flowers in July and August.
Known Distribution: Otero County, New Mexico, and adjacent Texas
Habitat: Gypseous ridges and flats, at about 1,250 m (4,000 ft.)
Ownership: Bureau of Land Management, private
Threats to Taxon: None known
Similar Species: The closest relatives of this species are shrubs in southern California. In New Mexico, it may be mistaken for a *Chrysothamnus* because of its narrow heads and matted hairs, but the three rounded bracts of the involucre on the heads distinguish it from that genus.
Remarks: This species was formerly considered to be a local endemic in extreme western Texas; it was first described and said to be rare in 1977. It was discovered in New Mexico in 1982, where it is locally abundant on a few small alkaline playas.

Important Literature:

Turner, B. L. *Lepidospartum burgessii* (*Asteraceae, Senecioneae*), a remarkable new gypsophilic species from Trans-Pecos Texas. Wrightia 5:354–55; 1977.

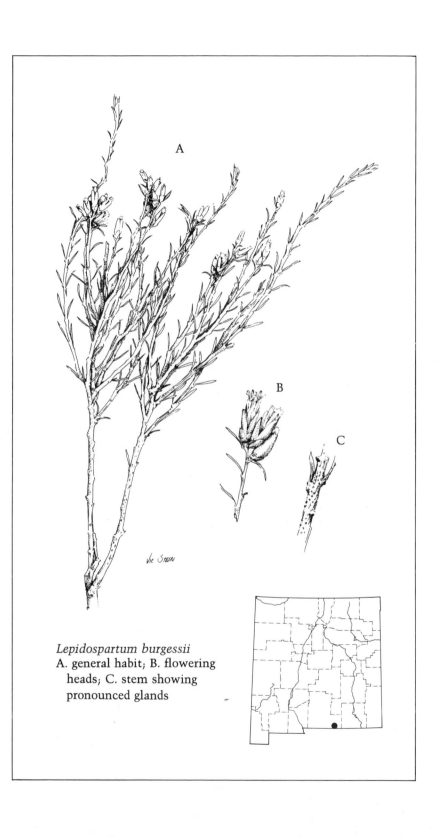

Lepidospartum burgessii
A. general habit; B. flowering
heads; C. stem showing
pronounced glands

Family: ASTERACEAE (Compositae)
Scientific Name: *Machaeranthera amplifolia* Woot. & Standl.
Common Name: Organ Mountain aster
Classification: State priority 1
Federal Action: None
Common Synonyms: *Aster amplifolius* (Woot. & Standl.) Kittell

Description: Erect biennial or perennial; stems to about 70 cm (27.5 in.) tall; leaves bright green, smooth or nearly so, to about 4 cm (1.5 in.) long and 2.5 cm (1 in.) wide, coarsely toothed, blunt at the tip; flower heads 10–12 mm (0.4–0.2 in.) high, rays blue-violet or violet, involucral bracts subtending the flower heads linear, the outer ones bent outward and downward. Flowers from June to October.
Known Distribution: Doña Ana County, New Mexico
Habitat: Rocky canyons in mountains; 1,825–2,125 m (6,000–7,000 ft.)
Ownership: Bureau of Land Management, Department of Defense, private, State of New Mexico
Threats to Taxon: None known
Similar Species: *Machaeranthera bigelovii,* a common species of the mountains, is densely glandular nearly throughout. *M. aquifolia* differs primarily in the leaves of the stem, which are not noticeably tapered to the base.
Remarks: Habitat alteration caused by recreational use and livestock grazing may affect the populations of this species. Its closest relatives respond in a positive manner to intermittent disturbance.

Important Literature:
Wooton, E. O., and P. C. Stanley. Descriptions of new plants preliminary to a report upon the flora of New Mexico. Contr. U.S. Nat. Herb. 16:109–96; 1913.

50

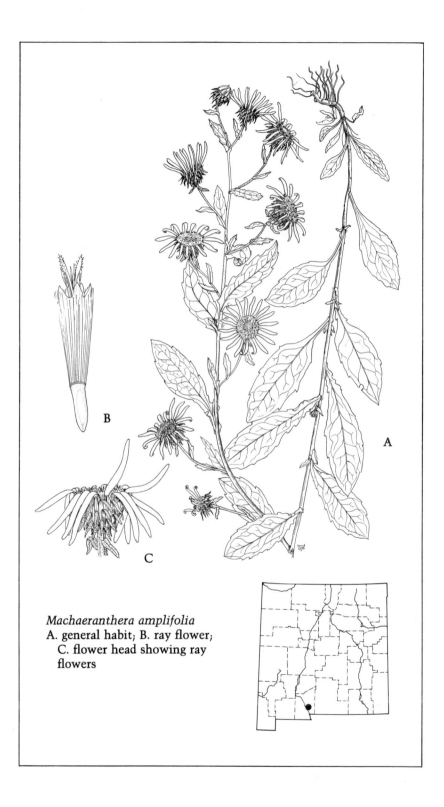

Machaeranthera amplifolia
A. general habit; B. ray flower;
  C. flower head showing ray
  flowers

Family: ASTERACEAE (Compositae)
Scientific Name: *Perityle cernua* (Greene) Shinners
Common Name: Nodding cliff daisy
Classification: Biologically threatened
Federal Action: Federal Register, 15 December 1980, candidate for federal protection
Common Synonyms: *Laphamia cernua* Greene
Pappothrix cernua (Greene) Rydb.

Description: Low, tufted perennials from a woody base, the stems leafy, to about 10 cm (4 in.) long; leaves petidate, the blades broadly rounded-triangular, thick, and fleshy, 2–3 cm (0.75–1.5 in.) wide, the margins toothed; flower heads yellow, rayless, solitary, held barely above the leaves on a bent stalk, with 15–20 involucral bracts about 8 mm (0.33 in.) long, and with 50–75 disk flowers; achenes with about 20 bristles at the summit. Flowers from June to September.
Known Distribution: Doña Ana County, New Mexico
Habitat: Cliffs of igneous rock; 1,525–2,680 m (5,000–8,800 ft.)
Ownership: Bureau of Land Management, Department of Defense, private
Threats to Taxon: None known
Similar Species: A number of cliff-dwelling species of *Perityle* are superficially similar. This one is distinguished by the numerous bristles on the achenes and the nodding head (when young). No other similar species occurs in the area of *P. cernua*.
Remarks: The relatively inaccessible habitat of this species affords it adequate protection. Human influences so far have apparently had little effect.

Important Literature:
Niles, W. E. Taxonomic investigations in the Genera *Perityle* and *Laphamia* (Compositae). Mem. New York Bot. Gard. 21:1–82; 1970.
Powell. A. M. Taxonomy of *Perityle* Section *Pappothrix* (Compositae-Peritylinae) Rhodora 72:58–93; 1969.

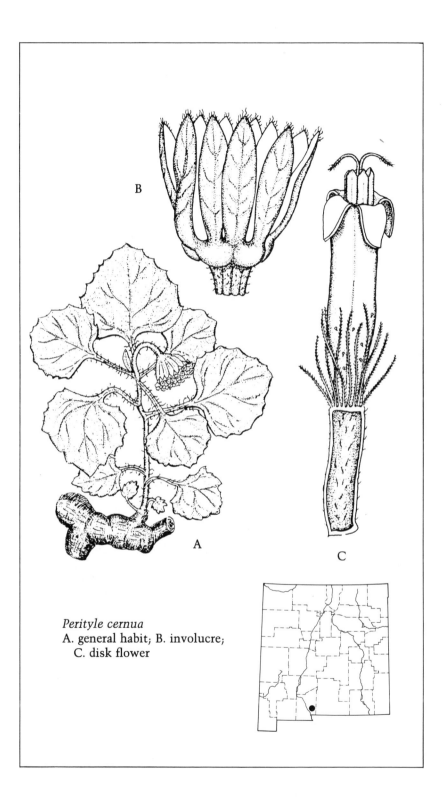

Perityle cernua
A. general habit; B. involucre;
  C. disk flower

Family: ASTERACEAE (Compositae)
Scientific Name: *Perityle quinqueflora* (Steyerm. & Shinners)
Common Name: Five-flowered rock daisy
Classification: State priority 1
Federal Action: None
Common Synonyms: *Laphamia quinqueflora* Steyerm.
Pappothrix quinqueflora (Steyerm.) Everly

Description: Tufted perennial from a woody base; stems to 30 cm (12 in.) tall; leaves opposite, broadly triangular to kidney shaped, 1.5–4.0 cm (0.6–1.6 in.) long, somewhat toothed to very shallowly lobed on the margins; flower heads in open clusters, yellow, 7–9 mm (0.30–0.35 in.) high, the involucral bracts five or six appearing as a single series; achenes with about 25–30 unequal bristles at the summit. Flowers from April to October.
Known Distribution: Eddy County, New Mexico, and adjacent Texas
Habitat: Limestone, or rarely igneous, cliffs; 1,525–1,830 m (5,000–6,000 ft.)
Ownership: Bureau of Land Management, Forest Service, National Park Service, private
Threats to Taxon: None known
Similar Species: None
Remarks: This species is unique owing to its relative rarity, striking appearance, and restricted habitat.

Important Literature:
Everly, M. L. A taxonomic study of the genus *Perityle* and related genera. Contr. Dudley Herb. 3:377–96; 1947.
Niles, W. E. Taxonomic investigations in genus *Perityle* and *Laphamia* (Compositae). Mem. New York Bot. Gard. 21:1–82; 1970.
Powell, A. M. Taxonomy of *Perityle* section *Pappothrix* (Compositae-Peritylineae) Rhodora 71:58–93; 1969.
Shinners, L. H. Species of *Laphamia* transferred to *Perityle* (Compositae-Helenieae). Southw. Nat. 4:204–6; 1959.

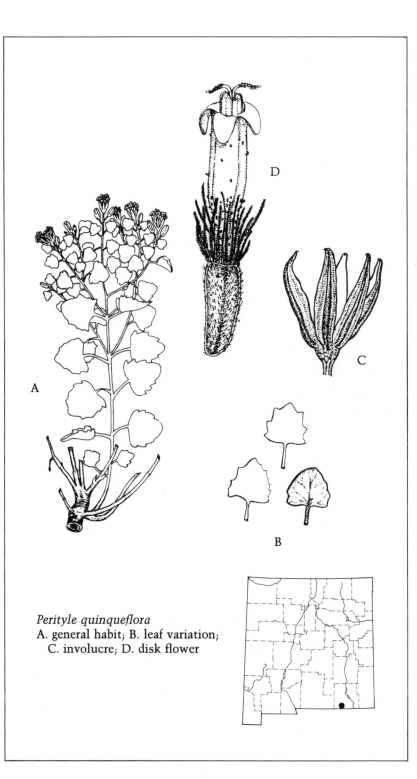

Perityle quinqueflora
A. general habit; B. leaf variation;
C. involucre; D. disk flower

Family: ASTERACEAE (Compositae)
Scientific Name: *Perityle staurophylla* (Barneby) Shinners
Common Name: None
Classification: State priority 1
Federal Action: Federal Register, 15 December 1980, removed from consideration for federal protection
Common Synonyms: *Laphamia staurophylla* Barneby

Description: Perennial herb from a woody base; stems many, to 30 cm (12 in.) long; leaves many, broadly oval to elliptic in outline, mostly deeply and narrowly three-lobed; flower heads terminal, solitary or in small clusters, somewhat bell shaped, involucral bracts lance shaped, about 4–5 mm (0.2 in.) long; ray flowers 0–8 (absent in var. *homoflora*), yellow, to 6 mm (0.25 in.) long; disk flowers 30–40, yellow, about 3 mm (0.12 in.) long; achenes usually bearing two stout awns at the summit. Flowers from June to September.
Known Distribution: Doña Ana, Otero, and Sierra counties, New Mexico
Habitat: Crevices in limestone cliffs and boulders, usually on protected north and east exposures at about 2,100 m (7,000 ft.)
Ownership: Bureau of Land Management, Department of Defense, Forest Service, private, State of New Mexico
Threats to Taxon: None known
Similar Species: *Perityle corropifolia* grows in the same region but has white rays.
Remarks: The var. *homoflora* is restricted to the north end of the San Andres Mountains. Both varieties are common in their limited habitat.

Important Literature:
Barneby, R. C. A new species of *Laphamia* from New Mexico. Leafl. West. Bot. 8:168–70; 1957.
Niles, W. E. Taxonomic investigations in the genera *Perityle* and *Laphamia*. Mem. New York Bot. Gard. 21:34–36; 1970.
Powell, A. H. Taxonomy of *Perityle* Section *Laphamia*. Sida (2):117–19; 1973.
Todsen, T. K. A new variety of *Perityle staurophylla* (Asteraceae) from New Mexico. Madroño 30:115–17; 1983.

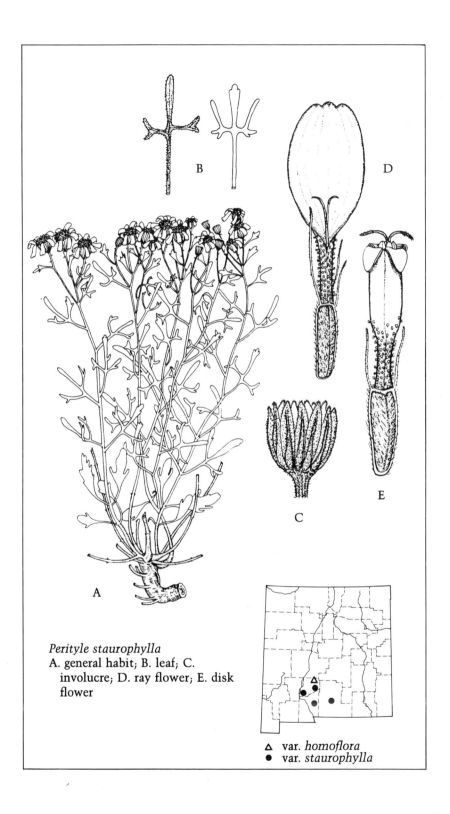

Perityle staurophylla
A. general habit; B. leaf; C. involucre; D. ray flower; E. disk flower

△ var. *homoflora*
● var. *staurophylla*

Family: ASTERACEAE (Compositae)
Scientific Name: *Senecio cardamine* Greene
Common Name: Heartleaf senecio
Classification: State priority 1
Federal Action: Federal Register, 15 December 1980, removed from consideration for federal protection
Common Synonyms: None

Description: Perennial smooth herb, with stems to 50 cm (20 in.) tall; leaves mostly basal, heart shaped to nearly round, to about 10 cm (4 in.) long and about as wide, the basal leaves with slender stalks, the few stem leaves small, without stalks, with clasping bases; flower heads few, mostly 4–6, 6–8 mm (0.25–0.33 in.) high; rays yellow. Flowers from April to August.
Known Distribution: Catron County, New Mexico, and adjacent Arizona
Habitat: Mature spruce-fir and Douglas fir forests, only on the colder north slopes at high elevations; 2,440–3,050 m (8,000–10,000 ft.)
Ownership: Forest Service, private
Threats to Taxon: Extensive opening of the forest canopy could alter habitat to the extreme of threatening individual populations.
Similar Species: This species is unmistakable; its broad, nearly round leaves are distinctive.
Remarks: This is an endemic of the climax forest vegetation of the higher southwestern mountains. Recent exploration of this vegetation type has resulted in the discovery of a number of populations.

Important Literature:
Barkley, T. M. *Senecio.* North American Flora, series 2, part 10, 50–139; 1978.

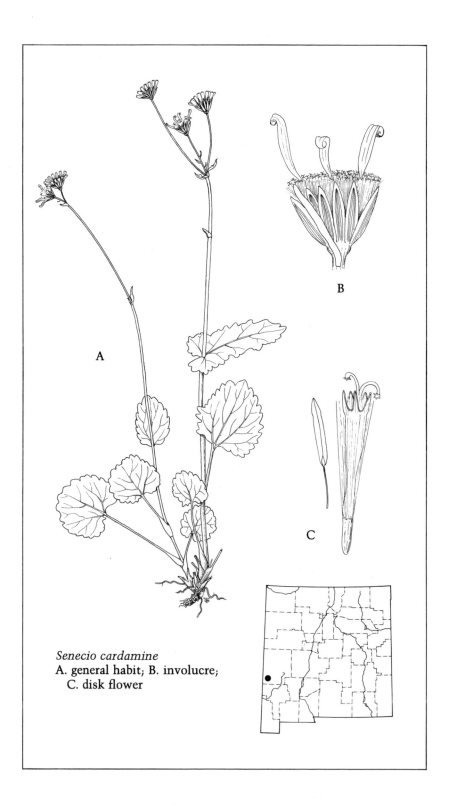

Senecio cardamine
A. general habit; B. involucre;
C. disk flower

Family: ASTERACEAE (Compositae)
Scientific Name: *Senecio quaerens* Greene
Common Name: Gila groundsel
Classification: Biologically endangered
Federal Action: Federal Register, 15 December 1980, candidate for federal protection
Common Synonyms: None

Description: Perennial, nearly glabrous, with erect stems 30–60 cm (12–24 in.) tall; leaves mostly basal, those oval, broadly rounded at the apex, the margins with shallow, rounded teeth, the few stem leaves deeply and regularly toothed, the terminal lobe larger than the others; flower heads 8–10 mm (0.5–0.4 in.) high, with 8–12 yellow ray flowers. Flowers from July to August.
Known Distribution: Catron County, New Mexico
Habitat: Wet meadows and streambanks; at about 2,440 m (8,000 ft.)
Ownership: Forest Service, private
Threats to Taxon: The species grows in an area subject to heavy recreational use. Modification of streamside habitat adversely affects this species.
Similar Species: *Senecio hartianus* can be differentiated in most instances by the presence of pubescence at least on the lower sides of the basal leaves, in the leaf axils, and among the flower heads.
Remarks: The species has limited distribution and is readily subject to decimation by any activities that disturb its habitat.

Important Literature:
Barkley, T. M. *Senecio.* North American Flora, series 2, part 10, 50–139; 1978.

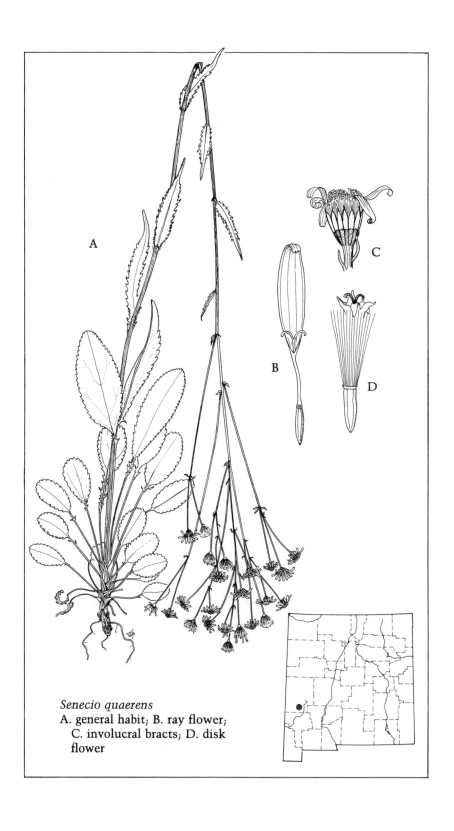

Senecio quaerens
A. general habit; B. ray flower;
C. involucral bracts; D. disk
flower

Family: ASTERACEAE (Compositae)
Scientific Name: *Senecio sacramentanus* Woot. & Standl.
Common Name: Sacramento groundsel
Classification: State priority 1
Federal Action: None
Common Synonyms: None

Description: Perennial, to about 70 cm (28 in.) tall, leafy throughout, but the leaves progressively reduced upward; leaves bright green, thin, lance shaped to narrowly triangular, to about 14 cm (5.5 in.) long and 5 cm (2 in.) wide, those at the base with petiole to 7 cm (2.75 in.) long, the stem leaves without petioles and often clasping the stem, abruptly sharp pointed at the tip, varying from heart shaped to tapered at the base, the margins coarsely toothed, upper surface without hairs, the lower sparsely hairy; flower heads about 10 mm (0.4 in.) high and nearly as wide, bent down; ray flowers absent. Flowers from July to September.
Known Distribution: Lincoln and Otero counties, New Mexico
Habitat: Mountain meadows; 2,440–3,550 m (8,000–11,000 ft.)
Ownership: Bureau of Indian Affairs, Forest Service, private
Threats to Taxon: None known
Similar Species: *S. bigelovii* is widespread in New Mexico; it is more robust than *S. sacramentanus* and has flower heads often more than 1 cm (0.4 in.) across.
Remarks: In some areas of New Mexico, forms of *S. bigelovii* approach those of *S. sacramentanus* and relationships are in need of clarification.

Important Literature:

Barkley, T. M. *Senecio.* North American Flora, series 2, part 10, 50–139; 1978.

Wooton, E. O., and P. C. Standley. New Plants from New Mexico. Contr. U.S. Nat. Herb. 16:109–96; 1913.

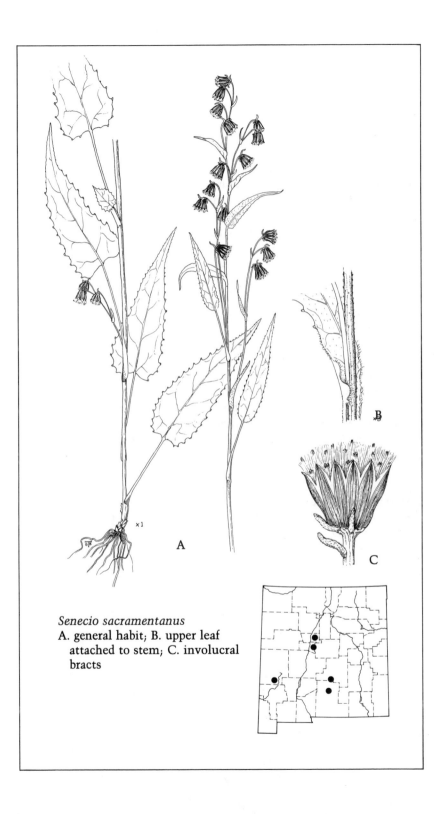

Senecio sacramentanus
A. general habit; B. upper leaf
 attached to stem; C. involucral
 bracts

Family: ASTERACEAE (Compositae)
Scientific Name: *Tetradymia filifolia* Greene
Common Name: Threadleaf horsebrush
Classification: State priority 1
Federal Action: None
Common Synonyms: None

Description: Much-branched, grayish shrub to about 1 m (40 in.) tall; leaves very narrow, 2.5–5.0 cm (1–2 in.) long, often covered with hairs, the larger leaves often with clusters of smaller leaves in their axils; flower heads very narrow, yellow, with four flowers; rays absent; involucral bracts 4.6–12.0 mm (0.25–0.50 in.) long; achenes with 80–100 tawny bristles at the summit. Flowers from July to September.
Known Distribution: Lincoln, Otero, Sandoval, Socorro, and Valencia counties, New Mexico; 1,825–2,215 m (6,000–7,000 ft.)
Habitat: Limestone or highly gypseous soils, usually in pinyon-juniper woodland
Ownership: Bureau of Land Management, Department of Defense, Forest Service, private, State of New Mexico
Threats to Taxon: None known
Similar Species: Some of the species of *Chrysothamnus* that have grayish hairy leaves look very similar to this. However, when in flower or fruit, the four involucral bracts of *Tetradymia* contrast with the four rows of bracts in *Chrysothamnus*. In vegetative condition, *Tetradymia* can be identified by the numerous clusters of small, almost needlelike leaves that grow in the axils of the longer, first-year leaves.

Important Literature:
Strother, J. L. Taxonomy of *Tetradymia* (*Compositae; Senecioneae*). Brittonia 26:177–202; 1974.

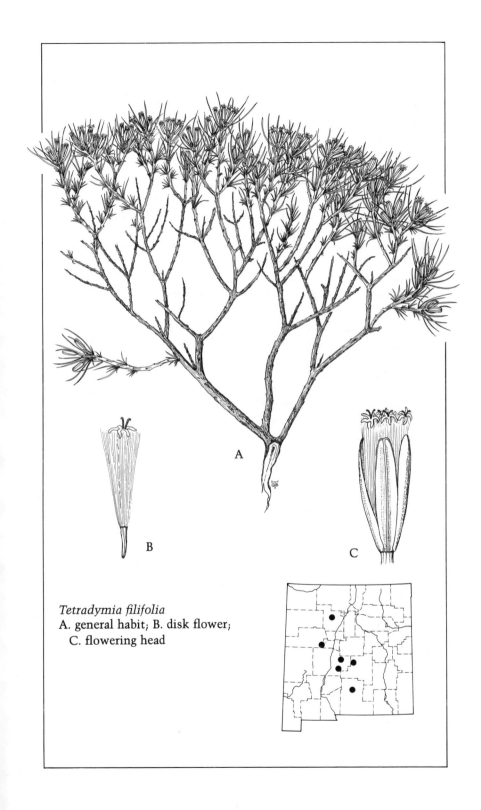

A

B

C

Tetradymia filifolia
A. general habit; B. disk flower;
C. flowering head

Family: BORAGINACEAE
Scientific Name: *Cryptantha paysonii* (Macbr.) I. M. Johnst.
Common Name: Payson's hiddenflower
Classification: State priority 1
Federal Action: None
Common Synonyms: *Oreocarya paysonii* Macbr.

Description: Stiffly hairy perennial; stems erect, mostly 10–15 cm (4–6 in.) tall; leaves broader toward the apex, tapering to the base, with stiff, appressed hairs on both surfaces; flower clusters loosely headlike, coiled; flowers white, about 10–12 mm (0.4–0.5 in.) wide, without crests inside at the base of the corolla tube; fruits divided into four nutlets, each about 3 mm (0.12 in.) long, finely roughened on the surface, narrowly winged on the margins. Flowers from April to July.
Known Distribution: DeBaca, Lincoln, Otero, Sierra, and Socorro counties, New Mexico, and adjacent Texas
Habitat: Open slopes on limestone soils; 1,225–2,100 m (4,000–7,000 ft.)
Ownership: Bureau of Land Management, Forest Service, National Park Service, private
Threats to Taxon: None known
Similar Species: Three similar species of *Cryptantha* are found in the region. *Cryptantha palmeri* differs by its smooth and shiny nutlets. *Cryptantha oblata* does not have styles of different length. Neither have the dense, headlike cluster of flowers characteristic of *C. paysonii*. *Cryptantha jamesii* is frequent in the range of *C. paysonii*, but has smaller flowers, 8 mm (0.3 in.) or less wide, with a conspicuous ring of crests inside at the base of the corolla tube.
Remarks: This species has a breeding system that encourages cross-pollination. Some of the plants will have styles that are very short, the tip of the style below the anthers. Other plants in the same population will have long styles, the tip of the style positioned above the anthers. Accurate observation of this feature is necessary for identification.

Important Literature:

Higgins, L. C. A revision of *Cryptantha* subgenus Oreocarya. Brigham
    Young Univ. Sci. Bull., Biol. Ser. 13:1–63; 1971.
Johnston, I. M. The North American species of *Cryptantha*. Mem. Gray
    Herb. 74:1–114; 1925.
Payson, E. G. A monograph of the section Oreocarya of *Cryptantha*. Ann.
    Missouri Bot. Gard. 14:211–358; 1927.

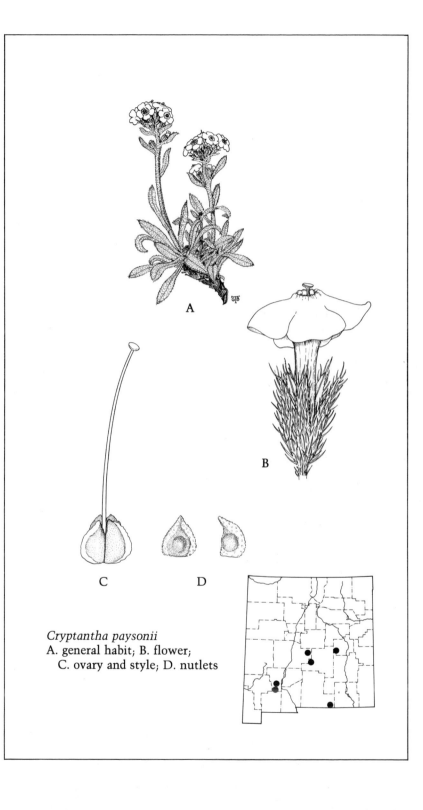

A

B

C

D

Cryptantha paysonii
A. general habit; B. flower;
 C. ovary and style; D. nutlets

Family: BORAGINACEAE
Scientific Name: *Mertensia viridis* A. Nels. var. *caelestina* (Nels. & Cockll.) L. O. Williams
Common Name: Alpine bluebell
Classification: State priority 1
Federal Action: None
Common Synonyms: *Mertensia caelestina* Nels. & Cockll.

Description: Nearly glabrous perennial, with stems to 35 cm (14 in.) tall; leaves lance shaped or ovate, thickish, the petioles sometimes longer than the blades; flower clusters densely coiled; petals blue, united, 12–18 mm (0.5–0.6 in.) long, the calyx 6–7 mm (0.25 in.) long; fruits divided into four nutlets each 2–3 mm (0.12 in.) long, wrinkled. Flowers from July to September.
Known Distribution: Rio Arriba, Santa Fe, and Taos counties, New Mexico
Habitat: Montane slopes; 3,650–3,950 m (12,000–13,000 ft.)
Ownership: Forest Service
Threats to Taxon: None known
Similar Species: *Mertensia alpina* is also a low-growing species of high elevations. *Mertensia viridis* has the filaments of the stamens attached near the throat of the corolla, the anthers projecting into the throat. Its styles are longer than the calyx. *Mertensia alpina* has the filaments attached in the corolla tube, the anthers projecting, at best, only slightly into the throat. Its style is about as long as the calyx.
Remarks: Other varieties of *M. viridis* occur in Colorado.

Important Literature:
Nelson, A., and T. D. A. Cockerell. Three new plants from New Mexico. Proc. Biol. Soc. Washington 16:45–46; 1903.
Williams, L. O. A monograph of the genus *Mertensia*. Ann. Missouri Bot. Gard. 24:17–159; 1937.

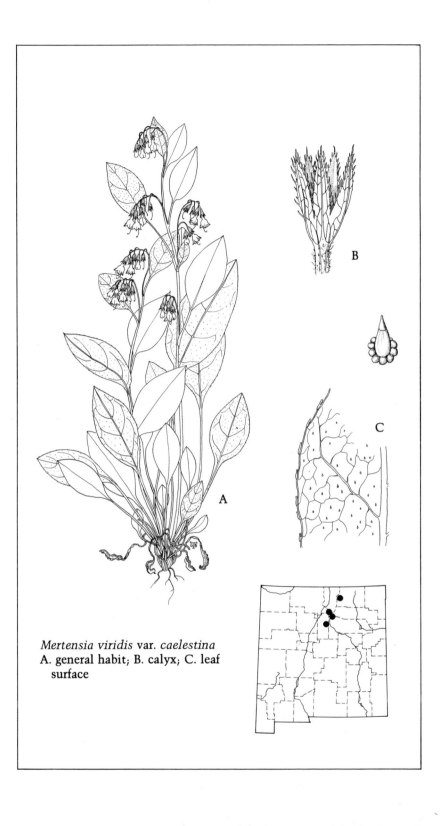

Mertensia viridis var. *caelestina*
A. general habit; B. calyx; C. leaf
surface

Family: BRASSICACEAE (Cruciferae)
Scientific Name: *Draba mogollonica* Greene
Common Name: Mogollon whitlowgrass
Classification: State priority 1
Federal Action: Federal Register, 15 December 1980, removed from consideration for federal protection
Common Synonyms: None

Description: Perennial, 15–25 cm (6–10 in.) tall; leaves mostly basal, 15–30 mm (0.6–1.2 in.) wide, toothed, with short-branched hairs; stem leaves, if any, much reduced; flowers yellow, four petals; fruits oblong, flat, twisted, hairy or not. Flowers from April to June.
Known Distribution: Catron, Grant, Sierra, and Socorro counties, New Mexico
Habitat: Moist cliff faces, rock cracks, crevices, and steep, shaded slopes with little soil development; 1,500–2,900 m (5,000–9,000 ft.)
Ownership: Forest Service, private
Threats to Taxon: None known
Similar Species: The much reduced or absent stem leaves and large basal leaves are characters that separate this perennial *Draba* from others in New Mexico.
Remarks: Only a few years ago, *Draba mogollonica* was known from perhaps a dozen collections. Since that time, the authors have encountered large populations in the mountains of central New Mexico.

Important Literature:
Greene, E. L. New species of plants from New Mexico. Bot. Gaz. 6:156–58; 1881.

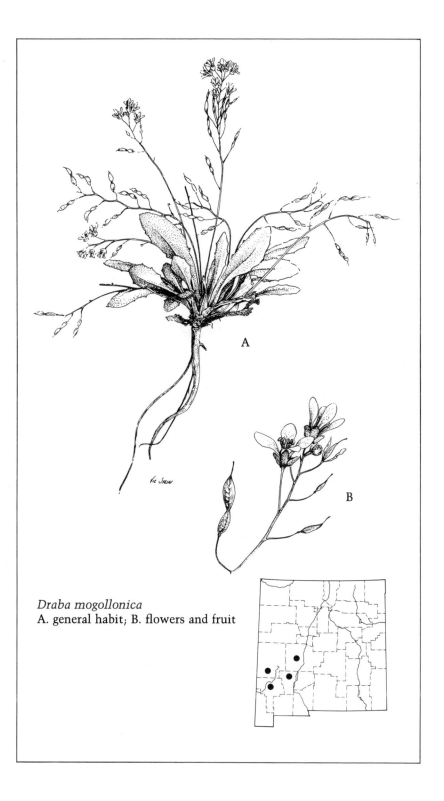

Draba mogollonica
A. general habit; B. flowers and fruit

Family: BRASSICACEAE
Scientific Name: *Lesquerella aurea* Woot.
Common Name: Golden bladderpod
Classification: Biologically threatened
Federal Action: Federal Register, 15 December 1980, candidate for federal protection
Common Synonyms: None

Description: Densely hairy biennial or short-lived perennial; stems branched from the base, to about 60 cm (24 in.) tall; basal leaves with petioles variously toothed or incised, to about 2.5 cm (1 in.) long and 10 mm (0.4 in.) wide; stem leaves without petioles, 2–4 cm (0.75–1.5 in.) long, 10–30 mm (0.4–1.25 in.) wide; flowers usually numerous; four petals, yellow; pods globose, about 3 mm (0.12 in.) in diameter, slightly hairy or hairless; pedicels to 2 cm (0.75 in.) long, strongly recurved, the fruit hanging downward. Flowers from June to August.
Known Distribution: Lincoln and Otero counties, New Mexico
Habitat: Open rocky slopes in mixed-conifer vegetation type; 1,980–2,750 m (6,500–9,000 ft.)
Ownership: Forest Service, Mescalero Indian Reservation, State of New Mexico
Threats to Taxon: Any activities creating substantial surface disturbance would have at least an initial adverse effect on this species. While rare overall, it is known to have become established along some roadsides.
Similar Species: There are a number of yellow-flowered species of *Lesquerella* in New Mexico. This species may be distinguished from others in its range by the recurving fruit stalks and the densely leafy stems.
Remarks: This taxon appears to be very rare, but its frequency from year to year is dependent in large part on temperature and rainfall patterns. In some areas, it has colonized roadsides, where methods of road maintenance might affect the population.

Important Literature:
Rollins, R. C., and E. A. Shaw. The genus *Lesquerella* (*Cruciferae*) in North America. Cambridge, Mass.: Harvard Univ. Press; 1973.
Soreng, R. Status report on *Lesquerella aurea*. U.S. Fish and Wildlife Service; 1981.
Wooton, E. O. New plants from New Mexico. Bull. Torr. Bot. Club 25:257–64; 1898.

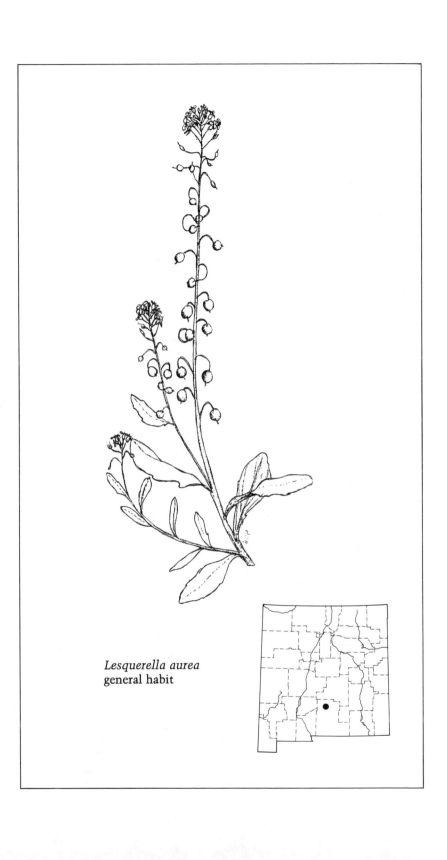

Lesquerella aurea
general habit

Family: BRASSICACEAE (Cruciferae)
Scientific Name: *Lesquerella gooddingii* Roll. & Shaw
Common Name: Goodding's bladderpod
Classification: State priority 1
Federal Action: Federal Register, 15 December 1980, candidate for federal protection
Common Synonyms: None

Description: Densely hairy annual or biennial; stems several, branching from the base, to 35 cm (14 in.) tall; stem leaves numerous, lying nearly flat against the stem, 1.0–2.5 cm (0.4–1.0 in.) long, 3–8 mm (0.12–0.25 in.) wide; four petals, yellow; pods hairy, 5 mm (0.2 in.) long, flattened, elliptic, with pedicels, S-shaped in fruit. Flowers from June to September.
Known Distribution: Catron, Grant, and Sierra counties, New Mexico, and probably adjacent Arizona
Habitat: Sandy areas in open ponderosa pine forest, dry arroyo bottoms, and on dry, rocky, open slopes of Gila conglomerate; 1,975–2,275 m (6,500–7,500 ft.)
Ownership: Forest Service, private, State of New Mexico
Threats to Taxon: None known
Similar Species: This is the only yellow-flowered species of *Lesquerella* in New Mexico with flattened pods.
Remarks: As with many taxa that occupy relatively open ground in the native habitat, this species frequently also inhabits roadsides. Methods and frequency of maintenance of roads can therefore significantly affect many populations. The amount of disturbance that this species can tolerate, or requires, is unknown. In different years it may be rare or common, presumably depending on temperature and rainfall patterns.

Important Literature:
Rollins, R. C., and E. A. Shaw. The genus *Lesquerella* (*Cruciferae*) in North America. Cambridge, Mass.: Harvard Univ. Press; 1973.

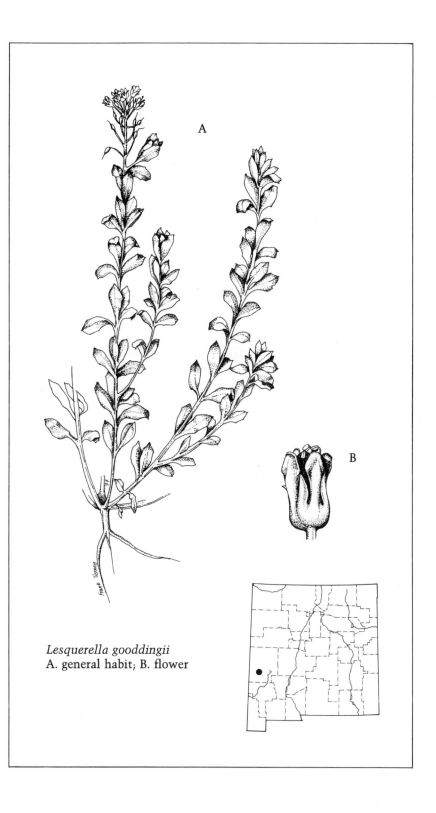

Lesquerella gooddingii
A. general habit; B. flower

Family: BRASSICACEAE (Cruciferae)
Scientific Name: *Sibara grisea* Roll.
Common Name: Gray sibara
Classification: Biologically threatened
Federal Action: None
Common Synonyms: None

Description: Small, annual, grayish green branching herb, glabrous throughout and slightly fleshy, growing up to 30 cm (12 in.) tall; leaves 3–7 cm (1.2–2.8 in.) long, 1.5–3.0 cm (0.6–1.2 in.) wide, deeply dissected into lobes; flowers minute, with sepals 2 mm (0.08 in.) long or less, and four white petals 3.5 mm (0.15 in.) long; fruit a long narrow pod 1.5–2.0 mm (0.6–0.8 in.) wide and 2–3 cm (0.8–1.2 in.) long; seeds small, yellow, and narrowly winged. Flowers in May and June.
Known Distribution: Otero County, New Mexico, and possibly adjacent Texas
Habitat: On and at the base of limestone cliffs; 1,350–1,800 m (4,500–6,000 ft.)
Ownership: Forest Service, Park Service
Threats to Taxon: None known
Similar Species: The nearest relative to *S. grisea* is *S. runcinata*, which does not occur in New Mexico
Remarks: This newly described species appears to be both rare and restricted in distribution. However, recent discoveries reported this taxon in the Guadalupe Mountains of Texas. If these reports are correct, this species may be more common than previously believed.

Important Literature:
Rollins, R. C. Species of *Draba, Lesquerella* and *Sibara*. Contr. Gray Herb. 211:111–14; 1981.

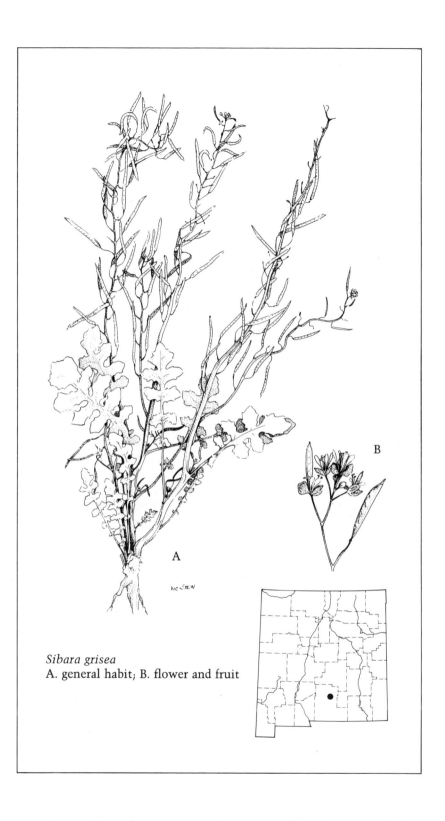

Sibara grisea
A. general habit; B. flower and fruit

Family: CACTACEAE
Scientific Name: *Cereus greggii* Engelm.
Common Name: Night-blooming cereus
Classification: Biologically threatened
Federal Action: Federal Register, 15 December 1980, candidate for federal protection
Common Synonyms: *Peniocereus greggii* (Engelm.) Britt. & Rose

Description: Stems slender, erect to reclining, strongly angled by the four to six low, broad ribs, to 2 m (6.5 ft.) long and 10–15 mm (0.4–0.5 in.) in diameter, usually from an enlarged root; spines mostly 11–13 per cluster, 1–3 mm (0.12 in.) long, swollen at the base; flowers white, opening at night, to about 20 cm (8 in.) long; fruit red, ovoid, somewhat spiny. Flowers in June.
Known Distribution: Doña Ana, Grant, Hidalgo, and Luna counties, New Mexico; southern Arizona, Texas, and northern Mexico
Habitat: Gravelly or silty areas in washes or flats; 900–1,600 m (3,000–5,000 ft.)
Ownership: Bureau of Land Management, private
Threats to Taxon: Once discovered, most populations are quickly decimated by cactus poachers. Heavy grazing probably also reduces populations because of habitat alteration and the destruction of the brittle stems by trampling.
Similar Species: There are no similar species in New Mexico. The narrow-stemmed species of *Opuntia* can be immediately distinguished by the presence of pale needlelike spines on the aeroles.
Remarks: The species has a wide distribution, extending some distance into Mexico, where its status is unknown. The more local variant, *transmontanus*, seems rare and is in need of study.

Important Literature:

Benson, L. The Cacti of Arizona. Tucson: University of Arizona Press; 1969.

Correll, D. S., and M. C. Johnston. Manual of the vascular plants of Texas. Renner, Texas: Texas Research Foundation; 1970.

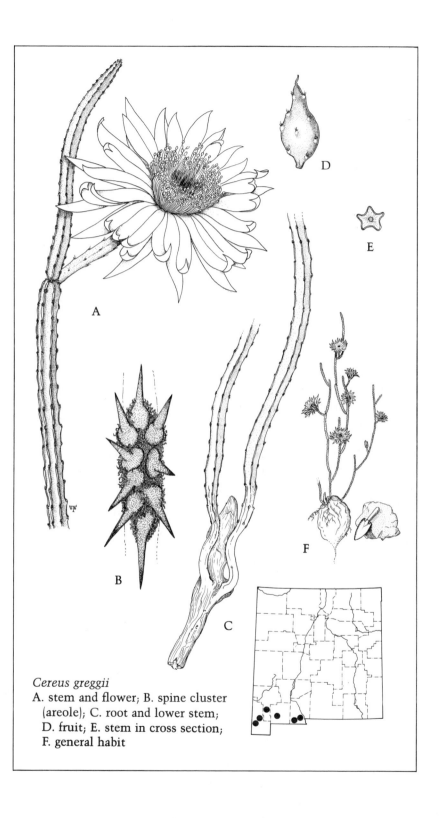

Cereus greggii
A. stem and flower; B. spine cluster
(areole); C. root and lower stem;
D. fruit; E. stem in cross section;
F. general habit

Family: CACTACEAE
Scientific Name: *Coryphantha duncanii* (Hester) L. Benson
Common Name: Duncan's pincushion cactus
Classification: Biologically threatened
Federal Action: Federal Register, 15 December 1980, candidate for federal protection
Common Synonyms: *Escobaria duncanii* (Hester) L. Benson
Escobesseya duncanii Hester

Description: Stems solitary or rarely two to three together, to about 6 cm (2.4 in.) high and about as wide; spines very numerous, completely obscuring the stem, not clearly differentiated into radials and centrals, 30–75 per aerole, to about 20 mm (0.75 in.) long, white; flowers about 1.5 cm (0.4 in.) long, the petaloid parts pink; fruits red; seeds black. Flowers from May to July.
Known Distribution: Sierra County, New Mexico, and adjacent Texas
Habitat: Limestone hills; 900–1,500 m (3,000–5,000 ft.)
Ownership: Bureau of Land Management
Threats to Taxon: Overcollecting is the primary factor affecting all of the state's rarer cacti.
Similar Species: Further study is needed in order to understand more fully the relationship of southern New Mexico's limestone inhabiting members of the genus *Coryphantha*, all of which are closely related and are difficult to differentiate based on the current literature.
Remarks: Future investigation may reveal new locations for *C. duncanii* in the southern portion of New Mexico.

Important Literature:
Correll, D. S., and M. C. Johnston. Manual of the vascular plants of Texas. Renner, Texas: Texas Research Foundation; 1970.

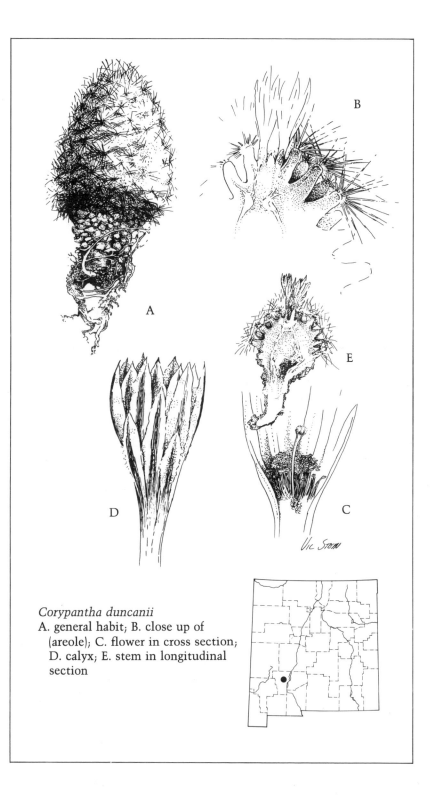

Corypantha duncanii
A. general habit; B. close up of (areole); C. flower in cross section; D. calyx; E. stem in longitudinal section

Family: CACTACEAE
Scientific Name: *Coryphantha organensis* D. Zimmerman
Common Name: Organ Mountain pincushion cactus
Classification: Biologically threatened
Federal Action: None
Common Synonyms: *Escobaria organensis* (D. Zimmerman) Castetter, Pierce, and Schwerin

Description: Stems clumped, usually 10 or more per cluster; spines yellowish, often reddish brown at the tip, mostly 41–47 per cluster, about 10–20 mm (0.4–0.75 in.) long; flowers pink, often tinged with violet or purple, about 1.5–2.5 cm (0.6–1.0 in.) long and about as wide; outer perianth parts fringed; fruits cylindric, yellowish green, to about 14 mm (0.62 in.) long. Probably flowers in May and June.
Known Distribution: Doña Ana County, New Mexico
Habitat: Gravelly slopes in open woods; at about 2,225 m (7,300 ft.)
Ownership: Bureau of Land Management, Department of Defense
Threats to Taxon: Overcollection
Similar Species: *Coryphantha dasyacantha* (Engelmann) Orcutt, *C. sandbergii* Castetter, Pierce, and Schwerin, *C. sneedii* var. *sneedii* (Britton and Rose) Berger, and *C. strobiliformis* (Poselger) Moran form a complex of taxa with great similarities. Characters presently utilized in separating these entities overlap sufficiently to preclude clear differentiation.
Remarks: A reassessment of *Coryphantha* may shed light on the delimitation of this difficult group. For the purpose of this work, the prudent course is to summarize and illustrate those taxa in this group that have been described and await a systematic revision that is both comprehensive and analytical.

Important Literature:
Castetter, Pierce, and Schwerin. A reassessment of the genus *Escobaria*. Cactus and Succ. Jour. 47:60–70; 1975.

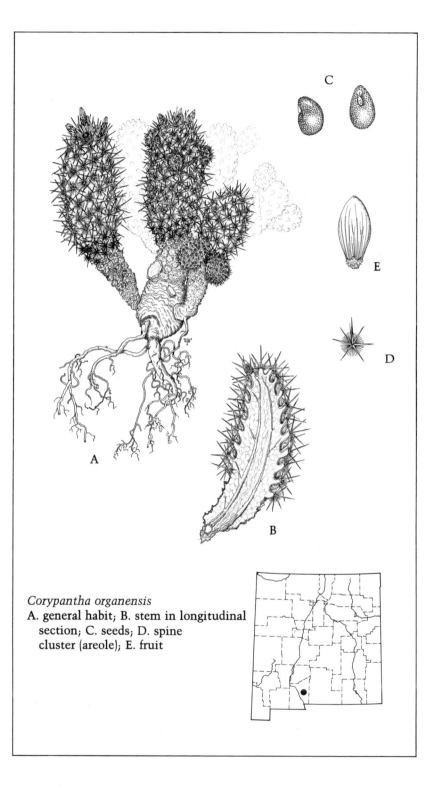

Corypantha organensis
A. general habit; B. stem in longitudinal
  section; C. seeds; D. spine
  cluster (areole); E. fruit

Family: CACTACEAE
Scientific Name: *Coryphantha scheeri* (O. Ktze.) L. Benson
Common Name: Scheer's pincushion cactus
Classification: Biologically endangered
Federal Action: None
Common Synonyms: *Coryphantha muehlenpfordtii* (Poselger) Britt. & Rose

Description: Var. *scheeri*—stems solitary or rarely in clusters, to 18 cm (7 in.) long and 10 cm (4 in.) in diameter; radial spines usually 6–12, yellowish white, except sometimes reddish or pinkish at the tip, attached at the apex of spirally arranged tubercles that are 25–38 cm (1.0–1.5 in.) long, the apex of the new tubercles not woolly, central spines 1–4 cm (1.6 in.) long; flowers to about 5.5 cm (2 in.) long and 7 cm (2.75 in) wide, petals yellow, with streaks of red; fruit elliptic, greenish, without scales. Flowers from June to September.
Var. *valida*—description same as above with the following exceptions: new tubercles densely woolly at the apex, 1–4 central spines to 4 cm (1.6 in.) long; petals yellow, lacking prominent red streaks.
Known Distribution: Var. *scheeri*—Dona Ana, Eddy, Hidalgo, Luna, and Sierra counties, New Mexico
Var. *valida*—Eddy County, New Mexico
Habitat: Open plains and flats, often in alluvial soils, at about 900–1,600 m (3,000–5,000 ft.)
Ownership: Bureau of Land Management, private, State of New Mexico
Threats to Taxon: Overcollection
Similar Species: *Coryphantha macromeris* has tubercles nearly as long as *C. scheeri* but does not have scales on the fruit.
Remarks: Several varieties of this species may be regarded as rare and threatened. In particular, var. *robustispina* and var. *uncinata* are prized by cactus collectors and dealers. Neither of these varieties has been found in New Mexico to date, but they occur in adjacent Arizona and Texas and may eventually be located in New Mexico.

Important Literature:
Benson, L. The Cacti of Arizona. Tucson: University of Arizona Press; 1969.
Britton, N. L. and J. N. Rose. Cactaceae. Carnegie Institute of Washington, Pub. No. 248; 1920.

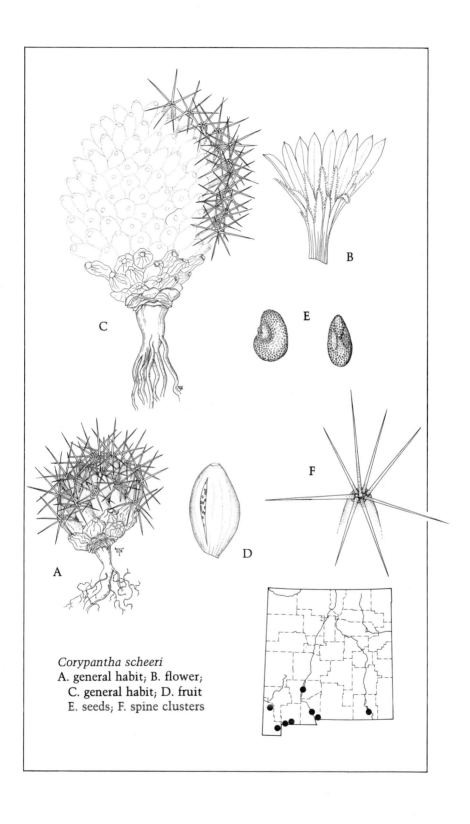

Corypantha scheeri
A. general habit; B. flower;
C. general habit; D. fruit
E. seeds; F. spine clusters

Family: CACTACEAE
Scientific Name: *Coryphantha sneedii* (Britt. & Rose) Berger var. *leei* (Rose) L. Benson
Common Name: Lee's pincushion cactus
Classification: Biologically threatened
Federal Action: Federal Register, 25 October 1979, federally threatened

Common Synonyms: *Escobaria leei* Boedeker

Description: Plants growing densely clustered, with as many as 100 or more stems in a clump; stems 1.5–3.0 cm (0.65–1.24 in.) tall and 1–2 cm (0.38–0.75 in.) in diameter; spines numerous, whitish; flowers pinkish; fruits green to reddish green. Flowers in the spring and fall.
Known Distribution: Eddy County, New Mexico
Habitat: Limestone slopes, ledges, and ridgetops; 1,250–1,780 m (4,100–5,900 ft.)
Ownership: National Park Service
Threats to Taxon: Illegal and widespread collection is a major threat to this taxon.
Similar Species: The closely related *C. sneedii* var. *sneedii* differs by having individual stems up to 12.5 cm (5 in.) tall.
Remarks: The large, matted clumps that this species forms are attractive to collectors.

Important Literature:
Castetter, E. F., and P. Pierce. *Escobaria leei* Boedeker rediscovered in New Mexico. Madroño 18:137–40; 1966.

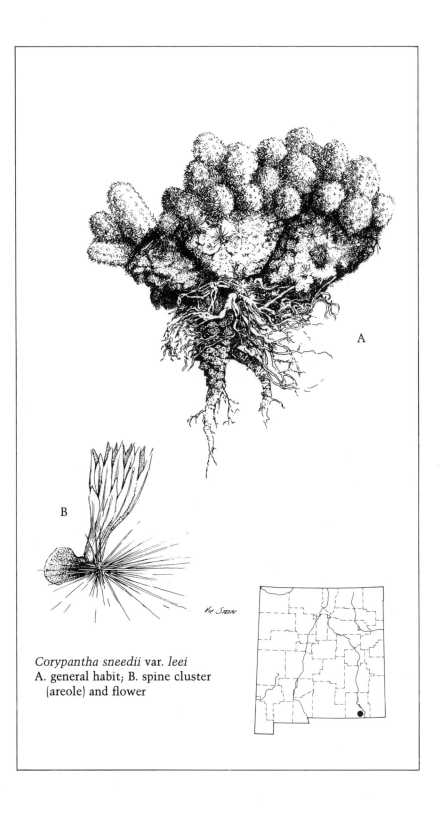

Corypantha sneedii var. *leei*
A. general habit; B. spine cluster
(areole) and flower

Family: CACTACEAE
Scientific Name: *Coryphantha sneedii* (Britt. & Rose) Berger var. *sneedii*
Common Name: Sneed's pincushion cactus
Classification: Biologically endangered
Federal Action: Federal Register, 7 November 1979, federally endangered
Common Synonyms: *Escobaria sneedii* Britt. & Rose

Description: Stems densely clustered, to about 12.5 cm (5 in.) tall, 1.0–2.5 cm (0.4–1.0 in.) in diameter, often with small offsets surrounding one or more of the larger stems; central spines 6–8; radial spines 25–35, white, nearly obscuring the surface of the stem; flowers small, pink to white; fruits green or greenish brown; seeds brown. Flowers from April to September.
Known Distribution: Doña Ana and Eddy counties, New Mexico, and adjacent Texas
Habitat: Rocky slopes of limestone mountains; 1,220–1,800 m (4,000–6,000 ft.)
Ownership: Bureau of Land Management, Department of Defense, Forest Service, private
Threats to Taxon: Poaching by cactus collectors is the major threat to this taxon.
Similar Species: *Coryphantha strobiliformis* grows in the same region as *C. sneedii*, and the populations often intermix. Where intergradation appears to occur, the two can be difficult to distinguish. The former taxon is said to have the radial spines on the upper surface of the areole not markedly longer than those on the lower, and has bright red fruit.
Remarks: Those populations of *C. sneedii* var. *sneedii* recently discovered in the Guadalupe Mountains need further study.

Important Literature:

Britton, N. L., and J. N. Rose. Cactaceae, Carnegie Institute of Washington, Pub. No. 248; 1920.
Champie, C. *Escobaria sneedii* further described. Cact. and Succ. Jour. 32:138–40; 1960.

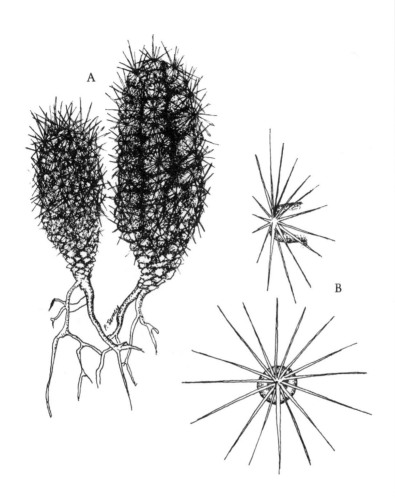

A

B

Corypantha sneedii var. *sneedii*
A. general habit; B. comparison of
  C. sneedii var. *leei* (top) and
  C. sneedii var. *sneedii* (bottom)
spine clusters (areole)

Family: CACTACEAE
Scientific Name: *Echinocerus fendleri* Engelm. var. *kuenzleri* (Castetter, Pierce & Schwerin) L. Benson
Common Name: Kuenzler's hedgehog cactus
Classification: Biologically endangered
Federal Action: Federal Register, 26 October 1979, federally endangered
Common Synonyms: *Echinocerus kuenzleri* Castetter, Pierce & Schwerin

Description: Stems usually solitary, cylindroid, mostly 7.5–25 cm (3–10 in.) tall, to 10 cm (4 in.) in diameter, with prominent ribs and tuberculate projection; spines stout, twisted, contorted, central spines absent, radial spines 0.9–1.2 cm (0.35–0.5 in.) long, the lower spine longer than the others and slightly curved. Flowers in May.
Known Distribution: Eddy, Otero, and Lincoln counties, New Mexico
Habitat: Limestone ledges, rock cracks, and gentle slopes in or just below juniper woodland, at about 1,800 m (6,000 ft.)
Ownership: Bureau of Land Management, Forest Service, private, State of New Mexico
Threats to Taxon: Overcollection is known to have seriously endangered the survival of this taxon, causing its near extinction in the wild.
Similar Species: Variety *kuenzleri* can be distinguished from var. *fendleri* by a lack of the central spine on the former. Also, its spines are somewhat angular, bulbous, twisted, and contorted; they possess a soft white felt coating and become chalky white in age.
Remarks: This is the rarest known cactus in New Mexico, and in the few years since its discovery, it has been collected to near extinction.

Important Literature:
Castetter, E. F., P. Pierce, and K. H. Schwerin. A new cactus species and two new varieties from New Mexico. Cact. and Succ. Jour. 68:77–78; 1976.

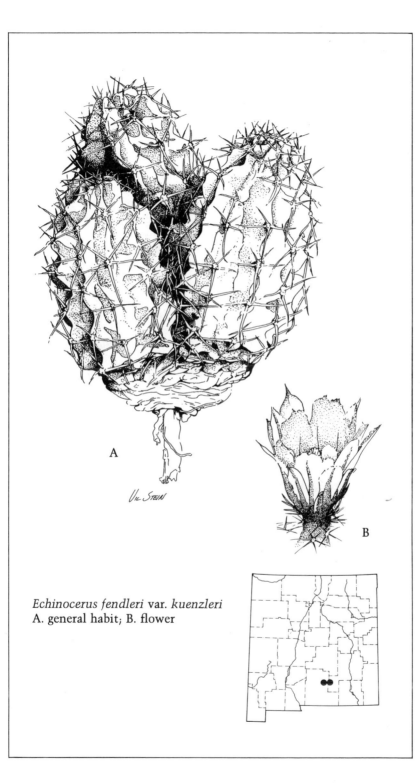

Echinocerus fendleri var. *kuenzleri*
A. general habit; B. flower

Family: CACTACEAE
Scientific Name: *Escobaria orcuttii* (Rose *ex.* Orcutt) Castetter, Pierce, and Schwerin var. *koenigii* Castetter, Pierce, and Schwerin
Common Name: Koenig's pincushion cactus
Classification: Biologically threatened
Federal Action: None
Common Synonyms: None

Description: Stems solitary or 2–3 per cluster, to 15 cm (6 in.) tall, the surface obscured by the numerous spines; spines mostly 35–56 per cluster, on projections of the stem (tubercles) up to 12 mm (0.5 in.) long, spines usually white, sometimes the central spines brownish or reddish brown; flowers pink or brownish pink, about 2 cm (0.75 in.) long, not quite as wide; fruits cylindric, about 1 cm (0.4 in.) long. Flowers from May to June.
Known Distribution: Luna County, New Mexico
Habitat: Rocky hillsides, at about 1,525 m (5,000 ft.)
Ownership: Private
Threats to Taxon: The known population is small and therefore is threatened by collectors.
Similar Species: *Coryphantha orcuttii* var. *orcuttii*, which differs in its darker-colored spines and larger fruits
Remarks: All of the pincushion cacti tend to be attractive to cactus enthusiasts and, as a result, are often overcollected. This variety has not been transferred to the genus *Coryphantha*.

Important Literature:
Castetter, Pierce, and Schwerin. A reassessment of the genus *Escobaria*. Cact. and Succ. Jour. 47:60–70; 1975.

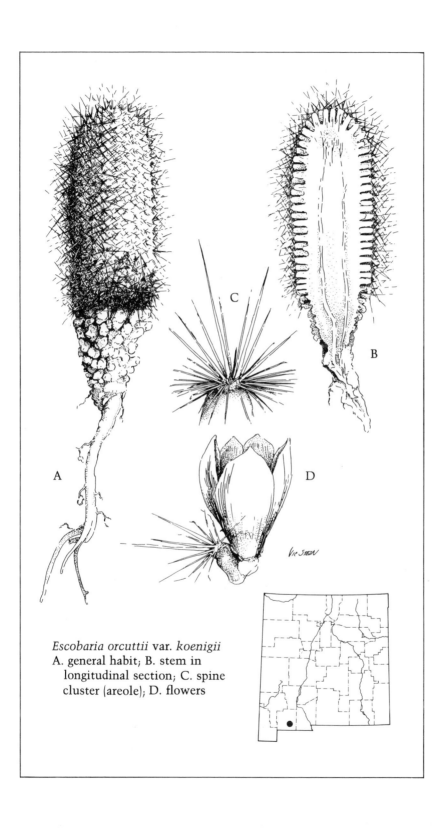

Escobaria orcuttii var. *koenigii*
A. general habit; B. stem in
   longitudinal section; C. spine
   cluster (areole); D. flowers

Family: CACTACEAE
Scientific Name: *Escobaria orcuttii* (Rose *ex.* Orcutt) Boedeker var. *macraxina* Castetter, Pierce, and Schwerin
Common Name: Big hatchet pincushion cactus
Classification: Biologically threatened
Federal Action: None
Common Synonyms: None

Description: Stems solitary or 1–6 per cluster, to about 12 cm (4.8 in.) tall; spines tending to be short and somewhat bristlelike, usually about 40–60 per cluster, those at the base of the stem usually blackish; flowers white to very pale pink, mostly about 2 cm (0.8 in.) or longer, and about as wide; fruits cylindric but tapering to each end, to 2 cm (0.8 in.) long. Probably flowers in May and June.
Known Distribution: Hidalgo County, New Mexico
Habitat: On limestone, at about 2,150 m (7,000 ft.)
Ownership: Private
Threats to Taxon: The only known population of this variety is small and threatened by overcollection.
Similar Species: This variety is distinguished from its relatives by the rather steeply angled spines arranged in at least four series.
Remarks: The taxonomy of this genus is controversial at all levels. Benson (1969, p. 204) considers *C. orcuttii* to be a variety of *C. strobiliformis*. Zimmerman (1972) views the differences between these taxa to be significant enough to separate them into species. This variety has not been transferred to the genus *Coryphantha*.

Important Literature:
Benson, L. The Cacti of Arizona. Tucson: University of Arizona Press; 1969.
Castetter, Pierce, and Schwerin. A reassessment of the genus *Escobaria*. Cact. and Succ. Jour. 47:60–70; 1975.
Zimmerman, D. Comments on certain southwestern *Coryphanthas* of the subgenus Escobaria. Cact. and Succ. Jour. 44:155–58; 1972.

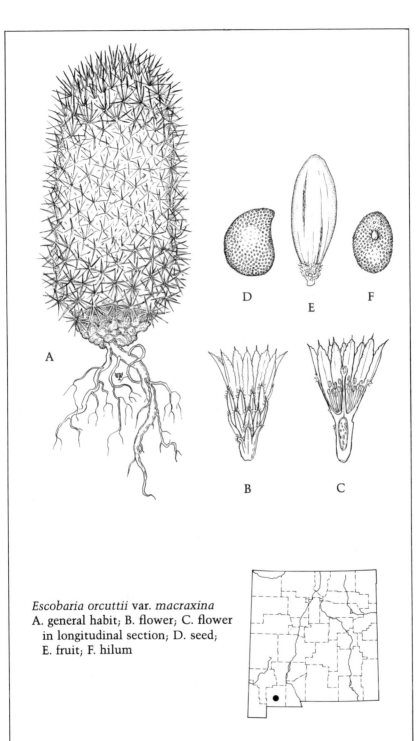

Escobaria orcuttii var. *macraxina*
A. general habit; B. flower; C. flower
   in longitudinal section; D. seed;
   E. fruit; F. hilum

Family: CACTACEAE
Scientific Name: *Escobaria sandbergii* Castetter, Pierce, and Schwerin
Common Name: Sandberg's pincushion cactus
Classification: Biologically threatened
Federal Action: None
Common Synonyms: None

Description: Stems clustered, often 20 or more per cluster, cylindric, densely spiny, to 15 cm (6 in.) tall; spines usually white with reddish brown tips, mostly 29–70 per cluster, usually 10–30 mm (0.38–1.0 in.) long; flowers pink, but usually tinged with violet or purple, mostly 1.5–2.5 cm (0.5–1.0 in.) long and about as wide; fruits cylindric to elliptic, to 2 cm (0.75 in.) long, 6 mm (0.25 in.) in diameter, greenish. Probably flowers in May and June.
Known Distribution: Doña Ana and Sierra counties, New Mexico
Habitat: Rocky hillsides; 1,825–2,275 m (6,000–7,500 ft.)
Ownership: Department of Defense
Threats to Taxon: Its habitat, lying completely within the San Andres Mountains, is closely protected and managed by Department of Defense personnel, and few individuals are allowed to enter the area. There is some danger of inadvertent destruction owing to military-related activities.
Similar Species: *Coryphantha organensis*, *Escobaria sandbergii*, and *E. villardii* form a complex of taxa with great similarities. These entities, in turn, are closely related to *C. strobiliformis*, *C. orcuttii*, *C. sneedii*, and *C. dasyacantha*. Characteristics presently utilized in distinguishing these species overlap sufficiently to preclude clear differentiation.
Remarks: This group requires a complete biological assessment of the taxonomic entities mentioned above and a careful review of the significance of the characters being utilized to distinguish them. It is not sufficiently clear how the first three listed taxa differ from each other, or, for that matter, from the remainder of the species listed above.

Important Literature:
Castetter, Pierce, and Schwerin. A reassessment of the genus *Escobaria*.
  Cact. and Succ. Jour. 47:60–70; 1975.

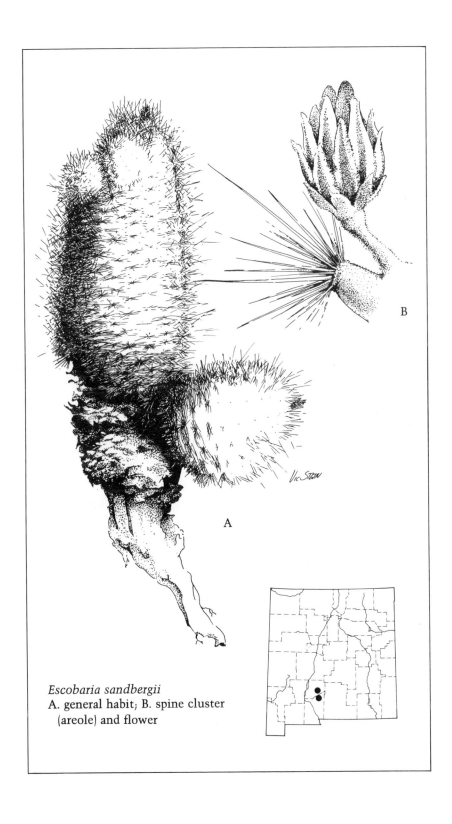

B

A

Escobaria sandbergii
A. general habit; B. spine cluster
   (areole) and flower

Family: CACTACEAE
Scientific Name: *Escobaria villardii* Castetter, Pierce, and Schwerin
Common Name: Villard's pincushion cactus
Classification: Biologically threatened
Federal Action: None
Common Synonyms: None

Description: Stems clustered, somewhat rounded to club shaped, to about 15 cm (6 in.) tall; spines dense, mostly whitish or straw colored except reddish brown at the tip, about 27–57 per cluster, to 20 mm (0.75 in.) long, the central spines longest and much darker than the peripheral ones; flowers pale pink to magenta, about 2–2.5 cm (0.75–1.0 in.) wide, the outer flower parts densely tangled-fringed; fruits cylindric, greenish, 1–2 cm (0.4–0.75 in.) long. Probably flowers in May and June.
Known Distribution: Otero County, New Mexico
Habitat: On limestone; 1,375–1,825 m (4,500–6,000 ft.)
Ownership: Forest Service
Threats to Taxon: Overcollection
Similar Species: *Coryphantha strobiliformis* is similar but does not have the longer, darker central spines. *Coryphantha organensis* has spines with a yellowish cast. (See comments under similar species on *C. sandbergii*.)
Remarks: The tangled-fringed outer perianth parts add to the novelty of this species. This species has not been transferred to the genus *Coryphantha*.

Important Literature:

Castetter, Pierce, and Schwerin. A reassessment of the genus *Escobaria*. Cact. and Succ. Jour. 47:60–70; 1975.

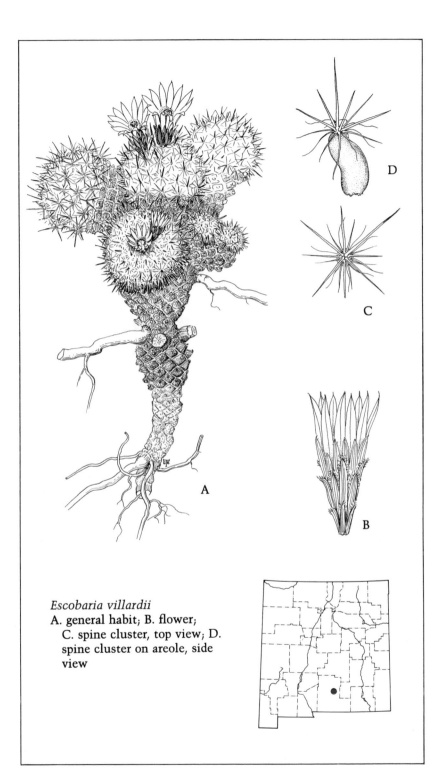

Escobaria villardii
A. general habit; B. flower;
C. spine cluster, top view; D.
spine cluster on areole, side
view

Family: CACTACEAE
Scientific Name: *Ferocactus wislizenii* (Engelm.) Britt.
Common Name: Southwestern barrel cactus
Classification: State priority 1
Federal Action: None
Common Synonyms: *Echinocactus wislizenii* Engelm.

Description: Stems usually solitary, cylindric to ovoid, to 2 m (6.5 ft.) tall, and 60 cm (2 ft.) in diameter, with numerous ribs; spines grayish to reddish, mostly 16–24 per cluster, often flattened, to 5 cm (2 in.) long, the central spines conspicuously transversely ribbed, some hooked at the tip; flowers yellow, 5–6 cm (2.0–2.4 in.) long and about as wide; fruit ovoid, yellowish, scaly. Flowers in June and July.
Known Distribution: Dona Ana, Eddy, Grant, Hidalgo, Lea, Luna, Otero, and Sierra counties, New Mexico, and adjacent Texas, Arizona, and Mexico
Habitat: Rocky, sandy, or gravelly slopes in deserts, grasslands, or canyons; 1,000–1,500 m (3,000–5,000 ft.)
Ownership: Bureau of Land Management, Department of Defense, Forest Service, private, State of New Mexico
Threats to Taxon: Overcollection
Similar Species: *Ferocactus hamatacanthus*, also an overcollected species, is smaller and has more slender spines.
Remarks: Although this cactus has a wide distribution in the Southwest, it is one of the most popular cacti of the region, in high demand for desert landscaping. Areas where it was once common near developing urban areas are now devoid of it.

Important Literature:
Benson, L. The Cactaceae of the United States and Canada. Stanford: Stanford University Press; 1982.

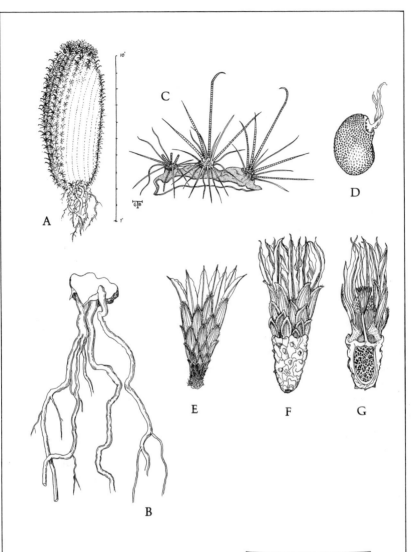

Ferocactus wislizenii
A. general habit; B. root; C. spine
  cluster (areole); D. seed; E. flower;
  F. early fruit; G. mature fruit

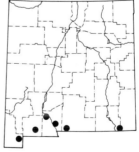

Family: CACTACEAE
Scientific Name: *Mammillaria wrightii* Engelm. var. *wilcoxii* (Toumey *ex.* Schumann) W. T. Marshall
Common Name: Wilcox's pincushion cactus
Classification: State priority 1
Federal Action: None
Common Synonyms: *Neomammillaria wilcoxii* Britt. & Rose
Chilita wilcoxii Orcutt.
Ebernella wilcoxii F. Buxbaum
Mammillaria wilcoxii Toumey

Description: Stems solitary, globose to turbinate, to about 10 cm (4 in.) tall and 5 cm (2 in.) wide; tubercles mostly 10–20 mm (0.4–0.75 in.) long; spines 10–15, 1–5 central spines, hooked, reddish brown, as many as 30 radial spines, tan or gray, spreading, straight, to about 1 cm (0.4 in.) long; flowers mostly 2–4 cm (0.75–1.5 in.) long, about 2–5 cm (0.75–1.5 in.) wide, broadly bell shaped, the petaloid parts pink to purple; fruit subglobose to ovoid, 1–2 cm (0.4–0.75 in.) long, to 15 mm (0.6 in.) in diameter. Flowers from August to October.
Known Distribution: Grant and Hidalgo counties, New Mexico, and adjacent Arizona and Mexico
Habitat: Rocky or gravelly slopes and canyons; 925–1,525 m (3,000–5,000 ft.)
Ownership: Bureau of Land Managment, Forest Service, private
Threats to Taxon: Overcollection
Similar Species: *Mammillaria viridiflora* is quite similar but has smaller flowers which are either dusky pink or green.
Remarks: Until recently, there was some question to the validity of var. *wilcoxii* and its relationship to *M. wrightii*. However, extensive fieldwork by Dale and Allan Zimmerman indicates that *M. wilcoxii* should be maintained as a variety of *M. wrightii*.

Important Literature:
Benson, L. Lectotype or neotype designation for *Mammillaria wilcoxii* Cact. and Succ. Jour. 48:34–35; 1977.
Benson, L. The Cactaceae of the United States and Canada. Stanford: Stanford University Press; 1982.

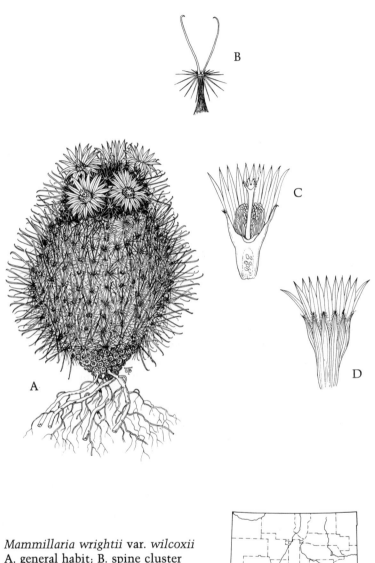

Mammillaria wrightii var. *wilcoxii*
A. general habit; B. spine cluster
(areole); C. flower in longtitudinal
section; D. flower

Family: CACTACEAE
Scientific Name: *Mammillaria wrightii* Engelm. var. *wrightii*
Common Name: Wright's pincushion cactus
Classification: Biologically threatened
Federal Action: None
Common Synonyms: *Ebnerella wrightii* F. Buxbaum
Neomammillaria wrightii Britt. & Rose
Chilita wrightii Orcutt.

Description: Stems solitary, to about 10 cm (4 in.) tall and 5 cm (2 in.)
wide; spines 10–15 per cluster, the outer spines tan or gray, the central
ones reddish brown and hooked, 10–12 mm (0.4–0.5 in.) long; flowers
pink to purple or tinged with white or yellow, mostly 2.5–5.0 cm (1–2
in.) long and somewhat wider than long; fruit rounded to ovoid, rust red.
Flowers from May through August.
Known Distribution: Bernalillo, Catron, Doña Ana, Guadalupe, Lincoln,
McKinley, Sandoval, Santa Fe, Socorro, Torrance, and Valencia counties,
New Mexico, and adjacent Texas and Arizona
Habitat: Gravelly hills or sandy hills or plains, desert grassland to
pinyon-juniper; 900–2,100 m (3,000–7,000 ft.)
Ownership: Bureau of Land Management, Forest Service, private
Threats to Taxon: This taxon has a wide, sporadic distribution and is
probably not in immediate danger. However, a number of populations are
in decline, owing to overcollection and habitat alteration.
Similar Species: *Mammillaria viridflora*, which is distinguished by its
smaller dusky pink or green flowers
Remarks: This species is very cryptic, and at one time was thought to be
extinct in New Mexico. However, recent fieldwork has revealed far more
populations than previously believed.

Important Literature:
Benson, L. The Cactaceae of the United States. Stanford: Stanford
    University Press; 1982.
Zimmerman, Allan D., and Dale A. Zimmerman. A revision of the
    United States taxa of the *M. wrightii* complex with remarks on the
    northern Mexico populations. Cact. and Succ. Jour. 49:23–35; 1977.

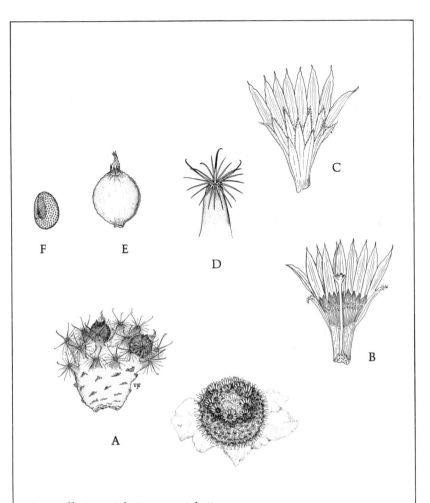

Mammillaria wrightii var. *wrightii*
A. general habit; B. flower in longitudinal section; C. flower; D. spine
cluster (areole); E. fruit; F. seed

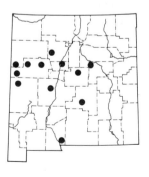

Family: CACTACEAE
Scientific Name: *Mammillaria viridiflora* (Britt. & Rose) Boedeker
Common Name: Green-flowered pincushion cactus
Classification: Biologically threatened
Federal Action: Federal Register, 15 December 1980, candidate for federal protection
Common Synonyms: *Mammillaria chavezei* Cowper
Mammillaria orestera L. Benson
Mammillaria wilcoxii var. *viridiflora* Britt. & Rose

Description: Stems solitary, rounded to ovoid, to about 10 cm (4 in.) high and 7 cm (2.75 in.) in diameter, the surface usually nearly obscured by spines; spines at least 16–25 per cluster, light tan to reddish brown, the outer spines in a cluster spreading nearly parallel to the stem, the inner or central spines erect, and at least one of them hooked; flowers greenish, sometimes striped with pink, or pale pinkish, usually 1.5–2.5 cm (0.5–1.0 in.) wide; fruits nearly globose to oblong, 10–20 mm (0.4–0.75 in.) long. Flowers in June and July.
Known Distribution: Dry slopes in arid grasslands or along margins of deserts; 1,375–1,975 m (4,500–6,500 ft.)
Ownership: Bureau of Land Management, Forest Service, private
Threats to Taxon: Overcollection
Similar Species: *Mammillaria wrightii* var. *wilcoxii*, which can be distinguished by its larger, more intensely colored flowers.
Remarks: Although this species has often been considered conspecific with *M. wrightii* var. *wilcoxii*, recent studies by Allan and Dale Zimmerman indicate that hybridization between *M. wrightii* and *M. viridiflora* does not occur; therefore, each must be considered as separate entities.

Important Literature:
Zimmerman, Allan D., and Dale A. Zimmerman. A revision of the *M. wrightii* complex with remarks on the northern Mexico populations. Cact. and Succ. Jour. 49:23–35, 51–62; 1977.
Zimmerman, Dale A. *Mammillaria orestera* Benson in New Mexico. Cact. and Succ. Jour. 48:113–15; 1975.

106

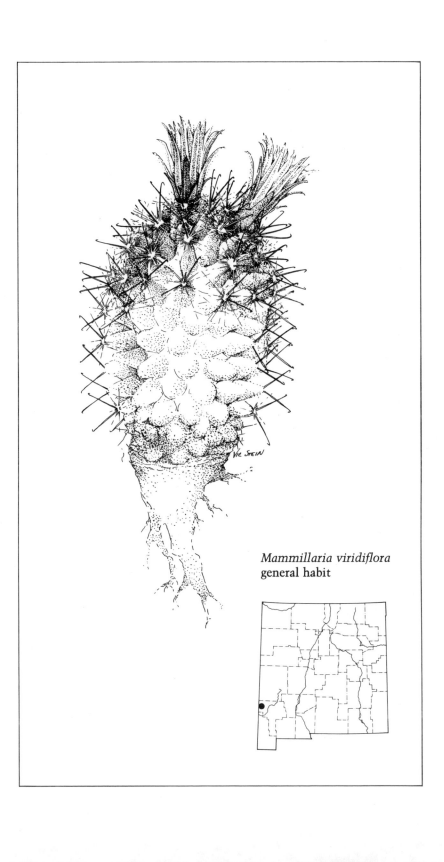

Mammillaria viridiflora
general habit

Family: CACTACEAE
Scientific Name: *Opuntia arenaria* Engelm.
Common Name: Sand prickly pear
Classification: Biologically threatened
Federal Action: Federal Register, 15 December 1980, candidate for federal protection
Common Synonyms: None

Description: Stems jointed, less than 30 cm (12 in.) high but forming clumps up to 1.5 m (4.9 ft.) broad, bearing roots with clusters of tiny spines; joints broadest above the middle, tapering to the base, or sometimes elliptic or ovate, to 8 cm (3 in.) long and 2–3 cm (0.8–1.0 in.) wide, and at least half as thick as wide; 5–7 spines per cluster, mostly white or gray or tinged with red, to about 30 mm (1.2 in.) long; flowers yellow, 4–6 cm (1.5–2.4 in.) wide; fruit green, broadly club shaped, bearing whitish spines. Flowers in May and June.
Known Distribution: Doña Ana County, New Mexico, and adjacent Texas and Mexico
Habitat: On and among sandy dunes, or on sandy floodplains in arroyos, at about 1,160 m (3,600 ft.)
Ownership: Bureau of Land Management, private
Threats to Taxon: Some populations have been lost to urban development, and others are threatened. Collectors also have reduced some populations to near extinction.
Similar Species: *Opuntia polyacantha*, in general, has larger stem joints, which are relatively thinner, rarely more than one-fourth as thick as wide.
Remarks: The digging of plants by collectors is unfortunate and unnecessary, as plants will readily root and grow rapidly from detached stems.

Important Literature:
Correll and Johnston. Manual of the vascular plants of Texas. Renner, Tex.: Texas Research Foundation; 1970.

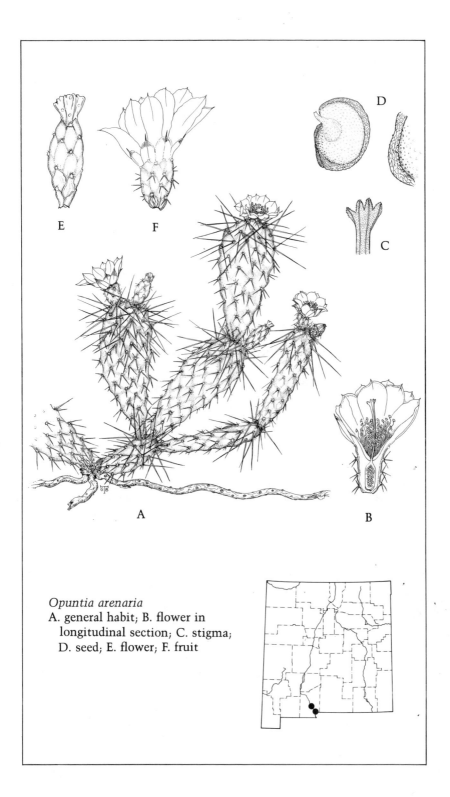

Opuntia arenaria
A. general habit; B. flower in
  longitudinal section; C. stigma;
  D. seed; E. flower; F. fruit

Family: CACTACEAE
Scientific Name: *Opuntia clavata* Engelm.
Common Name: Dagger-thorn cholla
Classification: State priority 1
Federal Action: None
Common Synonyms: None

Description: Low mat-forming cholla, usually not more than 10 cm (4 in.) tall, forming clumps up to 1 m (39 in.) in diameter; the stems composed of numerous club-shaped joints, each about 4–5 cm (1.6–2.0 in.) long, and about 2.5 cm (1 in.) wide; the tubercles large, up to 12 mm (0.5 in.) long, each bearing a cluster of 10–20 conspicuous white spines, the largest of these up to 2.5 cm (1 in.) and conspicuously daggerlike; flowers yellowish green, 3–5 cm (1.2–2.0 in.) wide and about 5 cm (2 in.) long; fruit yellow, up to 4 cm (1.6 in.) long, fleshy, smooth, covered with minute yellow to tan-colored spines (glochids); seeds yellow, about 5 mm (0.2 in.) long. Flowers in June.
Known Distribution: Bernalillo, Cibola, Doña Ana, Guadalupe, Lincoln, Otero, Rio Arriba, Sandoval, San Miguel, Santa Fe, Socorro, Torrance, and Valencia counties, New Mexico
Habitat: Sandy soils of valleys and grassland; 1,800–2,400 m (6,000–8,000 ft.)
Ownership: Bureau of Indian Affairs, Bureau of Land Management, Department of Defense, Fish and Wildlife Service, Forest Service, private, State of New Mexico
Threats to Taxon: None known
Similar Species: None very similar in its range
Remarks: This is an unusual species in that it is exceedingly common in the Rio Grande Valley and adjacent drainages, but it has not been documented outside of New Mexico.

Important Literature:
Benson, L. The Cactaceae of the United States and Canada. Stanford: Stanford University Press; 1982.

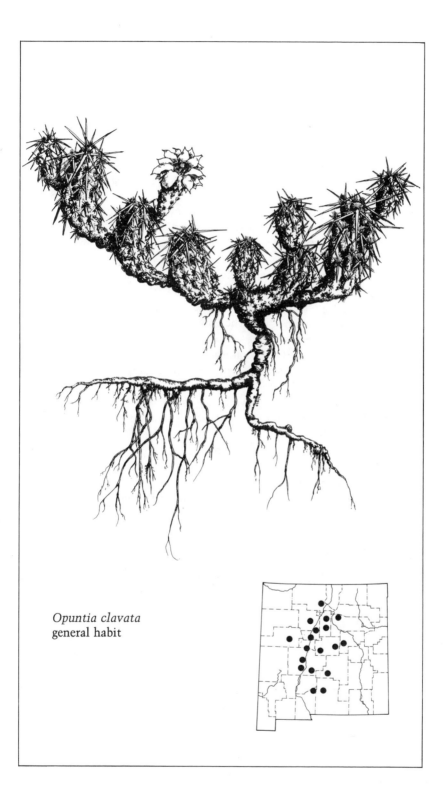

Opuntia clavata
general habit

Family: CACTACEAE
Scientific Name: *Opuntia viridiflora* Britt. & Rose
Common Name: Santa Fe cholla
Classification: Biologically threatened
Federal Action: None
Common Synonyms: *Opuntia whipplei* Engelm. & Bigel. var. *viridiflora*
(Britt. & Rose) L. Benson
Opuntia arborescens var. *viridiflora* (Britt. & Rose) Weniger

Description: Low-growing, much-branched shrub; stems cylindric, 30–
100 cm (1–3 ft.) tall, joints of the current year 1.5–2.0 cm (0.4–0.75 in.)
in diameter; spines variable in number, spreading, brownish, sheathed;
areoles circular or oval, with gray or yellow wool; flowers 2.5–5.0 cm (1–
2 in.) in diameter, not opening widely; perianth parts coral pink within,
greenish or yellowish on the outside; stamens with green filaments and
yellow anthers; stigmas with eight or nine lobes; fruits usually less than
2.5 cm (1 in.) in diameter, spiny when young, becoming naked at
maturity. Flowers in early July.
Known Distribution: Santa Fe County, New Mexico
Habitat: South- and west-facing slopes in pinyon-juniper at about 2,200
m (7,200 ft.)
Ownership: City of Santa Fe, private
Threats to Taxon: The Santa Fe population is in an urban area. The most
immediate possibilities for destruction appear to be road construction,
vandalism, and expansion of the city park.
Similar Species: *Opuntia davisii* has longer spines (up to 2 inches long)
and longer tubercles (up to 1 inch long), and differs in its mat-forming
nature, its conspicuously shiny spine sheaths, and its greenish stigmas.
Remarks: It has long been suspected that *O. viridiflora* is a hybrid of *O.
imbricata* and some other cylindopuntia. The most likely candidates for
such a hybrid are *O. davisii*, *O. whipplei*, and *O. imbricata*. There is also
speculation that *O. viridiflora* may be sterile, reproducing only be
vegetative means. Both of these theories need to be tested by future
researchers.

Important Literature:
Benson, L. The Cactaceae of the United States and Canada. Stanford:
    Stanford University Press; 1982.
Britton, N. L., and J. N. Rose. The Cactaceae. Carnegie Institute of
    Washington, Pub. No. 248; 1963.

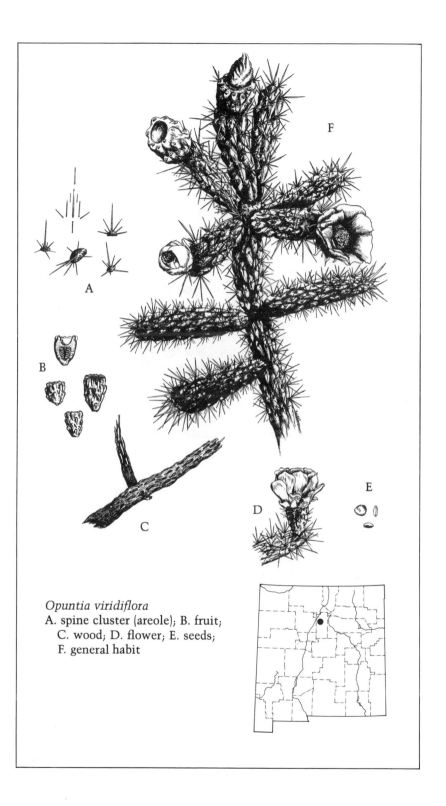

Opuntia viridiflora
A. spine cluster (areole); B. fruit;
   C. wood; D. flower; E. seeds;
   F. general habit

Family: CACTACEAE
Scientific Name: *Pediocactus knowltonii* L. Benson
Common Name: Knowlton's cactus
Classification: Biologically endangered
Federal Action: Federal Register, 29 October 1979, federally endangered
Common Synonyms: None

Description: Stems inconspicuous, solitary or clustered, to 3 cm (1.25 in.) tall and 2 cm (0.75 in.) in diameter; about 20 spines per cluster, to about 1.4 mm (0.6 in.) long, inconspicuous; flowers pink, about 2 cm (0.75 in.) wide when fully open; fruit green to light brown. Flowers in April and May.
Known Distribution: San Juan County, New Mexico, and possibly adjacent Colorado
Habitat: Alluvial hills; 1,800–2,000 m (6,000–6,500 ft.)
Ownership: Bureau of Land Management, private
Threats to Taxon: Poaching by collectors, gas exploration and development, wood cutting with related road use and habitat alteration.
Similar Species: No similar-looking species occur in the general area. Some of the *Pediocacti* are very small, but these either have central spines and/or longer radial spines.
Remarks: This species has been reduced to near extinction in the wild because of persistent collecting during the past 20 years. Plants are very small and shrink into the ground during dormant periods, becoming difficult to find.

Important Literature:

Benson, L. A new *Pediocactus*. Cact. and Succ. Jour. 32:193; 1960.
Benson, L. A revision of *Pediocactus* I. Cact. and Succ. Jour. 33:49–54; 1961.
Benson, L. A revision of *Pediocactus* II. Cact. and Succ. Jour. 34:17–19; 1962.
Benson, L. A revision of *Pediocactus* IV. Cact. and Succ. Jour. 34:163–68; 1962.

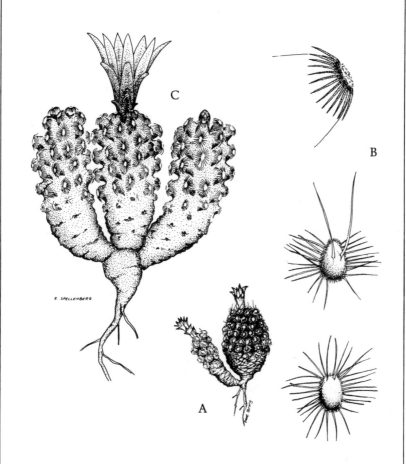

R. SPELLENBERG

Pediocactus knowltonii
A. general habit; B. spine cluster
(areole); C. growth habit and flower

Family: CACTACEAE
Scientific Name: *Sclerocactus mesae-verdae* L. Benson
Common Name: Mesa Verde cactus
Classification: Biologically threatened
Federal Action: Federal Register, 30 October 1979, federally threatened
Common Synonyms: *Coloradoa mesae-verdae* Boiss., *Echinocactus mesae-verdae* L. Benson

Description: Stems solitary or in clusters, about 6 cm (2.4 in.) high, globose; ribs 13–17, continuous, in a spiral or nearly vertical; spines 8–10 per cluster, about 10 mm (0.4 in.) long; central spines absent; flowers vertical or nearly so, developing from just above an immature spine-producing areole at apex of stem, to 3.5 cm (1.25 in.) long; petaloid parts yellow to greenish white, the outer parts brownish; base of flower naked or with a few scales; fruits smooth; seeds large, about 4 mm (0.16 in.) long, black. Flowers from March to November.
Known Distribution: San Juan County, New Mexico, and adjacent Colorado
Habitat: Barren Mancos shale and at least one place on Fruitland clay badlands; 1,200–1,600 m (4,000–5,300 ft.)
Ownership: Bureau of Land Management, Navajo Indian Reservation, private
Threats to Taxon: Poaching by collectors, recreational use of the badlands with off-road vehicles, urbanization of the habitat, rangeland development for cattle grazing, and coal mining. A moth larva has been noted to attack and kill numerous individual cacti.
Similar Species: *Sclerocactus parviflorus* (*S. whipplei* of manuals for the area) is the most similar and grows in the same area. Unlike *S. mesae-verdae*, it has a strong, hooked central spine and pinkish purple flowers.
Remarks: Species that grow on severe habitats, such as these shale formations, ordinarily withstand little disturbance. It is reported in the literature that *S. mesae-verdae* does not transplant well.

Important Literature:
Benson, L. A revision of *Sclerocactus*. Cact. and Succ. Jour. 38:50–57; 1966.
Bolssevain and Davidson. Colorado Cacti. Pasadena: Abbey Garden Press; 1940.
Gray, E., and B. Gray. A cactophiles guide to the Four Corners. Cact. and Succ. Jour. 39:67–78; 1967.

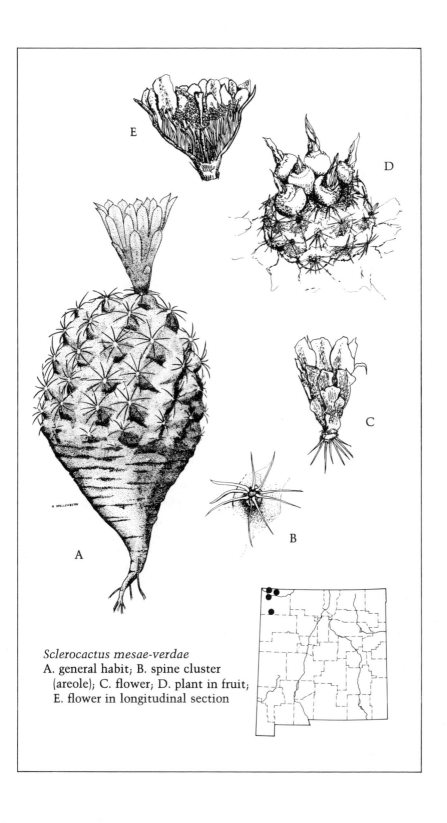

Sclerocactus mesae-verdae
A. general habit; B. spine cluster
   (areole); C. flower; D. plant in fruit;
   E. flower in longitudinal section

Family: CACTACEAE
Scientific Name: *Sclerocactus whipplei* (Engelm. & Bigel.) Britt. & Rose
var. *heilii* Castetter, Pierce, and Schwerin
var. *reevesii* Castetter, Pierce, and Schwerin
Common Name: Hard wall cactus
Classification: Biologically endangered
Federal Action: Federal Register, 15 December 1980, candidate for federal protection
Common Synonyms: None

Description: Var. *heilii*—stems cylindrical, usually not clustered, to 17.5 cm (7 in.) tall and 5–6 cm (2.0–2.4 in.) wide, prominently ribbed; radial spines smooth, straight or curved, numerous, at least some of them light brown or straw-colored and brown-tipped, central spines 8–9, nearly white above and darker on the lower surface; flowers purplish, funnel shaped; fruits usually pear shaped, 1–2 cm (0.4–0.75 in.) long. Flowers in May.
Var. *reevesii* differs from the above description by having 6–9 central spines and by being more massive in stature, up to 35 cm (14 in.) tall. Flowers in May.
Known Distribution: San Juan County, New Mexico
Habitat: Gravelly or sandy ground, often in pinyon-juniper association; 1,525–2,125 m (5,000–7,000 ft.)
Ownership: Bureau of Land Management
Threats to Taxon: Overcollection
Similar Species: *Sclerocactus whipplei* var. *intermedius* from which it is almost indistinguishable
Remarks: There is some doubt as to the validity of these varieties. It appears that *S. whipplei* is a highly variable species that takes many forms throughout its range. A more careful study needs to be undertaken to establish the relationships between all members of the genus *Sclerocactus* in New Mexico. In Lyman Benson's most recent work, *The Cactaceae of the United States and Canada,* he places all elements of *S. whipplei* in New Mexico under *S. parviflorus.*

Important Literature:
Castetter, Pierce, and Schwerin. A new cactus species and two new
    varieties from New Mexico. Cact. and Succ. Jour. 48:77–82; 1976.
Clover, E. U., and L. Jotter. Cacti of the canyon of the Colorado River and
    tributaries. Bull. Torr. Bot. Club 68:419; 1941.

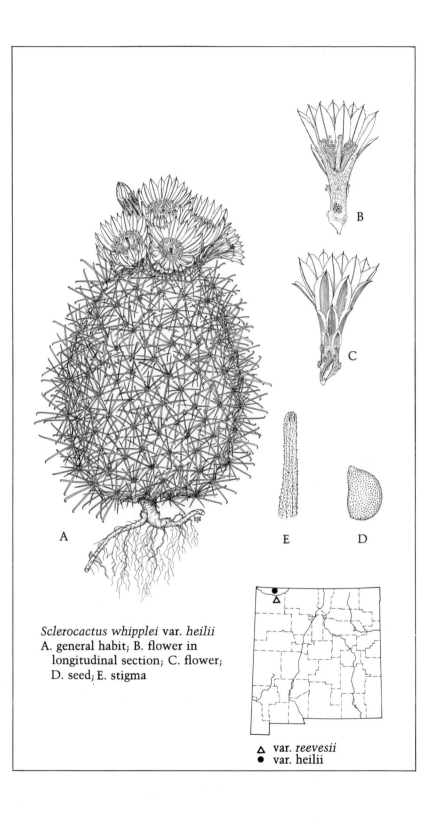

Sclerocactus whipplei var. *heilii*
A. general habit; B. flower in
longitudinal section; C. flower;
D. seed; E. stigma

△ var. *reevesii*
● var. heilii

Family: CACTACEAE
Scientific Name: *Toumeya papyracantha* (Engelm.) Britt. & Rose
Common Name: Grama grass cactus
Classification: Biologically threatened
Federal Action: Federal Register, 15 December 1980, candidate for federal protection
Common Synonyms: *Mammillaria papyracantha* Engelmann
Echinocactus papyracanthus Engelmann
Pediocactus papyracanthus (Engelm.) L. Benson

Description: Stems solitary, ribbed, 2.5–20 cm (1–8 in.) tall; central spines elongate, flexible, grooved, flattened, resembling dry grass blades; radial spines short, straight; flowers white, not spreading widely when open; fruit round, tan, dry when mature, up to 18 mm (0.75 in.) long. Flowers from April to June.
Known Distribution: Bernalillo, Cibola, Doña Ana, Grant, Los Alamos, Otero, Rio Arriba, Sandoval, Santa Fe, Socorro, Torrance, and Valencia counties, New Mexico, and adjacent Arizona
Habitat: Grama grass and galleta grasslands, usually where soil is sandy, rarely on gypseous soils; 1,525–2,225 m (5,000–7,300 ft.)
Ownership: Bureau of Land Management, Department of Defense, Forest Service, private, State of New Mexico
Threats to Taxon: Overcollection, overgrazing, and destruction of habitat by urbanization are the major threats to this species.
Similar Species: No other species in this area is similar.
Remarks: This cactus was probably, at one time, quite abundant in central New Mexico. However, degradation of rangeland and overgrazing have sharply reduced the abundance of this species throughout its range. *Toumeya* is preferred over *Pediocactus* as *T. papyracantha* seems discordant in the genus *Pediocactus*.

Important Literature:
Benson, L. A revision and amplification of *Pediocactus* II. Cact. and Succ. Jour. 35:57–61; 1962.
Benson, L. The Cactaceae of the United States and Canada. Stanford: Stanford University Press; 1982.

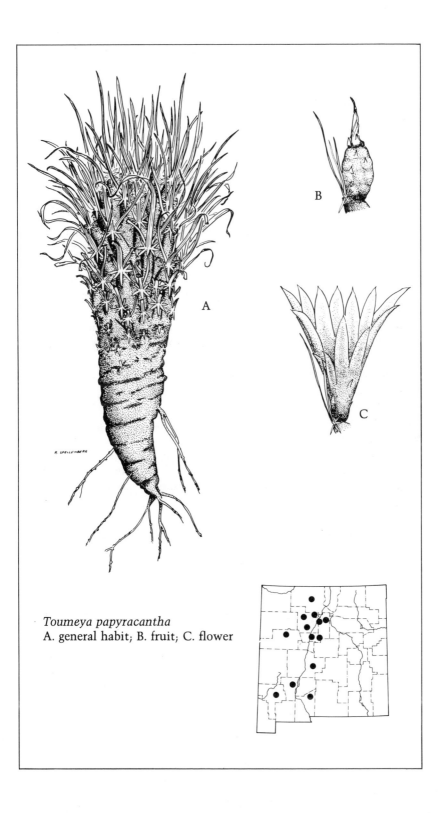

Toumeya papyracantha
A. general habit; B. fruit; C. flower

Family: CAPPARIDACEAE
Scientific Name: *Cleome multicaulis* DC.
Common Name: Slender spiderflower
Classification: State priority 1
Federal Action: Federal Register, 15 December 1980, candidate for federal protection
Common Synonyms: *Cleome sonorae* Gray
Peritoma sonorae (Gray) Rydb.

Description: Plants annual, the stems slender, erect, to about 60 cm (24 in.) tall; leaves sessile or with short stalks, compound, the leaflets digitately arranged, slender, folded, 1–2 cm (0.4–0.75 in.) long; flowers in the axils of the stem leaves, the petals pink or white, 4–6 mm (to 0.25 in.) long; pods elongate, to about 20 mm (8 in.) long and 4 mm (0.12 in.) wide, smooth, circular in cross section, bent abruptly downward. Flowers in August and September.
Known Distribution: Grant County, New Mexico; south-central Colorado to southeastern Arizona, western Texas, and Mexico; 1,200–2,100 m (4,000–7,000 ft.)
Habitat: Saline or alkaline soils, often in and around alkali sinks, or in alkaline meadows or old lake beds
Ownership: Private
Threats to Taxon: None known
Similar Species: None
Remarks: The species is known in New Mexico from only one collection made in 1851 and may be extinct in the state. Extensive use of mesic, alkaline land may have altered much of its formerly suitable habitat.

Important Literature:
Iltis, H. Studies in the Capparidaceae V. Capparideaceae of New Mexico. Southw. Nat. 3:133–44; 1958.

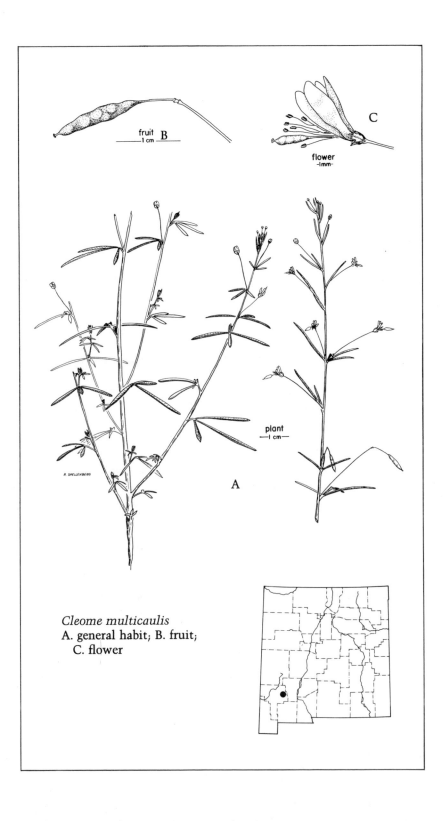

fruit B
— 1 cm —

flower
-1mm-

C

plant
— 1 cm —

A

R. SPELLENBERG

Cleome multicaulis
A. general habit; B. fruit;
C. flower

Family: CARYOPHYLLACEAE
Scientific Name: *Silene plankii* Hitchc. & Maguire
Common Name: Plank's catchfly
Classification: State priority 1
Federal Action: Federal Register, 15 December 1980, candidate for federal protection
Common Synonyms: None

Description: Low, clumped perennial from a woody rootstock; 10–15 cm (4–6 in.) tall, finely hairy, glandular, and sticky near the flowers; stem leaves in 5–8 pairs, linear to narrowly lance shaped 1.5–2.5 cm (0.5–1.0 in.) long; flowers few, scarlet, to 2.5 cm (1 in.) long, petals united, forming a tubular base, the three petal ties spreading at right angles to the tube; 10 stamens; fruit a capsule. Flowers from July to September.
Known Distribution: Bernalillo, Doña Ana, Sandoval, Sierra, and Socorro counties, New Mexico, and adjacent Texas
Habitat: Crevices and pockets in protected cliff faces of igneous rock; 1,500–2,000 m (5,000–6,500 ft.)
Ownership: Bureau of Land Management, Department of Defense, Forest Service, private
Threats to Taxon: Browsed by bighorn sheep
Similar Species: It is most similar to *S. laciniata*, but differs in having fringed petals, not merely notched ones.
Remarks: Plank collected this species in 1895, probably near Socorro Peak. However, this species was not described until 1947. It was not collected again until 1965 in the Franklin Mountains of Texas. Since that time, it has been found in several locations in the mountains along the Rio Grande Valley.

Important Literature:
Correll, D. S. Some additions and corrections to the flora of Texas. Brittonia. 18:309; 1966.
Hitchcock, C. L., and B. Maguire. A revision of the North American species of *Silene*. Univ. Washington Pub. Biol. 13:1–73; 1947.

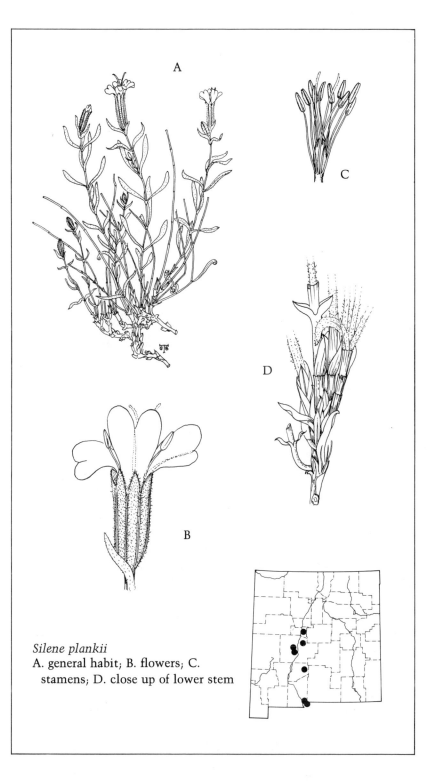

Silene plankii
A. general habit; B. flowers; C.
  stamens; D. close up of lower stem

Family: CARYOPHYLLACEAE
Scientific Name: *Silene wrightii* Gray
Common Name: Wright's catchfly
Classification: State priority 1
Federal Action: Federal Register, 15 December 1980, candidate for federal protection
Common Synonyms: None

Description: Perennial with several stems from a thick woody base, 10–70 cm (4–28 in.) tall; herbage densely glandular and sticky throughout, marked by a pungent odor; stems leafy; leaves lance shaped, 3–6 cm (1.25–2.4 in.) long, 4–14 mm (0.25–0.4 in.) wide; calyx tubular, 16–20 mm (0.4–0.85 in.) long, with five pointed teeth at the summit; flowers united into a tube with five white to pinkish petal lobes, each lobe cleft into several pointed segments; fruit a capsule. Flowers from July to September.
Known Distribution: Catron, Grant, Luna, Socorro, and Sierra counties, New Mexico
Habitat: Ledges and cracks of cliff faces, rarely on boulders; 1,950–2,880 m (6,400–9,600 ft.)
Ownership: Forest Service, private
Threats to Taxon: Mining is a threat to this taxon in the Mogollon Mountains. However, this plant is sufficiently widespread and abundant that its continued existence is not in jeopardy.
Similar Species: None
Remarks: This taxon was once thought to be extremely rare and restricted to the Mogollon Mountains. Since the summer of 1981, field investigators in the San Mateo Mountains have located extensive populations.

Important Literature:
Hitchcock, C. L., and B. Maguire. A revision of the North American species of *Silene.* Univ. Washington Pub. Biol. 13:1–73; 1947.
Spellenberg, R. Status report on *Silene wrightii.* U.S. Fish and Wildlife Service; 1981.

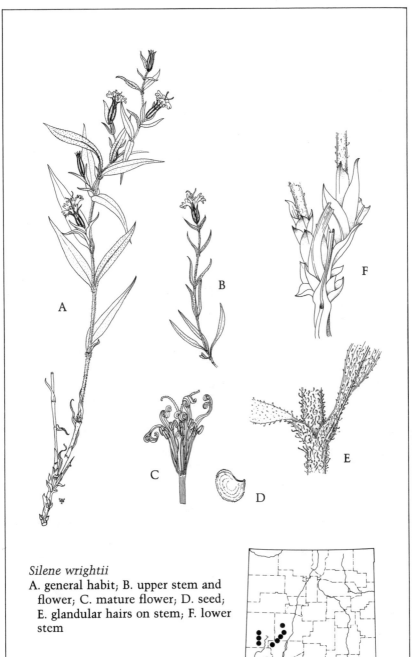

Silene wrightii
A. general habit; B. upper stem and
flower; C. mature flower; D. seed;
E. glandular hairs on stem; F. lower
stem

Family: CHENOPODIACEAE
Scientific Name: *Atriplex griffithsii* Standl.
Common Name: Griffith's saltbush
Classification: State priority 1
Federal Action: Federal Register, 15 December 1980, removed from consideration for federal protection
Common Synonyms: *Atriplex lentiformis* (Torr.) Wats. var. *griffithsii* (Standl.) L. Benson
Atriplex torreyi Wats. var. *griffithsii* (Standl.) Brown

Description: Shrub 30–100 cm (12–39 in.) tall, bark rough and gray on older stems; leaves alternate, short-stalked or stalkless, elliptic-ovate to narrowly oblong, 0.9–2.0 cm (0.35–0.8 in.) long, 0.3–1.2 cm (0.1–0.5 in.) wide, margins mostly entire; male and female flowers without petals, greenish, tiny, inconspicuous, on separate plants; fruiting bracts stalkless, heart shaped to kidney shaped 4–5 mm (0.2 in.) long and slightly wider. Flowers August and September, possibly later.
Known Distribution: Hidalgo and Luna counties, New Mexico, and adjacent Arizona
Habitat: Dry lakebeds, at about 1,280 m (4,200 ft.)
Ownership: Bureau of Land Management, State of New Mexico, private
Threats to Taxon: Farming and livestock use
Similar Species: The only other woody atriplex with similar habitat is the widespread *Atriplex canescens*. It has fruiting bracts with four well-developed wings.
Remarks: This species is common over almost 20,000 acres of dry lakebeds in southwest New Mexico but is otherwise known only from Wilcox Playa in adjacent Arizona.

Important Literature:
Wagner, W. L., and E. F. Aldan. Manual of the saltbushes (*Atriplex* ssp.) in New Mexico. Rocky Mt. Forest and Range Exp. Station, USDA, FS.

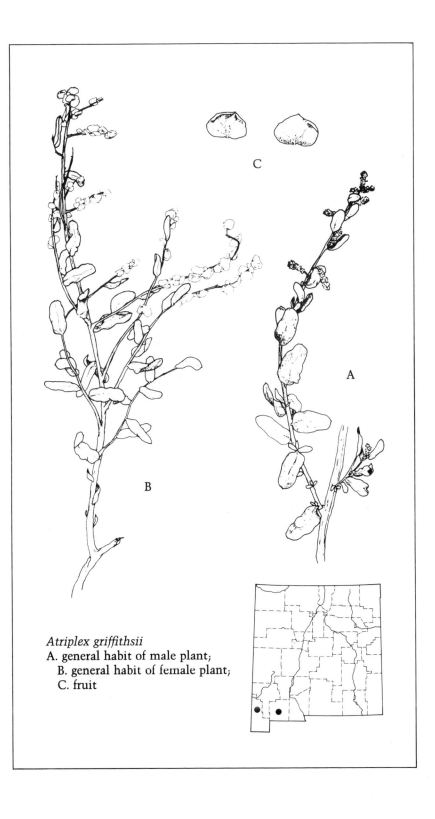

Atriplex griffithsii
A. general habit of male plant;
  B. general habit of female plant;
  C. fruit

Family: COMMELINACEAE
Scientific Name: *Tradescantia wrightii* Rose & Bush
Common Name: Wright's spiderlily
Classification: State priority 1
Federal Action: Federal Register, 15 December 1980, removed from consideration for federal protection
Common Synonyms: None

Description: Perennial; stems unbranched, erect, glabrous, to about 20 cm (8 in.) tall; leaves glabrous or nearly so, narrowly lance shaped, to about 10 cm (4 in.) long, elongate, tapering at the tip; flowers in loose terminal clusters, the clusters solitary at the apex of each stem and with leaflike bracts at the base; flowers rose-pink to purple, the petals about 10 mm (0.4 in.) long; fruit a capsule, 3–4 mm (0.04–0.15 in.) long. Flowers from June to September.
Known Distribution: Eddy, Lincoln, Otero, Socorro, and Torrance counties, New Mexico, and adjacent Texas
Habitat: Ledges, moist canyons, streambanks, usually on limestone substrate; 1,050–1,500 m (3,500–5,000 ft.)
Ownership: Bureau of Land Management, Forest Service
Threats to Taxon: The populations in New Mexico are small, local, and frequently grazed by rabbits.
Similar Species: *Tradescantia occidentale* differs from *T. wrightii* in having branching stems.
Remarks: The above-ground presence of this fleshy rooted perennial is dependent upon seasonal moisture.

Important Literature:

Anderson, E., and R. Woodson. The species of *Tradescantia* indigenous to the United States. Contr. Arn. Arb. 9:1–132; 1935.

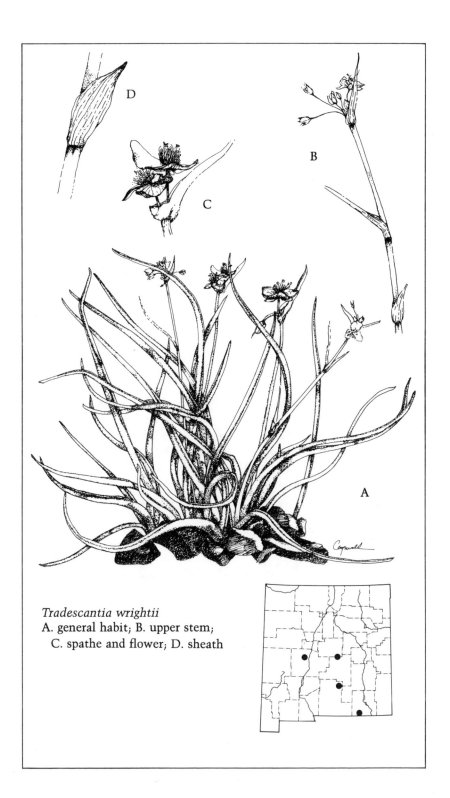

Tradescantia wrightii
A. general habit; B. upper stem;
C. spathe and flower; D. sheath

Family: CROSSOSOMATACEAE
Scientific Name: *Apacheria chiricahuensis* Mason
Common Name: Cliff brittlebush
Classification: State priority 1
Federal Action: Federal Register, 15 December 1980, candidate for federal protection
Common Synonyms: None

Description: Perennial, low-growing shrub up to 50 cm (20 in.) long, usually growing flat against cliff faces; leaves oblanceolate to spoon shaped, opposite, sometimes with three teeth at the apex, leaves usually 3.5–7.5 mm (0.14–0.3 in.) long, 1.0–2.3 mm (0.04–0.09 in.) wide; flowers white, the four petals 4–5 mm (0.16–0.2 in.) long, four sepals, 3.0–3.5 mm (0.12–0.13 in.) long, eight stamens; fruit with one or two minutely bumpy seeds 1.5 mm (0.6 in.) long. Flowers May through October.
Known Distribution: Sierra and Socorro counties, New Mexico, and the Chiricahua and Dragoon mountains of Arizona
Habitat: Crevices in cliff faces of rhyolitic rock; 1,785–2,460 m (5,800–8,000 ft.)
Ownership: Forest Service, National Park Service
Threats to Taxon: None known
Similar Species: *Fendlerella utahensis* may be mistaken for *Apacheria* but is distinguished by its erect growth form (up to 1 m tall).
Remarks: This genus with its single species was described from a few isolated spots in the Chiricahua Mountains of Arizona in 1975. In 1981–82, it was discovered in the San Mateo Mountains and in the Black Range of central New Mexico.

Important Literature:
Mason, C. T. *Apacheria chiricahuensis:* a new genus and species from Arizona. Madroño, 23(3):105–8; 1975.

132

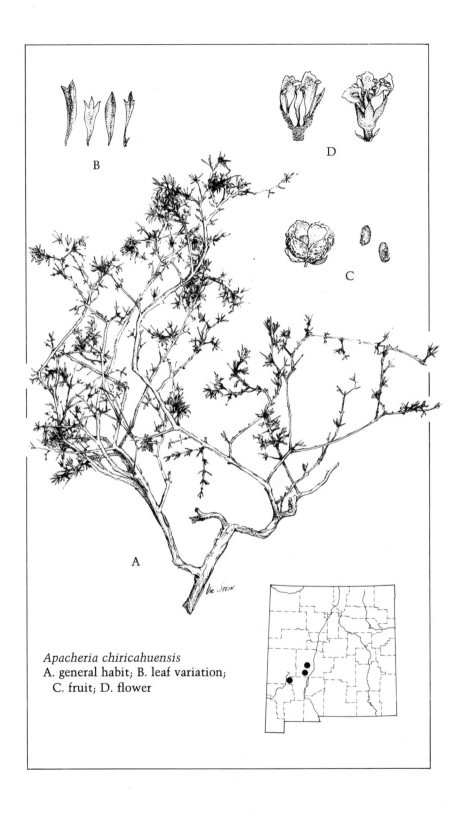

Apacheria chiricahuensis
A. general habit; B. leaf variation;
C. fruit; D. flower

Family: CUCURBITACEAE
Scientific Name: *Sicyos glaber* Wooton
Common Name: Smooth cucumber
Classification: State priority 1
Federal Action: None
Common Synonyms: None

Description: Vining annual; stems to 6 m (20 ft.) long, smooth except sticky-hairy at nodes and branch tips; tendrils stout at the base, with three or four branches; leaves relatively thin, 5–12 cm (2.0–4.75 in.) long, almost as wide; blades heart shaped at base, with five triangular-oval, coarsely toothed lobes, the midlobe longer than the others, acute, upper and lower surfaces sparsely and stiffly hairy; petioles 5–50 mm (0.2–2.0 in.) long, sticky-hairy; staminate (male) flowers yellow, in groups of 15–20; calyx teeth obscure; corolla bell-shaped to funnellike, parted into five oval segments; stamens united into a column 2 mm (0.1 in.) long; pistillate (female) flowers in 6- to 12-flowered clusters, greenish, about 4 mm (0.15 in.) long; fruit oval, 5 mm (0.18 in.) long, smooth, thin-walled, but tough. Flowers from July to September.
Known Distribution: Doña Ana County, New Mexico, and adjacent Texas
Habitat: Lower to middle elevations of the Organ Mountains; 1,525–2,100 m (5,000–6,000 ft.)
Ownership: Bureau of Land Management, Department of Defense, private
Threats to Taxon: None known
Similar Species: *Sicyos glaber* can be distinguished from all other species of *Sicyos* in New Mexico by its coarsely toothed leaves, and smooth fruit (all other NM *Sicyos* have large bristles on their fruits).
Remarks: This relative of the cucumber obtains great length of stem, considering its life cycle takes place in one year.

Important Literature:
Wooton, E. O. New plants from New Mexico, II. Bull. Torr. Bot. Club 25:310; 1898.

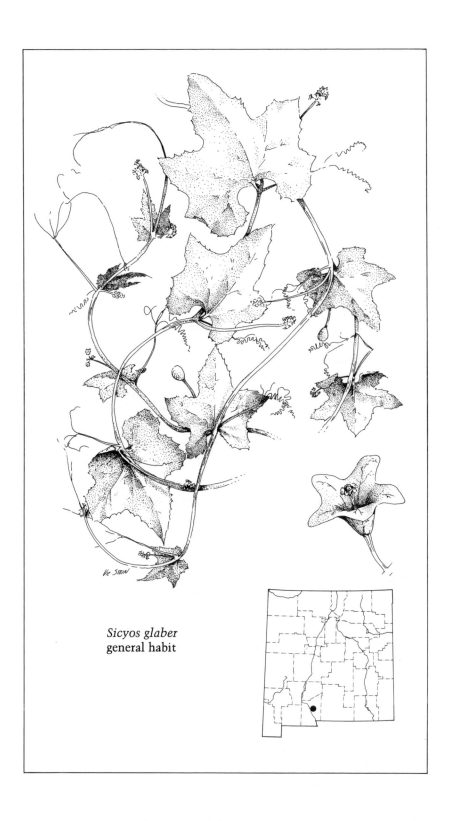

Sicyos glaber
general habit

Family: EUPHORBIACEAE
Scientific Name: *Euphorbia strictior* Holz.
Common Name: Tall plains spurge
Classification: State priority 1
Federal Action: Federal Register, 15 December 1980, candidate for federal protection
Common Synonyms: None

Description: Perennial herb; stems erect, diffusely branching from the base, 20–80 cm (8–24 in.) tall; leaves alternate, linear, 25–50 mm (1–2 in.) long, 2 mm (0.1 in.) wide; cups containing the flowers solitary in the upper axils of the leaves, with four or five yellowish glands; fruit well exerted from the cups below, three angled, with three conspicuous two-parted styles arising from the apex. Flowers from August and September.
Known Distribution: Chaves, Curry, and Roosevelt counties, New Mexico, and the Texas Panhandle
Habitat: Infrequent in sandy areas of the short grass plains; 900–1,400 m (3,000–4,500 ft.)
Ownership: Bureau of Land Managment, private
Threats to Taxon: None known
Similar Species: *Euphorbia strictior* is similar to *E. wrightii*. It differs in having whorled leaves at the top of the plant that are shorter than the stalks, which subtend the flowers.
Remarks: This species is closely related to the Christmas poinsettia.

Important Literature:
Correll, D. S., and M. C. Johnston. Manual of the vascular plants of Texas. Renner, Tex.: Texas Research Foundation; 1970.

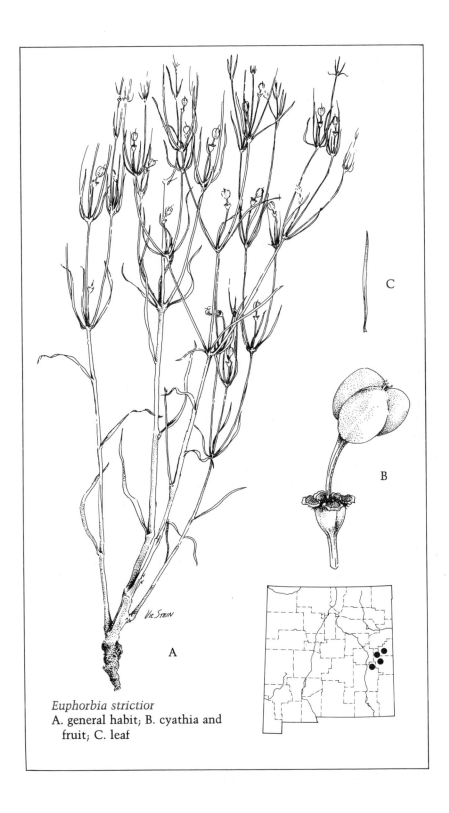

Euphorbia strictior
A. general habit; B. cyathia and
fruit; C. leaf

Family: FABACEAE (Leguminosae)
Scientific Name: *Astragalus accumbens* Sheld.
Common Name: Zuni milk-vetch
Classification: Biologically threatened
Federal Action: Federal Register, 15 December 1980, candidate for federal protection
Common Synonyms: None

Description: Low, tufted, grayish forb; leaves 1.0–6.5 cm (0.4–2.6 in.) long, pinnately divided into 7–15 oval leaflets; 3–14 small pealike flowers in short racemes; petals incurved, poorly graduated (hence the flower has a "squared-off" profile), pale yellowish white, often tinged with dull lilac, the veins generally dull lilac; upper petal (banner) 7–8 mm (0.3–0.4 in.) long, abruptly bent back at least 90°; pod straight, plump, 9–18 mm (0.35–0.7 in.) long, round at base, contracted into a short point at tip, persistent on the peduncle (often over winter). Flowers from May to August.
Known Distribution: Catron, Cibola, and McKinley counties, New Mexico
Habitat: On clay soils derived from Chinle Formation, at about 2,200 m (7,000 ft.)
Ownership: Forest Service
Threats to Taxon: This narrowly distributed species could be adversely affected by uranium mining, but it appears to be more abundant than had been thought.
Similar Species: In *A. missouriensis* var. *mimetes*, the closest relative, the banner is bent back less than 90°.
Remarks: The taxonomic status of this species requires further examination.

Important Literature:
Barneby, R. C. Atlas of North American *Astragalus*. Mem. New York Bot. Gard. 13:1–1188; 1964.

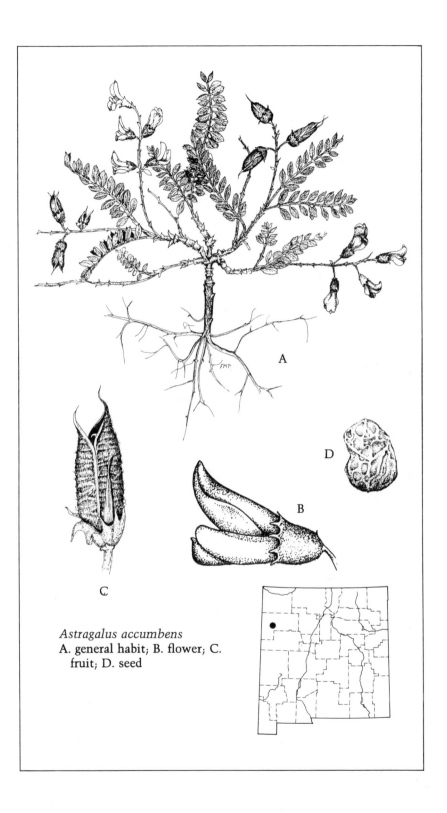

Astragalus accumbens
A. general habit; B. flower; C.
fruit; D. seed

Family: FABACEAE (Leguminosae)
Scientific Name: *Astragalus altus* Woot. & Standl.
Common Name: Tall milk-vetch
Classification: State priority 1
Federal Action: Federal Register, 15 December 1980, removed from consideration for federal protection
Common Synonyms: *Atelophragma altum* (Woot. & Standl.) Rydb.

Description: Perennial stems several, ascending, reddish to 1 m (39 in.) tall; leaves to 12 cm (4.9 in.) long, pinnately compound into 15–25 ovate leaflets each 3–12 mm (0.12–0.5 in.) long; flowers 15–45, nodding, pealike, pale cream to yellow about 1 cm (0.4 in.) long; pods hanging down, with a stalk 6–10 mm (0.2–0.4 in.) long between the calyx and the pod, about 15 mm (0.6 in.) long, triangular in cross section, grooved on the lower side. Flowers from late May to September.
Known Distribution: Otero County, New Mexico
Habitat: Limestone soils in the upper ponderosa and lower Douglas-fir vegetation types, on steep forest slopes or along roadcuts, 1,900–2,500 m (6,500–8,200 ft.)
Ownership: Forest Service, Mescalero Indian Reservation, private
Threats to Taxon: Road construction and maintenance, and general development of the Cloudcroft area
Similar Species: No other tall *Astragalus* with cream or yellow flowers occurs in the Sacramento Mountains.
Remarks: An early succession species that frequently colonizes roadsides. This species was lost since the 1890s, but was rediscovered in 1968.

Important Literature:
Barneby, R. C. Atlas of North American *Astragalus.* Mem. New York Bot. Gard. 13:1–1188; 1964.

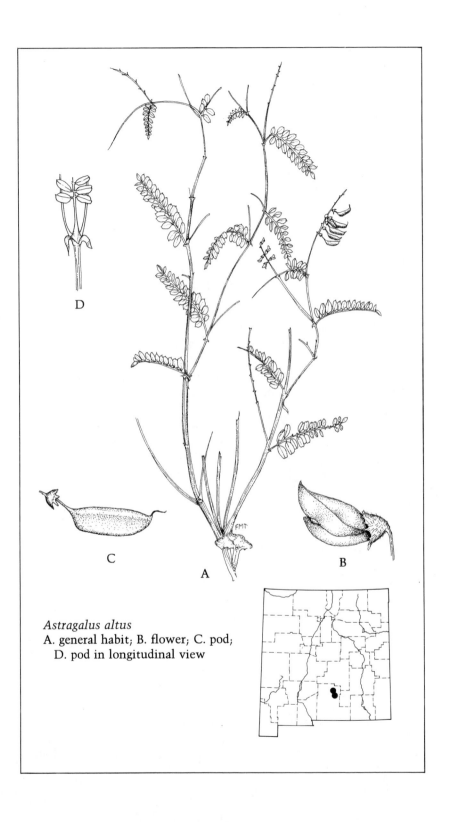

Astragalus altus
A. general habit; B. flower; C. pod;
  D. pod in longitudinal view

Family: FABACEAE (Leguminosae)
Scientific Name: *Astragalus castetteri* Barneby
Common Name: Castetter's milk-vetch
Classification: State priority 1
Federal Action: Federal Register, 15 December 1980, candidate for federal protection
Common Synonyms: None

Description: Perennial herb; stems spreading or ascending, to 40 cm (16 in.) long; leaves to 10 cm (4 in.) long, pinnately compound, with 13–25 oblong leaflets to 15 mm (0.6 in.) long; leaflets sparsely hairy on the upper surface, more densely so beneath, the hairs lying flat; flowers 8–18, pealike, spreading, pale purple, 14–20 mm (0.5–0.7 in.) long; pod spreading or drooping, bladderlike, 22–28 mm (0.8–1.1 in.) long, 11–16 mm (0.4–0.6 in.) wide, with a short stalk at the base and a triangular beak at the tip. Flowers from June through September.
Known Distribution: Doña Ana and Sierra counties, New Mexico
Habitat: Among pinyon and juniper, on limestone; 1,500–1,800 m (5,000–6,000 ft.)
Ownership: Bureau of Land Management, Department of Defense
Threats to Taxon: Some populations could be damaged by military operations.
Similar Species: *Astragalus hallii* Gray var. *fallax* (Wats.) Barneby, from southwestern New Mexico and eastern Arizona, has pods less than 12 mm broad, and shorter calyx teeth.
Remarks: Although restricted in distribution, this species is common within its preferred habitat.

Important Literature:
Barneby, R. C. Atlas of North American *Astragalus*. Mem. New York Bot. Gard. 13:1–1188; 1964.

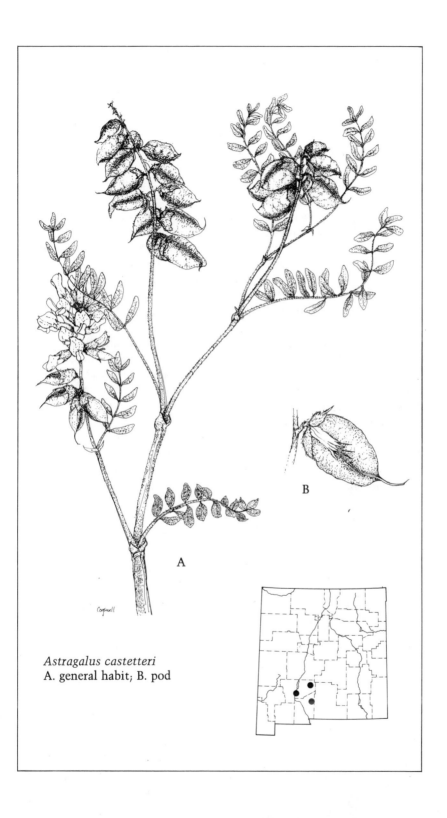

Astragalus castetteri
A. general habit; B. pod

Family: FABACEAE (Leguminosae)
Scientific Name: *Astragalus cyaneus* Gray
Common Name: Cyanic milk-vetch
Classification: State priority 1
Federal Action: None
Common Synonyms: None

Description: Low, tufted perennial covered with grayish hairs that lie flat; stems to 6 cm (2.4 in.) long, shorter than the leaves; leaves 6–18 cm (2.4–7.0 in.) long, pinnately compound, with 15–29 elliptic flat leaflets; flowers pealike, 9–22, pinkish purple, 18–22 mm (0.7–0.4 in.) long, upper petal (banner) shallowly notched at the tip and marked with a pale stripe; pod ascending or spreading upward, 25–50 mm (1–2 in.) long, gently curved, slightly flattened, broader than deep except near the pointed beak, covered with hairs, the wall thick and fleshy when green, becoming woody and with network pattern when dry, the middle "seam" strong and cordlike. Flowers from April to June.
Known Distribution: Found locally adjacent to the Rio Grande in Bernalillo, Rio Arriba, Santa Fe, and Taos counties, New Mexico
Habitat: With pinyon and juniper on sandy, or gravelly hillsides; 1,700–2,000 m (5,500–6,500 ft.)
Ownership: Bureau of Land Management, private
Threats to Taxon: None known
Similar Species: *Astragalus shortianus*, found from Santa Fe north to Wyoming, has less than 21 leaflets on the largest leaves.
Remarks: Additional studies may prove *A. cyaneus* to be a robust form of *A. shortianus*.

Important Literature:
Barneby, R. C. Atlas of North American *Astragalus*. Mem. New York Bot. Gard. 13:1–1188; 1964.

A. cyaneus –
- banner shellowly notched
- herbage greenish, pubescent on both sides, but brighter green on underside of leaflets

A. shortianus:
- banner not shallowly notched
- herbage silvery, rarely greenish. (both sides of leaflets silvery)

144

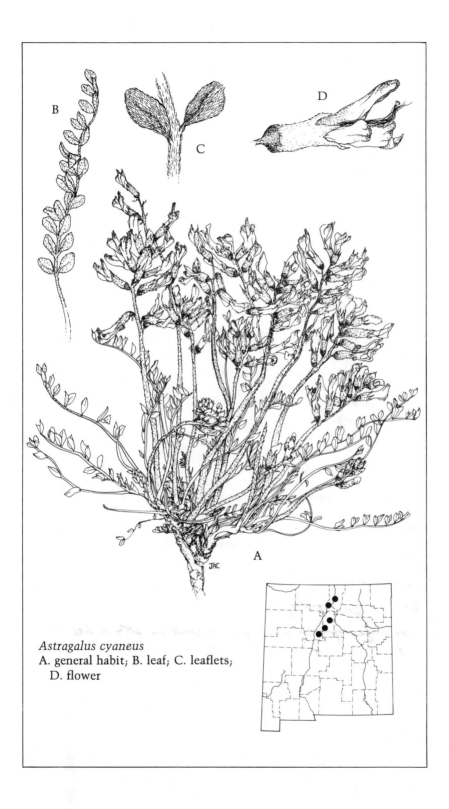

Astragalus cyaneus
A. general habit; B. leaf; C. leaflets;
  D. flower

Family: FABACEAE (Leguminosae)
Scientific Name: *Astragalus feensis* M. E. Jones
Common Name: Santa Fe milk-vetch
Classification: State priority 1
Federal Action: None
Common Synonyms: *Hamosa feensis* (Jones) Rydb.
Astragalus sanctae-fidei Tides

Description: Loosely tufted perennial; stems prostrate or spreading upward, to 10 cm (4 in.) long; leaves 2.5–9.5 cm (1.0–3.7 in.) long, pinnately compound, with 7–19 obovate, blunt, usually folded leaflets 3–13 mm (0.5 in.) long, the leaflets soft-hairy on the lower surface; flowers pealike, reddish purple, 13–16 mm (0.5–0.6 in.) long, the upper (banner) petal with a conspicuous whitish center; pod spreading upward, curved through a half circle, 13–30 mm (0.6–1.1 in.) long, elliptic, covered with hairs lying flat, three-sided in cross section. Flowers in May and June.
Known Distribution: Bernalillo, Santa Fe, and Torrance counties, New Mexico
Habitat: Dry slopes, usually in association with pinyons and junipers; 1,525–2,000 m (5,000–6,500 ft.)
Ownership: Bureau of Land Management, Forest Service, private
Threats to Taxon: None known
Similar Species: Similar *Astragalus* in the region, *A. cyaneus*, *A. missouriensis*, and *A. amphioxys* have pods with one chamber. In *A. feensis*, the pods are divided into two chambers.
Remarks: This species grows in a region that is extensively grazed. The effects of this activity on the species are unknown.

Important Literature:
Barneby, R. C. Atlas of North American *Astragalus*. Mem. New York Bot. Gard. 13:1–1188; 1964.

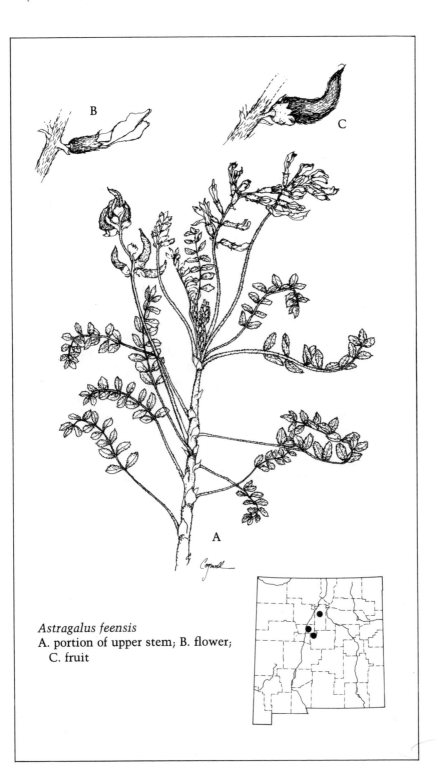

B

C

A

Astragalus feensis
A. portion of upper stem; B. flower;
  C. fruit

Family: FABACEAE (Leguminosae)
Scientific Name: *Astragalus gypsodes* Barneby
Common Name: Gypsum milk-vetch
Classification: State priority 1
Federal Action: None
Common Synonyms: None

Description: Perennial, stems stout, spreading upward, grayish, hairy, sometimes purplish, mostly 15–35 cm (6–14 in.) long; leaves 4–18 cm (1.5–7.0 in.) long, pinnately compound, with 11–29 elliptic flat, blunt leaflets, 5–20 mm (0.20–0.75 in.) long, the hairs straight, lying flat against the leaf surface; flowers pealike, 10–30, 16–24 mm (0.6–1.0 in.) long, pinkish purple when fresh, changing to bluish when dry; pods spreading or ascending, oblong, usually straight and plump, 25–50 mm (1–2 in.) long, two-chambered, the tip forming a small beak, walls green, thick, succulent, becoming spongy when ripe and often wrinkled in age. Flowers from March to May.
Known Distribution: Eddy County, New Mexico, and adjacent Texas
Habitat: Dry flats and slopes, on gypsum soils; 1,050–1,125 m (3,500–4,000 ft.)
Ownership: Bureau of Land Management, private
Threats to Taxon: Gypsum mining could jeopardize this species.
Similar Species: No *Astragalus* in this area has similar pods.
Remarks: This *Astragalus* requires a gypsum substrate.

Important Literature:

Barneby, R. C. Pugillus Astragalorum XVIII. Am. Midl. Nat. 55:499–500; 1956.

Barneby, R. C. Atlas of North American *Astragalus*. Mem. New York Bot. Gard. 13:1–1188; 1964.

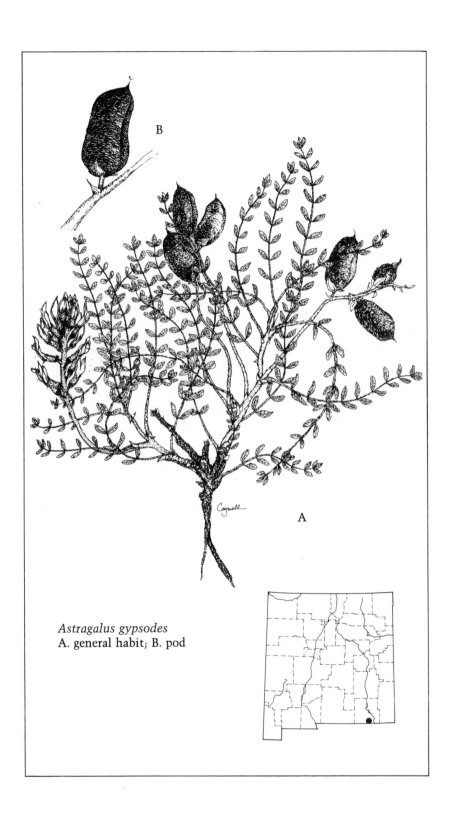

Astragalus gypsodes
A. general habit; B. pod

Family: FABACEAE (Leguminosae)
Scientific Name: *Astragalus humillimus* Gray *ex.* Brand.
Common Name: Mancos milk-vetch
Classification: Biologically endangered
Federal Action: Federal Register, 15 December 1980, candidate for federal protection
Common Synonyms: *Tragacantha humillima* (Gray) O. Kuntze
Phaca humillima (Gray) Rydb.

Description: Diminutive, tufted perennial forming clumps up to 30 cm (12 in.) across; crown with persistent, spiny leaf stalks; stems up to 1 cm (0.4 in.) long, leaves crowded, up to 4 cm (1.6 in.) long, with 7–11 oval leaflets, these 0.7–2.0 mm (up to 0.1 in.) long; flower branches short, 1–3 flowers; calyx about 3 mm (0.1 in.) long, withered leaves persistent as spiny protections from the stem base, petals lavender to purplish, with a conspicuous lighter-colored spot in the throat of the corolla tube; pod spreading, egg shaped, about 4.5 mm (0.2 in.) long, 2 mm (0.1 in.) wide. Flowers late April and early May.
Known Distribution: San Juan County, New Mexico, and adjacent Colorado
Habitat: Sandstone ledges or mesa tops often in cracks in the sandstone substrate or in shallow pockets of sandy soil. On sandstone of Cretaceous origin in the Mesa Verde series; 1,540–1,720 m (5,000–5,600 ft.)
Ownership: Navajo Indian Reservation
Threats to Taxon: Oil and gas development along the rimrock country of northwest New Mexico
Similar Species: No other mat-forming *Astragalus* has persistent spinescent leaf stalks.
Remarks: *Astragalus humillimus* was rediscovered near Farmington, New Mexico, in 1980, over a hundred years since the first collection. The original population discovered by Brandegee near Mesa Verde, Colorado has yet to be relocated.

Important Literature:
Barneby, R. C. Atlas of North American *Astragalus*. Mem. New York Bot. Gard. 13(2):1–1188; 1964.

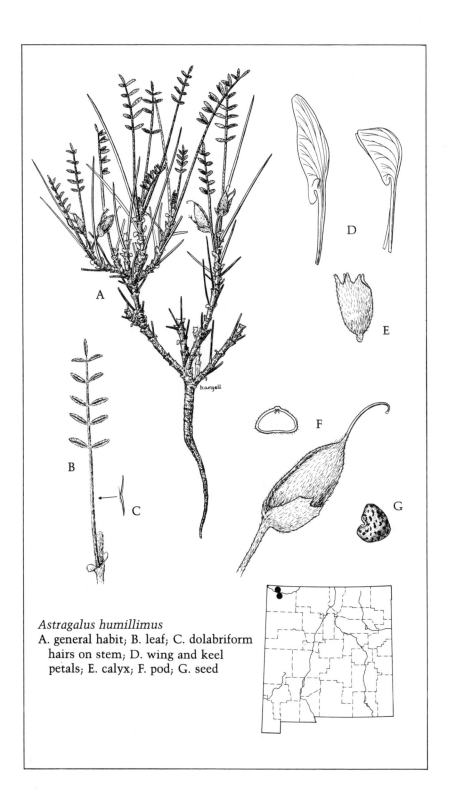

Astragalus humillimus
A. general habit; B. leaf; C. dolabriform
  hairs on stem; D. wing and keel
  petals; E. calyx; F. pod; G. seed

Family: FABACEAE (Leguminosae)
Scientific Name: *Astragalus kentrophyta* Gray var. *neomexicanus*
Barneby
Common Name: Spiny-leaf milk-vetch
Classification: State priority 1
Federal Action: None
Common Synonyms: None

Description: Low, bushy perennial, branched at the base, stems 4–30 cm
(1.6–12.0 in.) tall; the stems covered with stiff, prickly, greenish five-
foliate leaves, these 8–22 mm (0.3–0.9 in.) long, leaflets linear-elliptic, 3–
13 mm (0.1–0.5 in.) long, each with a minute spine 0.5–1.0 mm (0.02–
0.04 in.) long at the tip; petals whitish 4.8–5.2 mm (0.2 in.) long; the pod
egg shaped, 3–4 mm (0.1–0.2 in.) long, 1.8–2.4 mm (0.07–0.1 in.) wide.
Flowers from June to September.
Known Distribution: Bernalillo, Cibola, McKinley, San Juan, Sandoval,
Santa Fe, and Valencia counties, New Mexico, and adjacent Arizona
Habitat: Gullied bluffs, badlands, dunes, and roadsides; 1,650–2,150 m
(5,300–6,900 ft.)
Ownership: Bureau of Land Management, Forest Service, Navajo Indian
Reservation, private, State of New Mexico
Threats to Taxon: None known
Similar Species: No other species of *Astragalus* in New Mexico has
prickly, spine-tipped leaflets.
Remarks: This unusual milk-vetch is apparently endemic to the San Juan
Basin and adjacent rimrock country of northwest New Mexico. It is not
uncommon, and is often quite weedy in nature.

Important Literature:
Barneby, R. C. Atlas of North American *Astragalus*. Mem. New York Bot.
Gard. 13:1–1188; 1964.

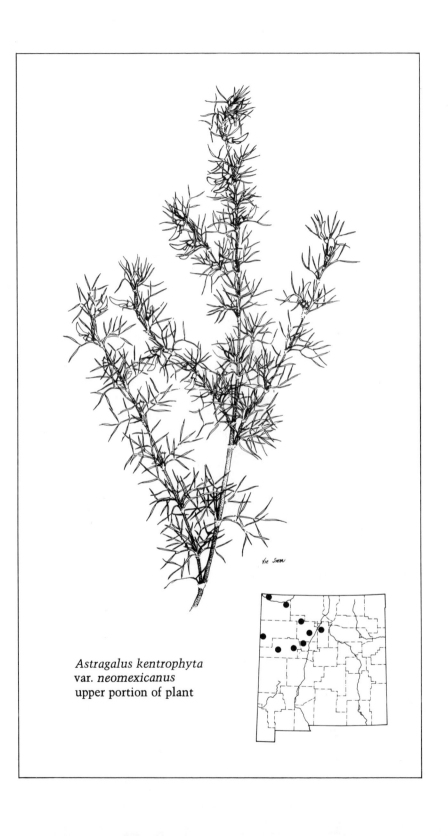

Astragalus kentrophyta
var. *neomexicanus*
upper portion of plant

Family: FABACEAE (Leguminosae)
Scientific Name: *Astragalus knightii* Barneby
Common Name: Knight's milk-vetch
Classification: Biologically threatened
Federal Action: None
Common Synonyms: None

Description: Small, tufted, perennial herb; with numerous ascending stems 1–5 cm (0.5–2.0 in.) long, arising from a taproot; leaves 2.5–8.5 cm (1.0–3.5 in.) long; stalks long, wiry, and sometimes persistent on the caudex; leaflets 9–15, elliptic or ovate-elliptic, 2–8 mm (0.1–0.4 in.) long; the 5–10 flowers drooping with age; calyx 3–4 mm (0.3 in.) long, bell shaped; petals whitish, lilac tinged along the margins, the lower petal purple tipped, the banner bent upward 45°, 5–6 mm (0.25 in.) long; pods hanging, narrowly obovoid-ellipsoid 8–14 mm (0.3–0.6 in.) long, 4–6 mm (0.4–0.5 in.) wide, red spotted. Flowers in May.
Known Distribution: Sandoval County, New Mexico
Habitat: Rimrock ledges of Dakota sandstone, in rock cracks and shallow pockets of soil; at about 1,750 m (5,700 ft.)
Ownership: Bureau of Land Management, Laguna Indian Reservation
Threats to Taxon: Development of coal and uranium reserves in the area
Similar Species: *Astragalus knightii* is similar to *A. ceramicus*. The latter can be distinguished by the presence of threadlike rhizomes, and the absence of a taproot.
Remarks: The growth form of *A. knightii* is similar to many of the rimrock *Astragalus* known from southeast Utah and the Four Corners area. *Astragalus knightii* may be evolved from *A. ceramicus*, with the resemblance to the more northern rimrock species being the result of parallel adaptation.

Important Literature:
Barneby, R. C. A new *Astragalus* from sandstone rimrock in New Mexico. Brittonia 35:109–10; 1983.

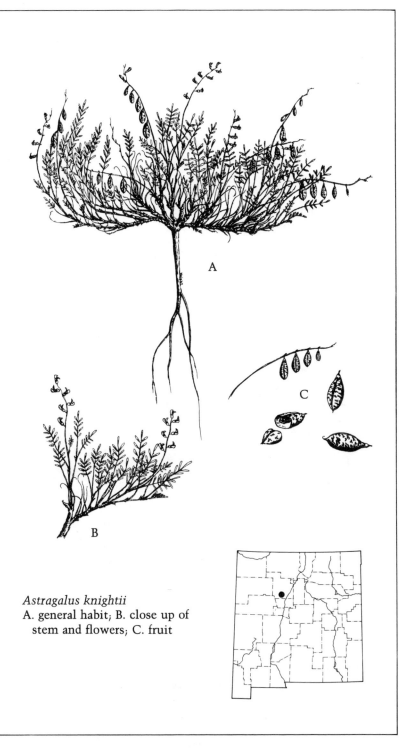

Astragalus knightii
A. general habit; B. close up of
stem and flowers; C. fruit

Family: FABACEAE (Leguminosae)
Scientific Name: *Astragalus micromerius* Barneby
Common Name: Chaco milk-vetch
Classification: State priority 1
Federal Action: None
Common Synonyms: None

Description: Perennial herb, silvery haired stems, prostrate, matted, 5–30 cm (2–12 in.) long; leaves 4–20 mm (0.1–0.7 in.) long, pinnately compound, the 3–9 leaflets 1–6 mm (to 0.25 in.) long, crowded; 1–5 flowers, pealike, whitish but tinged with purple, about 6 mm (0.25 in.) long, pods spreading, ovoid, 4–5 mm (0.15–0.20 in.) long, slightly broader than long, the tip forming a triangular, flattened beak. Flowering in July and August.
Known Distribution: McKinley, Rio Arriba, and San Juan counties, New Mexico
Habitat: Ledges of sandstone cliffs or on talus; 2,000–2,225 m (6,600–7,300 ft.)
Ownership: Bureau of Land Management, Forest Service, Navajo Indian Reservation, Zuni Indian Reservation
Threats to Taxon: None known
Similar Species: In this area, *A. humistratus* is the only similar species. It has hairs attached in the middle leaving both ends free, whereas the Chaco milk-vetch has hairs attached at one end.
Remarks: During drought, colonies of this species disappear, only to reappear under favorable conditions.

Important Literature:
Barneby, R. C. Atlas of North American *Astragalus.* Mem. New York Bot. Gard. 13:1–1188; 1964.

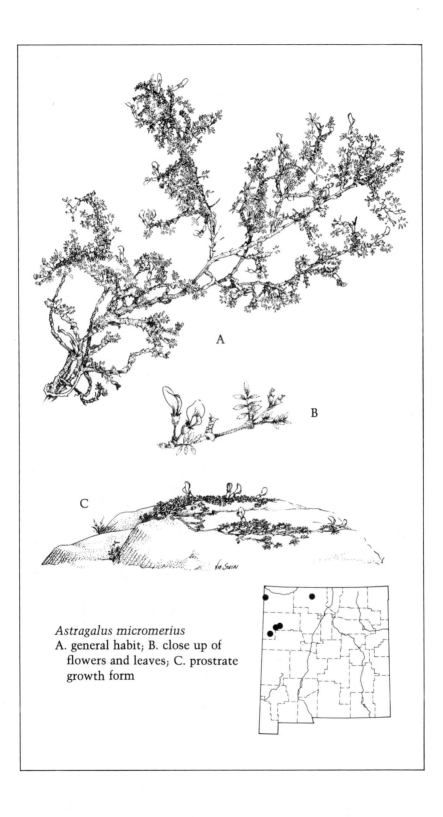

Astragalus micromerius
A. general habit; B. close up of
flowers and leaves; C. prostrate
growth form

Family: FABACEAE (Leguminosae)
Scientific Name: *Astragalus mollissimus* Torr. var. *mathewsii* (Wats.) Barneby
Common Name: Mathew's woolly milk-vetch
Classification: State priority 1
Federal Action: None
Common Synonyms: *Astragalus mathewsii* Wats. *A. bigelovii* var. *mathewsii* (Wats.) M. E. Jones

Description: Perennial herb, stems silky-hairy, tufted to 15 cm (6 in.) long; leaves 5–12 cm (2.0–4.75 in.) long, pinnately compound, with 11–29 broadly oval, blunt leaflets 10–20 mm (0.4–0.75 in.) long; flowers 5–12, pealike 18–22 mm (0.7–0.9 in.) long, pale purple or yellowish purple; pod abruptly curved upward, 12–18 mm (0.5–0.7 in.) long, plump, densely hairy, broadest near the base, the beak conical and two-chambered. Flowers from April to June.
Known Distribution: Cibola, McKinley, Santa Fe, and Sandoval counties, New Mexico
Habitat: Usually on open slopes and ridges in pinyon pine forests, but sometimes in canyons; 1,525–2,000 m (5,000–6,500 ft.)
Ownership: Bureau of Land Management, Forest Service, Navajo Indian Reservation, private
Threats to Taxon: None known
Similar Species: A number of species of *Astragalus* are similar. *A. mollissimus* is distinguished by its two-chambered pod and hairs on the foliage of two types, one short, curly, and entangled, the other longer and straighter. Of those varieties of *A. mollissimus* with hairy pods, the two-chambered beak on the pod, and the few flowers (5–12) distinguish the variety *mathewsii*.
Remarks: Populations are widely scattered, but at any one location there usually are few individuals. This variety occurs in heavily grazed areas, apparently without detriment.

Important Literature:
Barneby, R. C. Atlas of North American *Astragalus*. Mem. New York Bot. Gard. 13:1–1188; 1964.

158

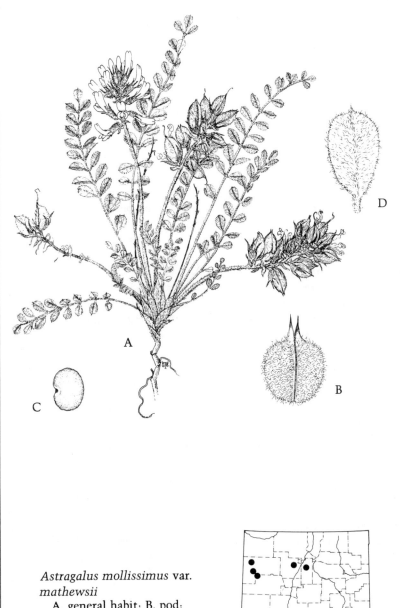

Astragalus mollissimus var.
mathewsii
    A. general habit; B. pod;
    C. seed; D. leaflet

Family: FABACEAE (Leguminosae)
Scientific Name: *Astragalus monumentalis* Barneby var. *cottamii* in ed.
Common Name: Cottam's milk-vetch
Classification: Biologically threatened
Federal Action: Federal Register, 15 December 1980, candidate for federal protection as *Astragalus cottamii*
Common Synonyms: *Astragalus cottamii* Welsh

Description: Perennial, slightly tufted, stem 1.5–4.0 cm (0.6–1.6 in.) long, branching beneath the ground surface; leaves 1–4 cm (0.4–1.6 in.) long, 9–19 leaflets, 1.0–4.2 mm (0.04–0.17 in.) wide, elliptic to oblanceolate, acute; 3–9 flowers, calyx 6.2–8.0 mm (0.24–0.32 in.) long, purplish; flowers 11–17 mm long, purplish or purple and white; pods spreading-descending, slightly curved, oblong to oblong-lanceolate, somewhat three-angled, two-chambered, hairy, usually purplish spotted. Flowers April and May.
Known Distribution: McKinley and San Juan counties, New Mexico, and southeastern Utah
Habitat: In weathered depressions and crevices of rimrock, on sandstone substrates of Cretaceous origin; 1,530–1,840 m (5,000–6,000 ft.)
Ownership: Bureau of Land Management, Navajo Indian Reservation, State of New Mexico
Threats to Taxon: Oil drilling along the rimrock sandstone formations near Farmington could be detrimental to this plant.
Similar Species: *Astragalus monumentalis* var. *cottamii* is distinguished from var. *monumentalis* by its longer stem, longer calyx, and larger flowers.
Remarks: This taxon is similar to *A. monumentalis* var. *monumentalis* and occupies much of the same range. In New Mexico, it is more common than var. *monumentalis*, but it is still highly restricted to specific rimrock outcrops in the northwest corner of the state.

Important Literature:
Welsh, S. An undescribed species of *Astragalus* from Utah. Rhodora 72:189–193; 1970.

A

B

Astragalus monumentalis var. *cottamii*
A. general habit; B. flowers

Family: FABACEAE (Leguminosae)
Scientific Name: *Astragalus monumentalis* Barneby var. *monumentalis*
Common Name: Monument Valley milk-vetch
Classification: Biologically threatened
Federal Action: Federal Register, 15 December 1980, candidate for federal protection
Common Synonyms: None

Description: Diminutive tufted perennial; herbage often grayish green with short hairs that lie flat; leaves 1.5–7.0 cm (0.6–2.75 in.) long, pinnately compound, with 5–12 leaflets 2–9 mm (0.06–0.4 in.) long and curved back along the midrib; 3–9 flowers, pealike, pinkish purple, 9–14 mm (0.4–0.6 in.) long, the upper (banner) petal slightly notched, the lower petal (keel) with a dark purple tip; pod spreading upward and inward, 1.5–3.0 cm (0.5–0.8 in.) long, somewhat triangular in cross section, two-chambered, the lower side with a deep groove. Flowers in April and May.
Known Distribution: McKinley and San Juan counties, New Mexico; also southeast Utah and northeast Arizona
Habitat: Rock cracks, sandy ledges, and slopes among pinyon and juniper; 1,530–1,840 m (5,000–6,000 ft.)
Ownership: Bureau of Land Management, Navajo Indian Reservation, State of New Mexico
Threats to Taxon: Oil drilling along the rimrock sandstone formations near Farmington could affect some population.
Similar Species: *Astragalus naturitensis* and *A. deterior*, both of which have white flowers
Remarks: This species was first discovered in New Mexico in 1977 in McKinley County. Since that time, additional populations have been located in San Juan County. This taxon is one of several endemic *Astragalus* adapted to the dry rimrock environment of the Four Corners area.

Important Literature:
Barneby, R. C. Atlas of North American *Astragalus*. Mem. New York Bot. Gard. 13:1–1188; 1964.

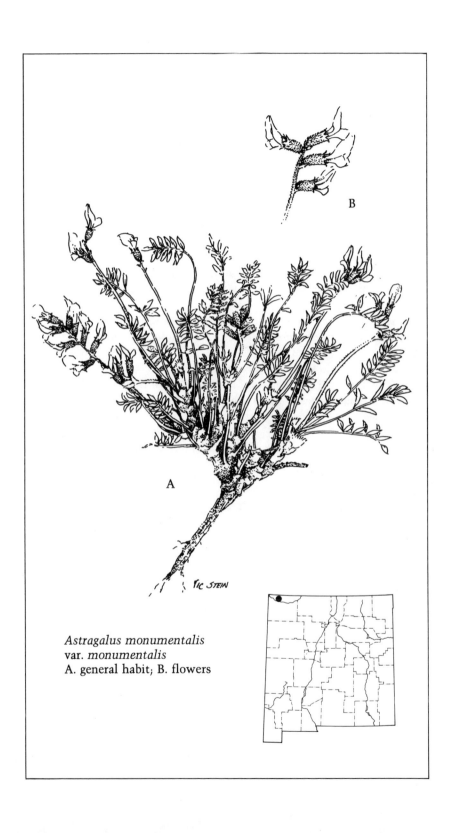

B

A

Pic Stein

Astragalus monumentalis
var. *monumentalis*
A. general habit; B. flowers

Family: FABACEAE (Leguminosae)
Scientific Name: *Astragalus naturitensis* Pays.
Common Name: Naturita milk-vetch
Classification: Biologically threatened
Federal Action: Federal Register, 15 December 1980, removed from consideration for federal protection
Common Synonyms: None

Description: Low-growing, spreading perennial, about 10 cm (4.0 in.) tall; leaves pinnate with 9–15 leaflets; flowers bicolored with a white upper petal and reddish purple lower petals; flower 14–15 mm (0.5–0.6 in.) long; calyx cylindrical 6–8 mm (0.25–0.3 in.); pods leathery, covered with short, stiff, flat-lying hairs. Flowers April and May.
Known Distribution: San Juan County, New Mexico, and adjacent Colorado
Habitat: Sandstone ledges and crevices of sandstone bedrock. In New Mexico, known only from sandstones of the Mesa Verde series; 1,650–1,900 m (5,400–6,200 ft.)
Ownership: Navajo Indian Reservation
Threats to Taxon: The population in New Mexico is small and limited in distribution. It is easily susceptible to mining activities.
Similar Species: *Astragalus deterior* is distinguished by its yellowish white flowers.
Remarks: This plant is a narrow endemic rare both in New Mexico and Colorado.

Important Literature:
Barneby, R. C. Atlas of North American *Astragalus*. Mem. New York Bot. Gard. 13:1–1188; 1964.

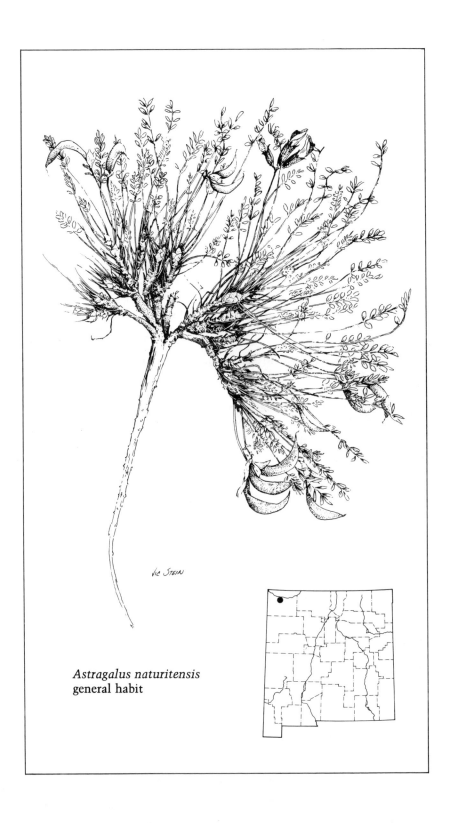

Astragalus naturitensis
general habit

Family: FABACEAE (Leguminosae)
Scientific Name: *Astragalus neomexicanus* Woot. & Standl.
Common Name: New Mexico milk-vetch
Classification: State priority 1
Federal Action: None
Common Synonyms: *Pisophaca neomexicana* (Woot. & Standl.) Rydb.

Description: Perennial, stems curving upward, to 30 cm (12 in.) long; leaves pinnately compound, 5–23 cm (2.0–8.75 in.) long, 19–39 leaflets, lance shaped to elliptic 3–20 mm (0.1–0.8 in.) long, somewhat hairy beneath; flowers pealike, dull pinkish lavender, 15–20 mm (0.6–0.8 in.) long, nodding, the upper petal (banner) notched at the tip; pod spreading or drooping downward, gently curved, mostly 20–30 mm (0.8–1.1 in.) long, 7–11 mm (0.3–0.4 in.) wide, one-chambered, hairy, wrinkled at maturity. Flowers from July to October.
Known Distribution: Lincoln and Otero counties, New Mexico
Habitat: Open, gravelly banks and montane slopes in yellow pine forest; 2,125–2,600 m (7,000–8,500 ft.)
Ownership: Forest Service, Mescalero Indian Reservation, private
Threats to Taxon: None known
Similar Species: *Astragalus flexuosus* is readily distinguished by the stipules at the base of each stem which form a "collar" closed on all sides. In *A. neomexicanus*, the "collar" is open on one side.
Remarks: This is a rather narrow but weedy endemic; within its range it is fairly common.

Important Literature:
Barneby, R. C. Atlas of North American *Astragalus*. Mem. New York Bot. Gard. 13:1–1188; 1964.

Astragalus neomexicanus
A. general habit; B. leaflets;
C. pod; D. flower

Family: FABACEAE (Leguminosae)
Scientific Name: *Astragalus oocalycis* M. E. Jones
Common Name: Arborales milk-vetch
Classification: Biologically threatened
Federal Action: Federal Register, 15 December 1980, removed from consideration for federal protection
Common Synonyms: *Diholocos oocalycis* (M. E. Jones) Rydb.
Astragalus urceolatus Greene

Description: Stout perennial, erect, stems to about 40 cm (16 in.) long, forming bushy clumps; leaves 5–17 cm (2.0–6.75 in.) long, pinnately compound into 9–27 linear or oblong leaflets, 1–4 cm (0.4–1.5 in.) long, flowers 35–60, cream-colored, 14–17 mm (0.6–0.7 in.) long, calyx expanding and forming a pale egg-shaped structure 11 mm (0.4 in.) in diameter; pod straight, 6–7 mm (0.25 in.) long, angled downward, with a 1 mm (0.05 in.) stalk between the pod and the base of the calyx, pod smooth at first, becoming wrinkled in age. Flowers in May and June.
Known Distribution: San Juan County, New Mexico, and southwestern Colorado
Habitat: In stiff, alkaline clay soils on slopes and along arroyos; 1,800–2,100 m (6,000–7,000 ft.)
Ownership: Bureau of Land Management, private
Threats to Taxon: None known
Similar Species: The inflated bladdery egg-shaped calyx of *A. oocalycis* separates it from all others.
Remarks: This species usually grows on selenium-bearing soils.

Important Literature:
Barneby, R. C. Atlas of North American *Astragalus*. Mem. New York Bot. Gard. 13:1–1188; 1964.

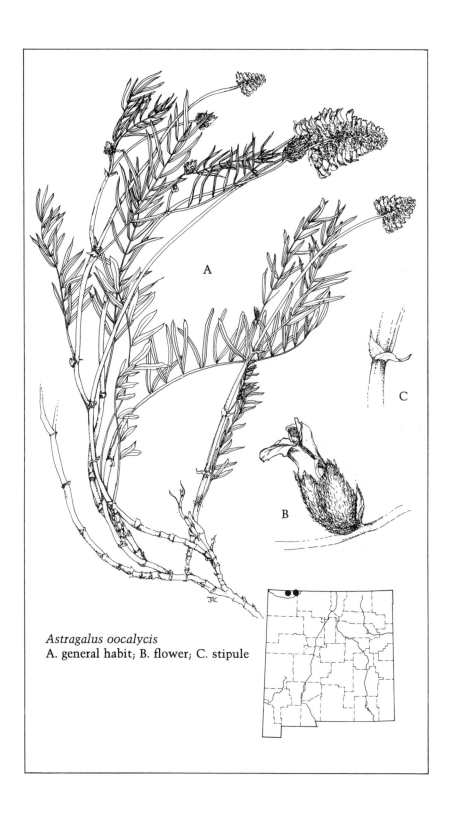

Astragalus oocalycis
A. general habit; B. flower; C. stipule

Family: FABACEAE (Leguminosae)
Scientific Name: *Astragalus puniceus* Osterh. var. *gertrudis* (Green) Barneby
Common Name: Taos milk-vetch
Classification: State priority 1
Federal Action: Federal Register, 15 December 1980, candidate for federal protection
Common Synonyms: *Astragalus gertrudis* Greene

Description: Perennial herb, stems spreading 20–50 cm (8–20 in.) long; leaves pinnately compound, 2–11 cm (0.75–4.5 in.) long, with 13–23 ovate leaflets 3–16 mm (0.1–0.6 in.) long; flowers pealike, pale to bright pink, 14–18 mm (0.6–0.7 in.) long; pod spreading, 15–24 mm (0.6–0.9 in.) long, 5.0–9.5 mm (0.2–0.4 in.) in diameter, nearly round in cross section, fleshy when green, red spotted and leathery when ripe. Flowers in May and June.
Known Distribution: Rio Arriba and Taos counties, New Mexico
Habitat: On open, loose soil among pinyon and juniper, at about 2,150 m (7,000 ft.)
Ownership: Bureau of Land Management, Forest Service, private
Threats to Taxon: None known
Similar Species: *Astragalus hallii* Gray var. *hallii* occurs in the same general area. It has a small stalk between the calyx and the base of the pod; this type of stalk is absent in *A. puniceus*.
Remarks: This variety is barely distinct from the more common variety *puniceus*, which occurs in northeastern New Mexico. It may be more common than supposed in the little-collected feeder canyons along the east side of the Rio Grande in southern Taos County.

Important Literature:
Barneby, R. C. Atlas of North American *Astragalus*. Mem. New York Bot. Gard. 13:1–1188; 1964.

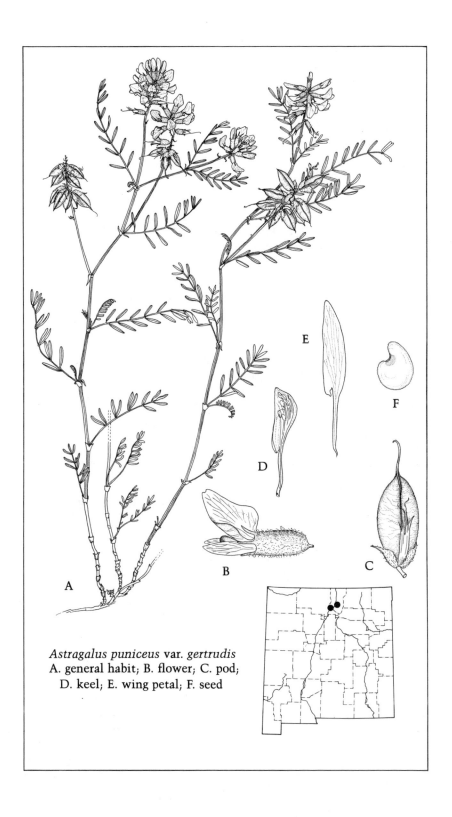

Astragalus puniceus var. *gertrudis*
A. general habit; B. flower; C. pod;
D. keel; E. wing petal; F. seed

Family: FABACEAE (Leguminosae)
Scientific Name: *Astragalus siliceus* Barneby
Common Name: Flint Mountains milk-vetch
Classification: State priority 1
Federal Action: Federal Register, 15 December 1980, candidate for federal protection
Common Synonyms: None

Description: Densely tufted, matted, grayish, hairy perennial; leaves pinnately compound, 5–30 mm (0.2–12 in.) long, 3–9 leaflets, crowded, elliptic, 1.5–5.0 mm (0.06–0.2 in.) long; 1–3 flowers, pealike, pale purple to vivid pinkish purple, 10–12 mm (0.4–1.2 in.) long, borne among the leaves; pod ascending or spreading, ovoid, 5.0–7.5 mm (0.2–0.3 in.) long, 2.8 mm (0.1 in.) in diameter, slightly compressed from the sides, the upper and lower "seams" forming low, narrow ridges. Flowers in May.
Known Distribution: Torrance County, New Mexico
Habitat: Rocky knolls, banks, and flats on high rolling plains, at about 1,850 m (6,000 ft.)
Ownership: State of New Mexico, private
Threats to Taxon: None known
Similar Species: *Astragalus wittmanii* can be distinguished by its solitary flowers, rounded pod, and larger leaves.
Remarks: This species is endemic to knolls and hills in the rolling grassland of east-central Torrance County. Although limited in distribution, it apparently increases with disturbance.

Important Literature:
Barneby, R. C. Four new species and one variety Pugillus Astragalorum XVII. Leafl. West. Bot. 8:14–16; 1956.

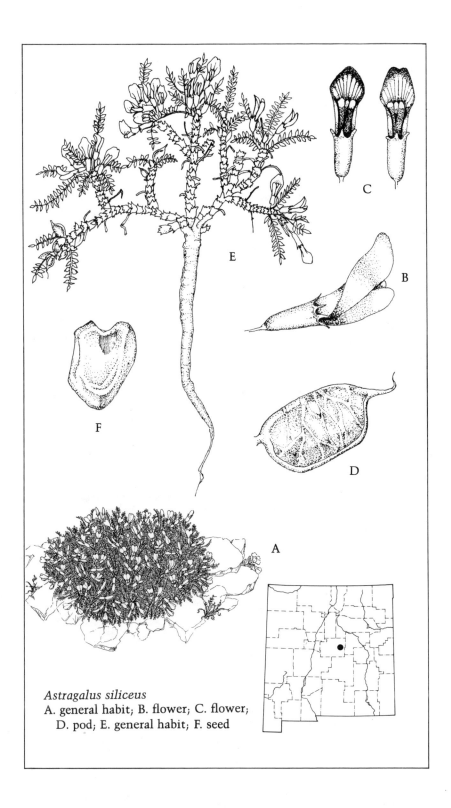

Astragalus siliceus
A. general habit; B. flower; C. flower;
D. pod; E. general habit; F. seed

Family: FABACEAE (Leguminosae)
Scientific Name: *Astragalus wittmanii* Barneby
Common Name: One-flowered milk-vetch
Classification: State priority 1
Federal Action: Federal Register, 15 December 1980, candidate for federal protection
Common Synonyms: None

Description: Diminutive mat-forming perennial, forming cushions to 30 cm (12 in.) across; leaves to 8 cm (3 in.) long, with 5–7 narrow leaflets; hairs of the foliage attached at the middle with the ends free; flowers solitary on each peduncle, nestled among the leaves, pealike, purple, about 15 mm (0.6 in.) long; pod plump, almost round, about 3 mm (0.1 in.) in diameter, hairy, with a minute beak at the tip. Flowers in May.
Known Distribution: Colfax, Harding, and Mora counties, New Mexico
Habitat: Limestone hills and knolls in open grassland, at about 2,000 m (6,500 ft.)
Ownership: Bureau of Land Management, Forest Service, private, State of New Mexico
Threats to Taxon: None known
Similar Species: *Astragalus siliceus*, which has 1–3 flowers on each stalk, ovoid fruits, and leaves no longer than 3 cm (1.25 in.)
Remarks: This plant appears to be localized on outcrops of Greenhorn limestone. Although this plant is rare, at least 20 populations have been located in northeastern New Mexico.

Important Literature:
Barneby, R. C. Dragma hippomanicum IV: new taxa of *Astragalus* sect. Humillimi. Brittonia 31:459–63; 1979.

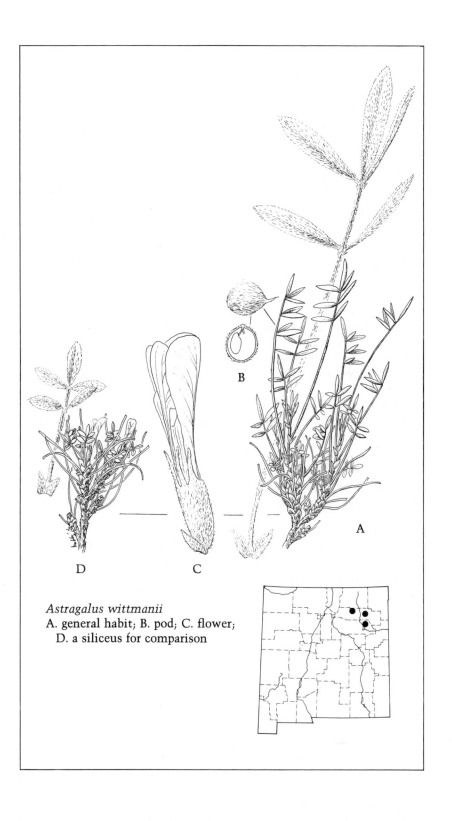

Astragalus wittmanii
A. general habit; B. pod; C. flower;
  D. a siliceus for comparison

Family: FABACEAE (Leguminosae)
Scientific Name: *Dalea scariosa* Wats.
Common Name: La Jolla prairie clover
Classification: State priority 1
Federal Action: Federal Register, 15 December 1980, removed from consideration for federal protection
(*Petalostemum scariosum*)
Common Synonyms: *Petalostemum scariosum*

Description: Stems spreading-ascending, 20–70 cm (0.8–2.8 in.) long; leaves bright green, gland dotted, 1–2.5 cm (0.4–1.0 in.) long, pinnately compound into 5–9 thick-textured leaflets 3–8 mm (0.12–0.25 in.) long, broadest near tips; flowers pealike, petals pale pink to pink-purple, 7–8 mm (0.22–0.25 in.) long, the calyx dotted with orange or reddish glands; pod 3–4 mm (0.12–0.16 in.) long, plump, with small glands like the calyx. Flowers August and September.
Known Distribution: Bernalillo, Sandoval, Socorro, and Valencia counties, New Mexico
Habitat: Sandy clay banks and bluffs, open sandy areas, and roadsides primarily in desert grassland or among junipers; 1,460–1,510 m (4,900–5,030 ft.)
Ownership: Bureau of Land Management, Laguna Indian Reservation, State of New Mexico, U.S. Fish and Wildlife Service
Threats to Taxon: Individual populations may be affected by highway rights-of-way grading and housing development.
Similar Species: None
Remarks: Seeds spread by mowing of highway rights-of-way appear to have increased the abundance of this species within its range.

Important Literature:
Barneby, R. C. Dalea imagines. Mem. New York Bot. Gard. 27:1–892; 1977.
Wemple, D. K. Revision of the genus *Petalostemum* (Leguminosae). Iowa State J. Sci. 45:1–102; 1970.

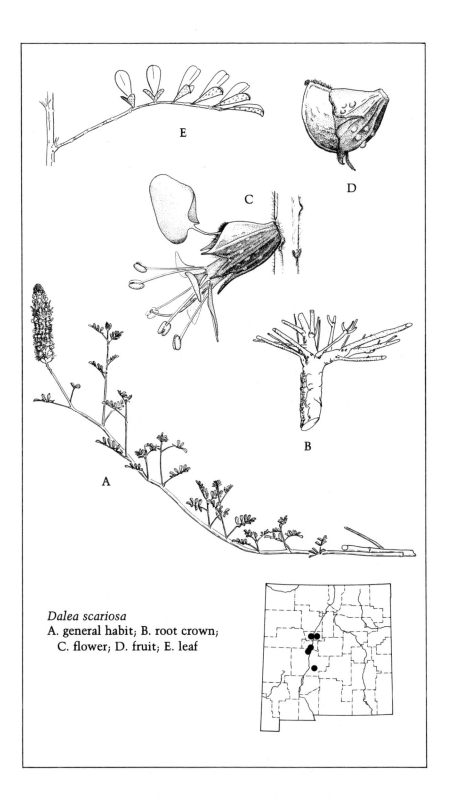

Dalea scariosa
A. general habit; B. root crown;
C. flower; D. fruit; E. leaf

Family: FABACEAE (Leguminosae)
Scientific Name: *Lupinus sierrae-blancae* Woot. & Standl.
Common Name: Sierra Blanca lupine
Classification: State priority 1
Federal Action: None
Common Synonyms: *Lupinus aquilinus* Woot. & Standl.

Description: Perennial herb; stems stout, to 1 m (3 ft.) or more tall, hairy, branched; leaves compound, with 7–9 sharply pointed leaflets, each 50–70 mm (2.0–2.75 in.) long, smooth above, hairy beneath, petiole about as long as the leaflets; corolla about 12 mm (0.5 in.) long, dull bluish, tinged with yellow, the upper petal (banner) with a large dark spot; pod 35 mm (1.4 in.) long, 5- to 7-seeded. Flowers June to September.
Known Distribution: Lincoln County, New Mexico
Habitat: Meadows, open slopes, and near streams; 2,100–3,040 m (7,000–10,000 ft.)
Ownership: Forest Service, Mescalero Indian Reservation, private
Threats to Taxon: None known
Similar Species: Until recently, *L. aquilinus* has been considered a distinct species, owing to its short raceme of flowers and blunt leaflets. However, it is now conidered the same as *L. sierrae-blancae.*
Remarks: This taxon is endemic to the Sacramento Mountains of south-central New Mexico. It appears to increase with disturbance.

Important Literature:
Wooton, E. O., and P. C. Standley. New plants from New Mexico. Contr. U.S. Nat. Herb. 16:109–96; 1913.

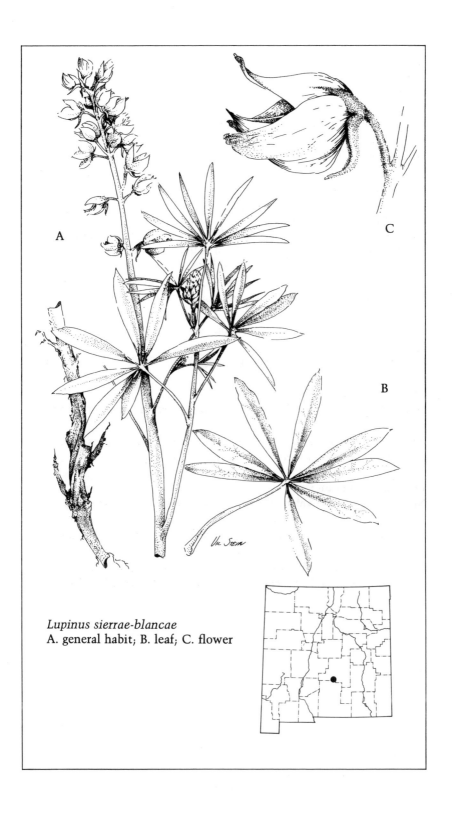

Lupinus sierrae-blancae
A. general habit; B. leaf; C. flower

Family: FABACEAE (Leguminosae)
Scientific Name: *Sophora gypsophila* var. *guadalupensis* Turner and Powell
Common Name: Guadalupe Mountain mescal bean
Classification: Biologically threatened
Federal Action: Federal Register, 15 December 1980, candidate for federal protection
Common Synonyms: None

Description: Shrub, about 1 m (3 ft.) tall; leaves pinnately compound, with 11–13 roundish, leathery, hairy leaflets; flowers purple, pealike, about 25 mm (1 in.) long; pod 5–14 cm (2.0–5.5 in.) long, 10–14 mm (0.4–0.6 in.) wide, slightly constricted between the seeds; seeds 7–10 mm (0.3–0.4 in.) long, 6–7 mm (0.3 in.) wide. Flowers in March and April.
Known Distribution: Eddy and Otero counties, New Mexico, and adjacent Texas
Habitat: Dry limestone slopes with one-seed juniper; 1,525–1,950 m (5,000–6,400 ft.)
Ownership: Bureau of Land Management, Forest Service, National Park Service
Threats to Taxon: None known
Similar Species: The leaflets of *S. secundiflora* are hairless on the under surface.
Remarks: This unpalatable and apparently poisonous taxon is probably a population left from a species formerly more widespread.

Important Literature:

Northington, D. K. Evidence bearing on the origin of infraspecific disjunction in *Sophora gypsophila*. Plant Syst. Evol. 125:233–44; 1976.

Rudde, V. E. *Leguminosae-Faboideae-Sophoreae*. N. A. Flora, Botanic Garden, series 2, part 7. New York; 1972.

Turner, B. L., and A. M. Powell. A new gypsophilic *Sophora* from north-central Mexico and adjacent Texas. Phytologia 22:419–23; 1972.

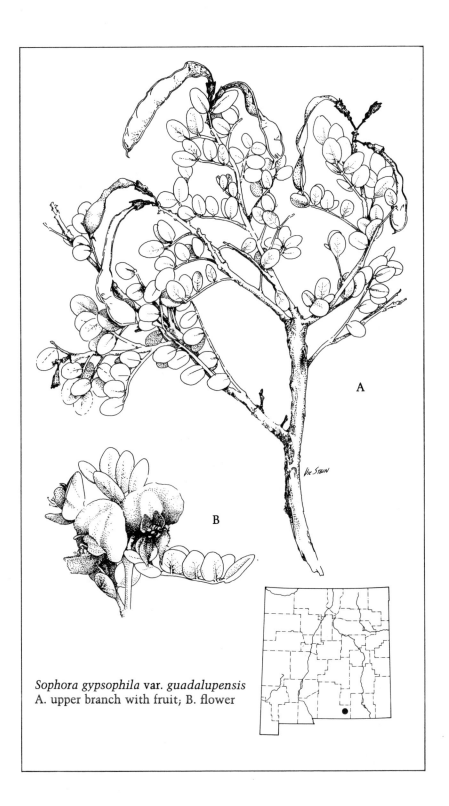

Sophora gypsophila **var.** *guadalupensis*
A. upper branch with fruit; B. flower

Family: FABACEAE (Leguminosae)
Scientific Name: *Trifolium longipes* Nutt. var. *neurophyllum* (Greene) Martin *ex.* Isely
Common Name: Mogollon clover
Classification: Biologically threatened
Federal Action: None
Common Synonyms: *Trifolium neurophyllum* Greene

Description: Perennial herb 50–80 cm (20–31 in.) tall; leaflets 10–35 mm (0.4–1.4 in.) long, narrowly lance shaped, sharp pointed, small toothed; flowers in globose clumps, the clumps on a hairy, leafless, bractless stalk; calyx tubular, ending in long teeth, hairy; flowers 10–20 mm (0.3–0.8 in.) long, purple, pods 3–6 seeded. Flowers August and September.
Known Distribution: Catron County, New Mexico, and adjacent Arizona
Habitat: Wet meadows and around springs; 2,400–2,750 m (8,000–9,000 ft.)
Threats to Taxon: Grazing by livestock, water development
Similar Species: Features that distinguish this plant are its height, purple flowers in heads on a long bractless and leafless stalk, and a hairy calyx.
Remarks: Historically, this plant is known from perhaps a half dozen collections; however, it may have been drastically reduced in numbers by intensive livestock use early in this century.

Important Literature:
Greene, E. L. New plants from southwestern mountains. Leafl. Bot. Obs. 1:154; 1905.
Isely, Duane. New combinations and one new variety in *Trifolium* (Leguminosae). Brittonia 32:55–57; 1980.

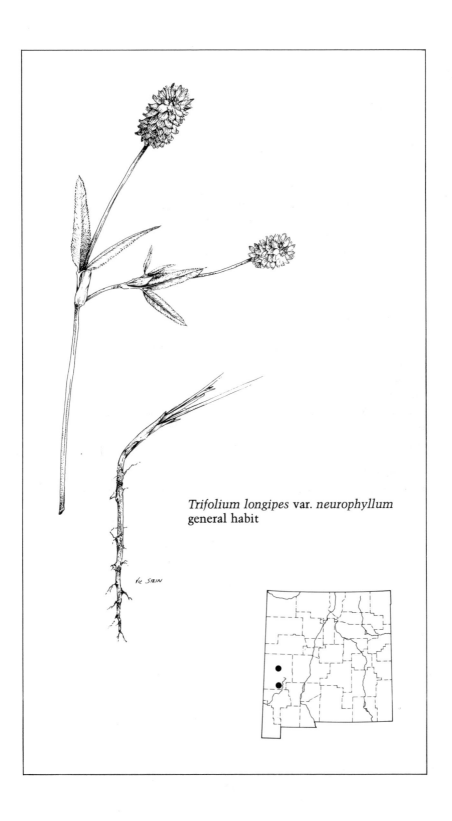

Trifolium longipes var. *neurophyllum*
general habit

Vic Stein

Family: HYDROPHYLLACEAE
Scientific Name: *Nama xylopodum* (Woot. and Standl.) Hitchc.
Common Name: Cliff nama
Classification: State priority 1
Federal Action: Federal Register, 15 December 1980, candidate for federal protection
Common Synonyms: *Marilaunidium xylopodum* Woot. and Standl.

Description: Tufted perennial herb from a woody root; stems numerous, slender, 10–12 cm (4.0–4.7 in.) long, coarse, hairy; leaves oblanceolate to spatulate, sharp pointed, to 2 cm (.8 in.) long and 2–4 mm (.08–.16 in.) wide; flowers funnel shaped, purple, blue to almost white, 7–10 mm (to 0.4 in.) long. Flowers from May to September.
Known Distribution: Otero and Eddy counties, New Mexico, and adjacent Texas
Habitat: Cracks and crevices of limestone boulders and scarps; 1,400–1,800 m (4,500–6,000 ft.)
Ownership: Bureau of Land Management, Forest Service, National Park Service, private
Threats to Taxon: None known
Similar Species: None
Remarks: *Nama xylopodum* is widely scattered, occurring here and there. However, it is a major member of the crevice and rockface community of the Guadalupe Mountains.

Important Literature:
Hitchcock, C. L. A taxonomic study of the genus *Nama*. Am. Jour. Bot. 20:415–30; 1933.

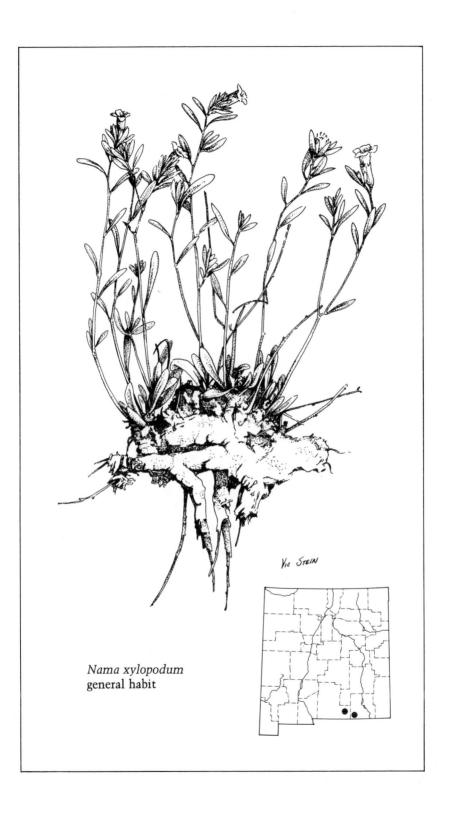

Vic Stein

Nama xylopodum
general habit

Family: LAMIACEAE (Labiateae)
Scientific Name: *Agastache cana* (Hook.) Woot. & Standl.
Common Name: Grayish white giant hyssop
Classification: State priority 1
Federal Action: None
Common Synonyms: *Cedronella cana* Hook.

Description: Perennial herb; stems very finely hairy, often grayish, 30–50 cm (12–20 in.); leaves lance shaped to triangular-ovate, to about 15 mm (0.6 in.) wide, the margins entire or with rounded or sharply pointed teeth; flowers in loose clusters 2–3 cm (0.75–1.25 in.) wide; calyx 8–10 mm (0.2–0.4 in.) long, the lobes triangular, sharp pointed, about 2 mm long; corolla 20–25 mm (0.75–1.0 in.) long, red, more than twice as long as the calyx. Flowers from mid-July to August.
Known Distribution: Bernalillo, Doña Ana, Grant, Lincoln, and Otero counties, New Mexico, and adjacent Texas
Habitat: In low mountains at middle elevations; 1,600–1,900 m (5,250–6,225 ft.)
Ownership: Bureau of Land Management, Forest Service
Threats to Taxon: None known
Similar Species: *Agastache rupestris*, which differs from this species by its linear leaves
Remarks: The record for the Sandia Mountains is questionable. Another record by Wooton and Standley in 1913, "Headwaters of the Pecos," is also anomalous. More study of this plant is needed.

Important Literature:
Lint, H., and Carl Epling. A revision of *Agastache*. Amer. Midl. Nat. 33:207–30; 1945.
Wooton, E. O., and P. C. Standley. Description of new plants preliminary to a report upon the flora of New Mexico. Contr. U.S. Nat. Herb. 16:109–96; 1913.

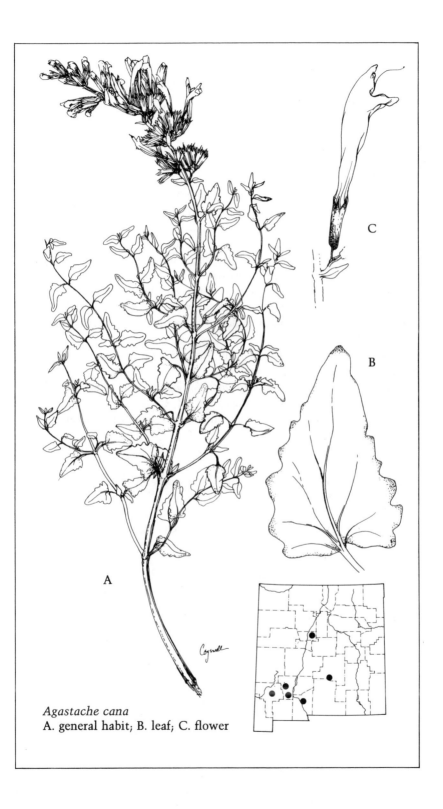

Agastache cana
A. general habit; B. leaf; C. flower

Family: LAMIACEAE (Labiateae)
Scientific Name: *Agastache mearnsii* Woot. & Standl.
Common Name: Mearns's giant hyssop
Classification: Biologically threatened
Federal Action: None
Common Synonyms: *Agastache pallidiflora* (Heller) Rydb. ssp. *mearnsii* (Woot. & Standl.) Lint and Epling

Description: Perennial, stems 50–70 cm (2.0–2.8 in.) tall, finely hairy leaves oval-triangular, coarsely toothed along edges, the blades longer than wide, finely hairy; flowering stems clustered; calyx purplish, 7–9 mm (0.3–0.4 in.) long, the lobes awl shaped to triangular; corolla purplish, 13–18 mm (0.5–0.7 in.) long, often more than twice as long as the calyx. Flowers from July to October.
Known Distribution: Suspected to occur in Hidalgo County, New Mexico, confirmed only from adjacent Mexico
Habitat: Slopes and valleys at middle to lower elevations; 1,300–1,950 m (4,500–6,500 ft.)
Ownership: Probably Bureau of Land Management, private
Threats to Taxon: None known
Similar Species: *Agastache pallidiflora* ssp. *havardii* has a shorter corolla, not more than half as long as the calyx.
Remarks: This plant is a Mexican endemic whose range may barely extend into New Mexico.

Important Literature:

Lint, H., and Carl Epling. A revision of *Agastache.* Amer. Midl. Nat. 33:207–30; 1945.

Wooton, E. O., and P. C. Standley. Description of new plants preliminary to a report upon the flora of New Mexico. Contr. U.S. Nat. Herb. 16:109–96; 1913.

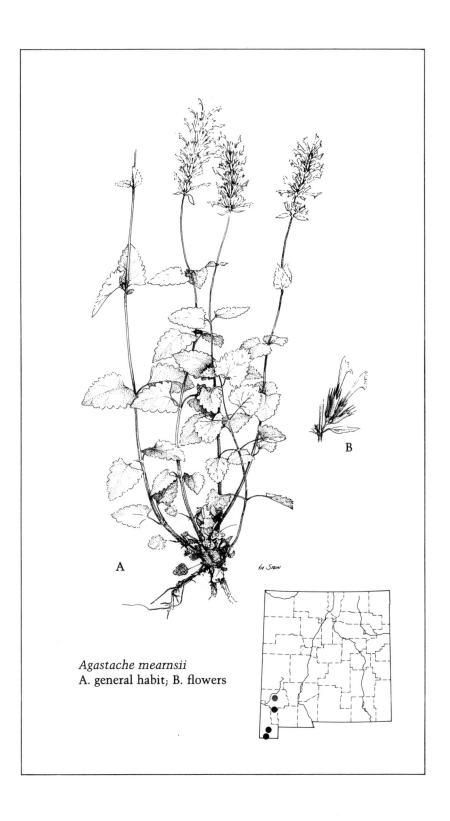

Agastache mearnsii
A. general habit; B. flowers

Family: LAMIACEAE (Labiateae)
Scientific Name: *Hedeoma apiculatum* Stewart
Common Name: McKittrick pennyroyal
Classification: Biologically threatened
Federal Action: Federal Register, 13 July 1982, federally threatened
Common Synonyms: None

Description: Low-growing, tufted perennial from a woody base; herbaceous stems bearing numerous small curled hairs; leaves opposite, crowded, to about 15 mm (0.6 in.) long, the margins without teeth, pointed at the tip; flowers 1–3 in the axils of leaves toward the summit of the stem, about 20 mm (0.8 in.) long, the lower lobe enlarged, about 10 mm (0.4 in.) wide. Flowers from July to August.
Known Distribution: Eddy County, New Mexico, and adjacent Texas
Habitat: Limestone crevices of canyon walls, and among rocks along watercourses and ridges, at about 1,825 m (6,000 ft.)
Ownership: Forest Service, National Park Service
Threats to Taxon: None known except possibly by trail use and development
Similar Species: None
Remarks: This unique pennyroyal is endemic to the Guadalupe Mountains.

Important Literature:

Correll, D., and M. Johnston. Manual of the vascular plants of Texas. Renner, Tex.: Texas Research Foundation; 1970.

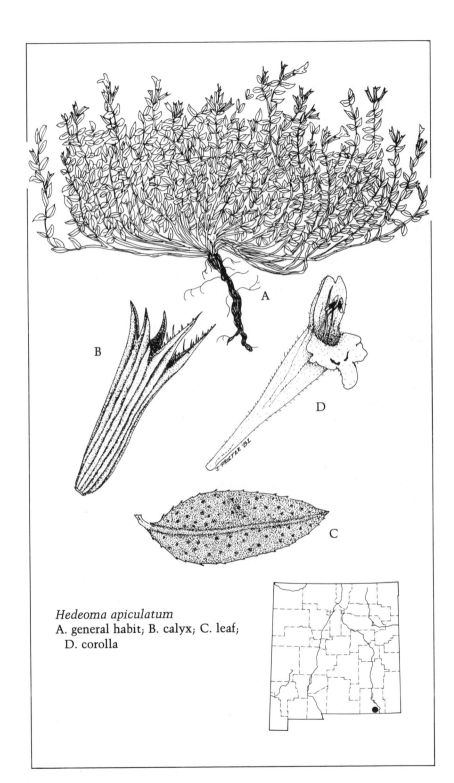

Hedeoma apiculatum
A. general habit; B. calyx; C. leaf;
  D. corolla

Family: LAMIACEAE (Labiateae)
Scientific Name: *Hedeoma pulcherrimum* Woot. & Standl.
Common Name: Mescalero pennyroyal
Classification: State priority 1
Federal Action: Federal Register, 15 December 1980, removed from consideration for federal protection
Common Synonyms: None

Description: Perennial, stems 20–30 cm (9–12 in.) tall; leaves elliptic to somewhat oblong, mostly 10–20 mm (0.4–0.8 in.) long, less than half as wide, blunt at the tip, minutely hairy, the margins without teeth; flowers clustered in the axils of the upper leaves, bluish purple, 12–14 mm (0.5–0.6 in.) long. Flowers from June to September.
Known Distribution: Lincoln and Otero counties, New Mexico
Habitat: Montane slopes, dry soil, among coniferous trees; 2,125–2,750 m (7,000–9,000 ft.)
Ownership: Forest Service, Mescalero Indian Reservation, private
Threats to Taxon: General development in the Cloudcroft area is continually reducing the habitat of this species. It may not tolerate livestock grazing.
Similar Species: None, however, *H. pulcherrimum* hybridizes naturally with *H. drummondii.*
Remarks: In spite of the listed threats, this plant does well in open, moderately disturbed habitat.

Important Literature:
Epling, C., and W. Stewart. A revision of *Hedeoma* with a review of allied genera. Repert. Sp. Nov. Bieh. 115:1–150; 1939.
Irving, R. S. Status report for *Hedeoma pulcherrimum*. U.S. Fish and Wildlife Service; 1980.

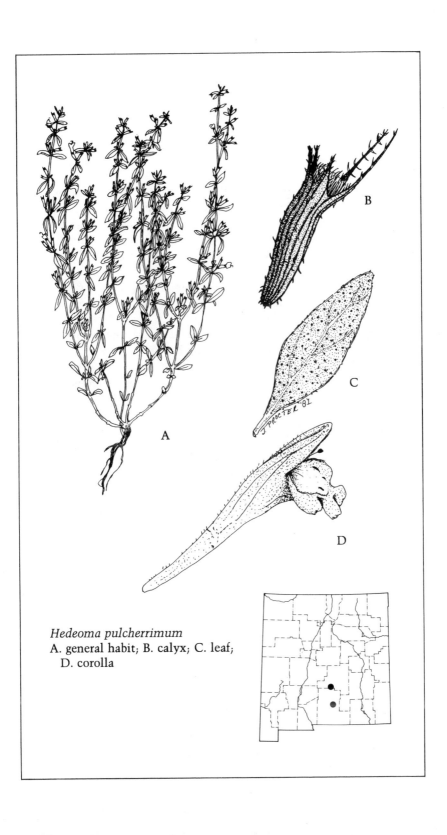

Hedeoma pulcherrimum
A. general habit; B. calyx; C. leaf;
  D. corolla

Family: LAMIACEAE (Labiateae)
Scientific Name: *Hedeoma todsenii* Irving
Common Name: Todsen's pennyroyal
Classification: Biologically threatened
Federal Action: Federal Register, 25 July 1980, federally endangered
Common Synonyms: None

Description: Low-growing perennial, 10–18 cm (4–7 in.) tall, stems several, clustered, somewhat woody at the base; leaves opposite, stiff, 8–14 mm (0.3–0.6 in.) long, blunt on end; few flowers, usually one or two on upper part of stem, tubelike, golden with red markings on the lips, up to 35 mm (1.5 in.) long. Flowers from July to September.
Known Distribution: Sierra County, New Mexico
Habitat: North- and east-facing 45° slopes, in gravelly gypseous limestone soil under scattered pinyon, at about 2,000 m (6,600 ft.)
Ownership: Department of Defense
Threats to Taxon: The poor reproductive potential of this species makes it especially susceptible to natural catastrophe.
Similar Species: None
Remarks: *Hedeoma todsenii* apparently represents an old evolutionary line in the genus.

Important Literature:
Irving, R. S. *Hedeoma todsenii* (Labiateae): A new and rare species from New Mexico. Madrono 26:184–87; 1979.
Irving, R. S. Status report from *Hedeoma todsenii*. U.S. Fish and Wildlife Service; 1980.

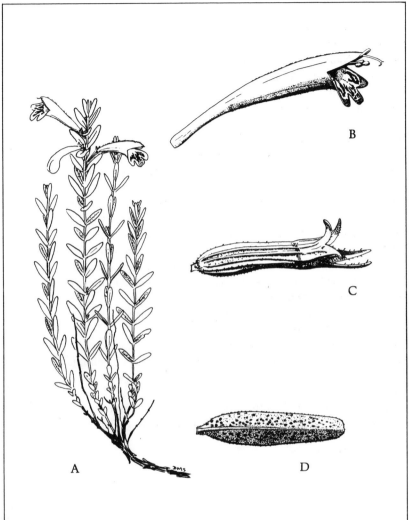

A

Hedeoma todsenii
A. general habit; B. corolla;
C. calyx; D. leaf

Family: LAMIACEAE (Labiateae)
Scientific Name: *Salvia summa* A. Nels.
Common Name: Supreme sage
Classification: Biologically threatened
Federal Action: None
Common Synonyms: None

Description: Perennial, several stems, weak (usually relying on surrounding vegetation or rocks for support) to 30 cm (12 in.) long; herbage glandular dotted, long-hairy; lower leaves pinnately lobed, the upper lobe largest; flowers few but showy, arising from the axils of the leaves; calyx two-lipped, the three teeth of the lower lip longer than the two of the upper; corolla pink to lavender, with red dots in the throat, slender, tubelike, 35–45 mm (1.3–1.6 in.) long, three-lipped on the upper side and two-lipped on the lower side. Flowers from March and April.
Known Distribution: Doña Ana, Eddy counties, New Mexico
Habitat: Shaded rock ledges and rock cracks on steep limestone canyon sides, at about 1,500 m (5,000 ft.)
Ownership: Department of Defense, Forest Service
Threats to Taxon: None known
Similar Species: *Salvia henryi* has a scarlet corolla.
Remarks: This species is scattered and rare within its habitat.

Important Literature:
Correll, D. S., and M. C. Johnston. Manual of the vascular plants of Texas. Renner, Tex.: Texas Research Foundation; 1970.

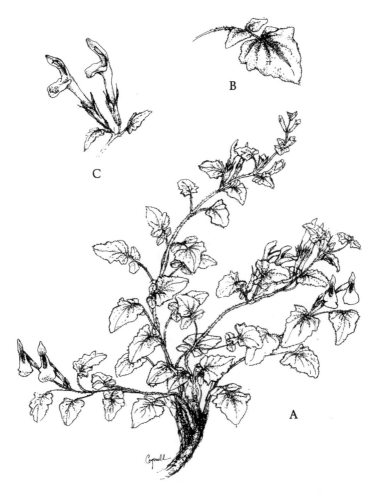

Salvia summa
A. general habit; B. leaf; C. flowers

Family: LILIACEAE
Scientific Name: *Allium gooddingii* Ownbey
Common Name: Goodding's onion
Classification: Biologically threatened
Federal Action: Federal Register, 15 December 1980, candidate for federal protection
Common Synonyms: None

Description: Perennial from bulbs terminating in short, thick rhizomes; leaves several, flat, to about 8 mm (0.4 in.) wide; flowering stalk to 45 cm (18 in.) tall; flowers about 20 per stalk, in a terminal cluster (umbel) subtended by conspicuous bracts; flowers deep red-violet, large, six petals, 8–10 mm (0.4 in.) long. Flowers from June to August.
Known Distribution: Catron County, New Mexico, and Arizona
Habitat: Moist shaded canyon bottoms in climax-conifer forest, at about 2,440 m (8,000 ft.) in New Mexico
Ownership: Forest Service
Threats to Taxon: Any activity creating a successional or disclimax state, such as grazing, or logging, will have an adverse effect on this species.
Similar Species: The deep red-violet flowers and broad leaves distinguish this onion from all others within this range.
Remarks: *Allium gooddingii* is our most attractive and easily eradicated species of onion.

Important Literature:
Ownbey, G. S. The genus *Allium* in Arizona. Res. St. State Coll. Washington 15:221–24; 1947.
Spellenberg, R. Status report on *Allium gooddingii*. U.S. Fish and Wildlife Service; 1982.

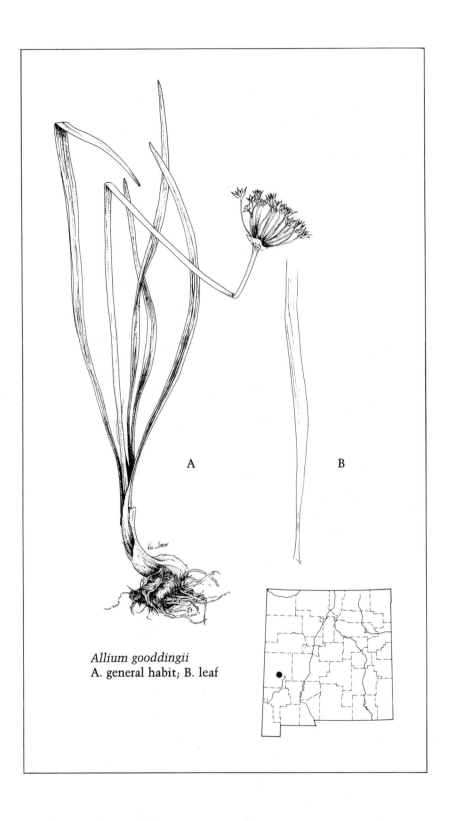

A

B

Allium gooddingii
A. general habit; B. leaf

Family: LOASACEAE
Scientific Name: *Mentzelia perennis* Woot.
Common Name: Gypsum blazing star
Classification: State priority 1
Federal Action: None
Common Synonyms: None

Description: Perennial herb, growing in clumps; stems 20–30 cm (8–12 in.) tall, whitish; herbage with numerous glands secreting a saltlike substance; leaves narrow, lobed or unlobed, 3–10 cm (1.2–4.0 in.) long, 2–3 mm (0.1 in.) wide; lower part of calyx tubelike, top shaped, 5 mm (0.2 in.) long, the upper part five-lobed, the lobes about 10 mm (0.6 in.) long; petals 10, pale yellow, 2 cm (0.75 in.) long, 5 mm (0.2 in.) wide; stamens numerous; capsule like an inverted cone, 1 cm (0.6 in.) long, 4 mm (0.12 in.) wide. Flowers in July and August.
Known Distribution: Cibola, Eddy, Lea, Otero, Socorro, and Torrance counties, New Mexico
Habitat: Gypsum deposits and limestone hills with gypsum lenses in the lower one-seed juniper vegetation type, at about 1,650 m (5,400 ft.)
Ownership: Bureau of Land Management, private
Threats to Taxon: None, perhaps mining of gypsum deposits
Similar Species: *Mentzelia humilus* is similar to *M. perennis*. It differs in having white, rather than yellow, flowers, and a shorter, more globular capsule.
Remarks: Hybridization and morphological variation is common in this species, and to fully understand this taxon, more studies are needed.

Important Literature:
Darlington, J. A monograph of the genus *Mentzelia*. Ann. Missouri Bot. Gard. 21:103–209; 1934.

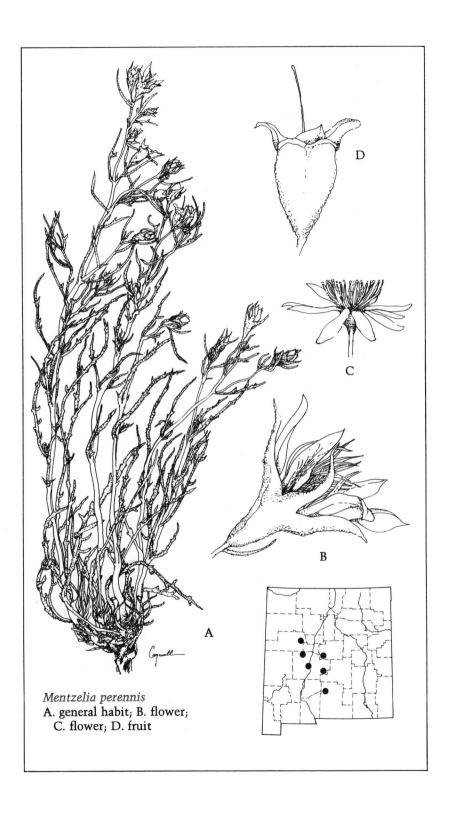

Mentzelia perennis
A. general habit; B. flower;
C. flower; D. fruit

Family: MALVACEAE
Scientific Name: *Iliamna grandiflora* (Rydb.) Wiggins
Common Name: Wild hollyhock
Classification: State priority 1
Federal Action: None
Common Synonyms: *Phymosia grandiflora* Rydb.
Sphaeralcea grandiflora Rydb.

Description: Perennial herb, stems to 1 m (40 in.) tall; leaves simple, hairy, petiolate, 10–15 cm (4–6 in.) in diameter, with 3–7 lobes and toothed margins; flowers white to rose-purple, mostly 3–5 cm (1.2–2.0 in.) wide, the base of the petals densely hairy; fruit divided into several segments arranged as pie-shaped structures around a central axis, each segment with 2–4 seeds. Flowers in July and August.
Known Distribution: Bernalillo, Santa Fe counties, New Mexico, and adjacent Colorado
Habitat: Damp montane meadows; 2,100–3,350 m (7,000–11,000 ft.)
Ownership: Forest Service
Threats to Taxon: None known
Similar Species: None in New Mexico
Remarks: There is confusion about the relationship between this species and *I. rivularis* of Colorado.

Important Literature:
Rydberg, P. A. A resurrection and revision of the genus *Iliamna*. Contr. Dudley Herb. 213–29; 1936.

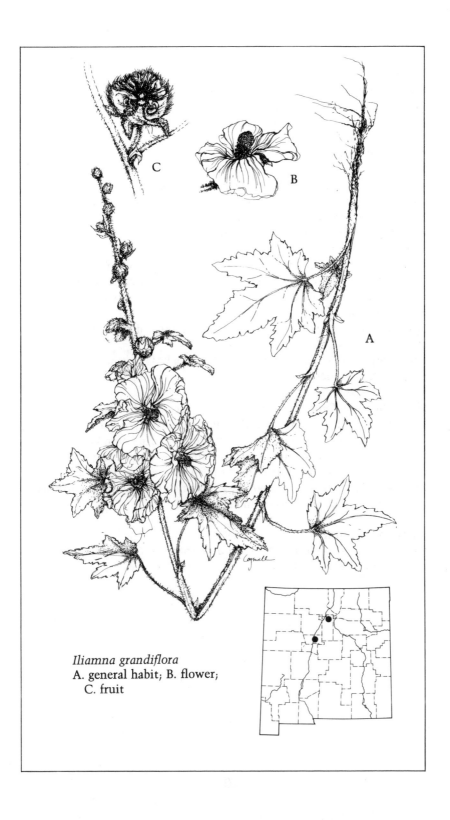

Iliamna grandiflora
A. general habit; B. flower;
   C. fruit

Family: MALVACEAE
Scientific Name: *Sphaeralcea procera* Porter
Common Name: Porter's globemallow
Classification: Biologically endangered
Federal Action: None
Common Synonyms: None

Description: Tall perennial, woody at the base; stem numerous, covered with tiny starlike hairs; leaves 1–5 cm long (0.5–2.0 in.), usually with a long terminal lobe and two basal lobes, the margins with a few irregular teeth; flowers numerous, with five lavender-pink petals, stamens many, united into a single column resembling a small shaving brush; fruits dividing into about ten pie-shaped segments each about 3 mm (0.12 in.) high, and each with a short point at the top, the netlike veins on the lower portion of their side walls coarse. Flowers from July to September.
Known Distribution: Luna County, New Mexico
Habitat: Sandy arroyos, but expected to be in other disturbed places, at about 1,350 m (4,500 ft.)
Ownership: Unknown, possibly Bureau of Land Management, private, or State of New Mexico
Threats to Taxon: None known
Similar Species: Other pink or lavender species of *Sphaeralcea* in southern New Mexico are *S. wrightii* and possibly *S. fendleri*. *Sphaeralcea wrightii* is short, rarely exceeding 75 cm (30 in.) tall. *Sphaeralcea fendleri* can have lavender-pink flowers. In that species, the fruit segments lack the short beaked tip, and the netlike veins are faint.
Remarks: This species is known only from a single collection northeast of Deming, and has not been found since 1943.

Important Literature:
Porter, C. L. A new species of *Sphaeralcea* from New Mexico. Bull. Torr. Bot. Club 70:531–32; 1943.

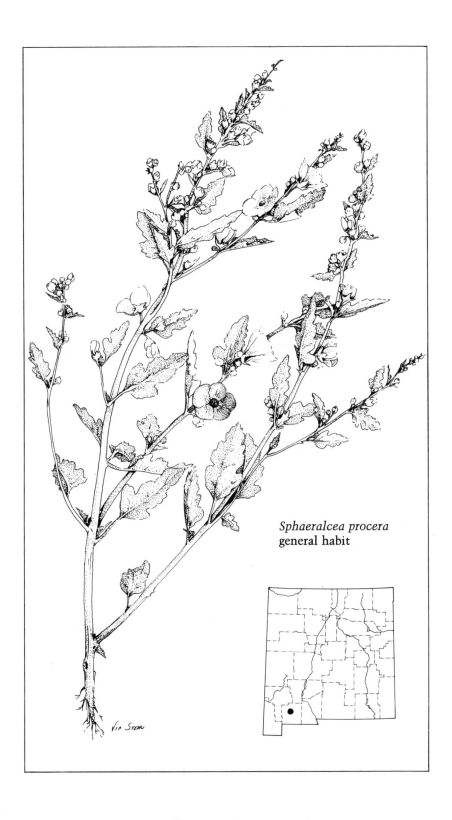

Sphaeralcea procera
general habit

Family: MALVACEAE
Scientific Name: *Sphaeralcea wrightii* Gray
Common Name: Wright's globemallow
Classification: Biologically threatened
Federal Action: None
Common Synonyms: None

Description: Grayish perennial, stems few to 75 cm (30 in.) tall; 2–4 cm
(0.75–1.5 in.) long, broadly ovate in outline with several wedge-shaped
lobes joined at the base; flowers with five lavender-pink or red-orange
petals, many stamens fused together so that they resemble a small
shaving brush; fruit dividing into 12–15 pie-shaped segments, about 4–5
mm (0.15 in.) high, and 3 mm (0.18 in.) wide, with a prominent, low,
blunt beak on the inside, the lower side walls are conspicuously marked
with netlike views. Probably flowering July to September.
Known Distribution: Doña Ana and Luna counties, New Mexico;
western Texas, southern Arizona, and northern Mexico
Habitat: Rocky slopes in arid grassland or desert; 1,100–1,500 m (4,000–
6,000 ft.)
Ownership: Bureau of Land Management, private, State of New Mexico
Threats to Taxon: None known
Similar Species: No other New Mexico *Sphaeralcea* with this leaf
arrangement have seeds completely filling the fruit segments.
Remarks: This is an uncommon endemic to the northern Chihuahuan
desert region, apparently just extending into southern New Mexico.

Important Literature:
Kearney, T. H. The North American species of *Sphaeralcea* subgenus
 Eusphaeralcea. Univ. Calif. Publ. Bot. 19:1–128; 1935.

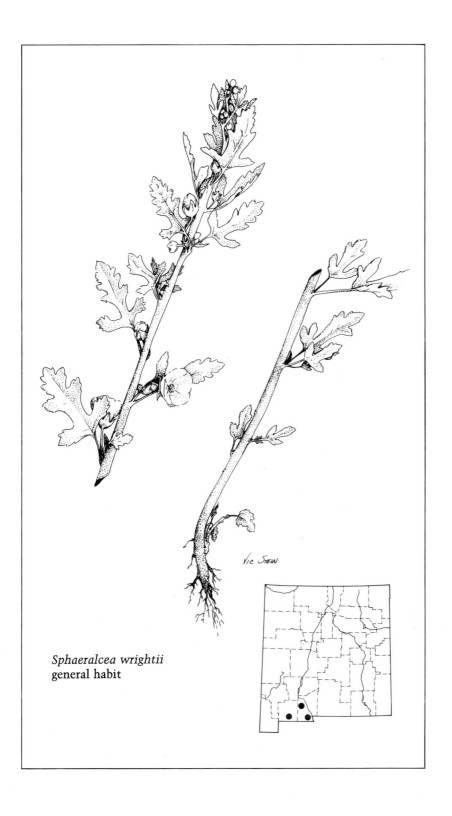

Sphaeralcea wrightii
general habit

Vic Stein

Family: MARTYNIACEAE
Scientific Name: *Proboscidea sabulosa* Correll
Common Name: Dune unicorn plant
Classification: Biologically threatened
Federal Action: Federal Register, 15 December 1980, candidate for federal protection
Common Synonyms: None

Description: Sticky-hairy annual; stems spreading, branched, about 1 m (40 in.) or more across; leaves long, stalked, the blades roughly triangular to rounded, heart shaped in outline, about 8–12 cm (3.2–4.8 in.) in diameter, wavy on the margins; flowers in small clusters, usually hidden by foliage, somewhat tubular with five irregular lobes, about 2 cm (0.8 in.) long and half as wide at the widest point, the base cream colored with small reddish spots or pale blotches on the inside, the lobes reddish purple; fruit oblong-ellipsoid, keeled on the back, to about 7 cm (2.8 in.) long and 2 cm (0.8 in.) wide, bearing a long, tapering, recurved tip, the tip splitting into two long, recurved claws when dry. Flowers in July and August.
Known Distribution: Eddy, Lea, and Socorro counties, New Mexico, and adjacent Texas
Habitat: Deep sands of mostly stabilized dunes, desert scrub, often with mesquite; 915–1,050 m (3,000–3,500 ft.)
Ownership: Bureau of Land Management, private, U.S. Fish and Wildlife Service
Threats to Taxon: None known
Similar Species: *Proboscidea louisianica* (Mill.) Thell. has substantially larger flowers.
Remarks: This species is a widely scattered, regional endemic adapted to dune regions.

Important Literature:
Correll, D., and M. Johnston. Manual of the vascular plants of Texas. Renner, Tex.: Texas Research Foundation; 1970.
Van Eseltine, G. A preliminary study of the unicorn plants. New York Agr. Exp. Sta. Tech. Bull. 149; 1929.

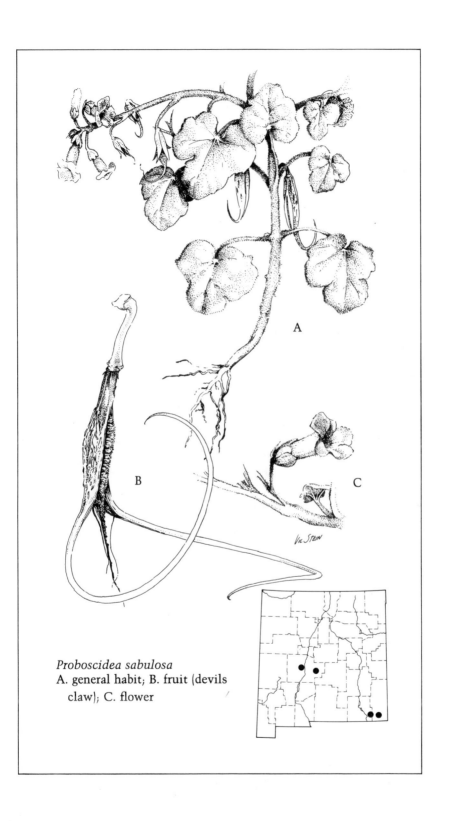

Proboscidea sabulosa
A. general habit; B. fruit (devils
  claw); C. flower

Family: NYCTAGINACEAE
Scientific Name: *Abronia bigelovii* Heimerl
Common Name: Tufted sand verbena
Classification: State priority 1
Federal Action: Federal Register, 15 December 1980, candidate for federal protection
Common Synonyms: None

Description: Tufted perennial herb, stems short, radiating out from a thickened base; leaves mostly at the base of the branches, linear to oblong, 1.5–3.0 cm (0.5–1.25 in.) long, 1.5–3.0 mm (to 0.12 in.) wide, blunt at the tip, smooth or with minute hairs, the margins devoid of teeth; flowering stems more or less erect, 5.0–7.5 cm (2–3 in.) long, forming headlike clusters of 20–30 flowers at the summit, the heads surrounded at the base with ovate papery bracts; flowers trumpet shaped, glandular, 1.5–2.0 cm (0.5–0.75 in.) long, with pink tube and small white lobes; fruit about 8 mm (3 in.) long, with four or five ridges. Flowers from April to August.
Known Distribution: Sandoval, Santa Fe, and Rio Arriba counties, New Mexico
Habitat: Hills and ridges of Todilto gypsum in central New Mexico, at about 1,850 m (6,000 ft.)
Threats to Taxon: Gypsum mining
Similar Species: *Abronia fragrans* grows in the same region as *A. bigelovii*. However, it does not form dense clumps and has larger, more broadly oblong leaves. No other New Mexico *Abronia* forms dense clumps.
Remarks: This species is entirely restricted to Todilto gypsum or the barren soils derived from this formation.

Important Literature:
Heimerl, A. Two new species of *Abronia*. Smiths. Misc. Coll. 52:197–98; 1908.

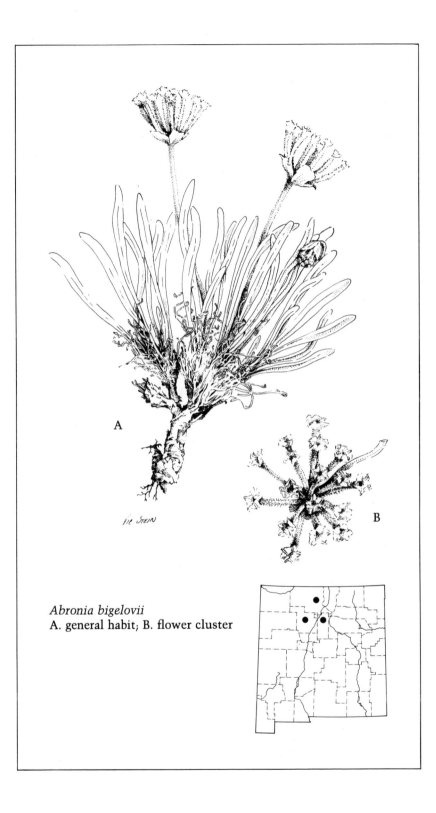

A

B

Abronia bigelovii
A. general habit; B. flower cluster

Family: ONAGRACEAE
Scientific Name: *Oenothera organensis* Munz
Common Name: Organ Mountain evening primrose
Classification: Biologically threatened
Federal Action: Federal Register, 15 December 1980, candidate for federal protection
Common Synonyms: *Oenothera macrosiphon* Wooton and Standley

Description: Perennial herbs; stems spreading or reclining, to about 60 cm (24 in.) long; herbage rough-hairy; leaves lance shaped, sometimes wavy toothed on the edges, without petioles or sometimes with a short-winged petioles; flowers yellow, becoming purple in age, the petals 50–60 mm (2.0–2.4 in.) long; flower tube beneath the petals conspicuous, as much as 19 cm (7.5 in.) long; pod 30–40 mm (1.2–1.6 in.) long, cylindrical, somewhat angled, slightly hairy. Flowers from June to September.
Known Distribution: Doña Ana County, New Mexico
Habitat: Restricted to seeps and springs; 1,700–2,280 m (5,700–7,600 ft.)
Ownership: Bureau of Land Management, Department of Defense, private
Threats to Taxon: Alteration of water tables could adversely affect this species.
Similar Species: None with this habitat
Remarks: This taxon has a limited range. It is dependent on seeps. Seed carried in deer droppings may play an important role in the distribution of this species.

Important Literature:
Munz, P. Studies in Onagraceae. Genetics 23:190–202; 1938.
Worthington, R. Status report for *Oenothera organensis*. U.S. Fish and Wildlife Service; 1981.

Oenothera organensis
A. upper stem and flower;
B. flower buds

Family: PAPAVERACEAE
Scientific Name: *Argemone pleiacantha* Greene ssp. *pinnatisecta* Ownbey
Common Name: Sacramento prickle-poppy
Classification: Biologically endangered
Federal Action: Federal Register, 15 December 1980, candidate for federal protection
Common Synonyms: None

Description: Perennial; stems numerous, commonly to 1.25 m (4 ft.) tall, branching from the base; stems and leaves prickly, with cream-colored sap; leaves pinnately dissected with divisions at right angles to the main axis of the leaf; petals white, the consistency of tissue paper; the anthers of the numerous stamens yellow, providing a striking contrast to the large, showy petals; capsule with many fine spines, none branched. Flowers May to August.
Known Distribution: Otero County, New Mexico
Habitat: Rocky canyon bottoms and slopes, and occasionally along roadsides; 1,500–2,100 m (5,000–7,000 ft.)
Ownership: Forest Service, private
Threats to Taxon: Road maintenance and excessive grazing
Similar Species: *Argemone pleiacantha* ssp. *pleiacantha* has yellow sap. Other species of *Argemone* in the region have fewer, coarser spines on the capsule.
Remarks: Activities creating major disturbances, such as road building, present initial adverse effects. However, its presence along roadsides indicates some degree of tolerance for such disturbances. The plant apparently does not have as great an ability to invade disturbed sites as do other prickle-poppies.

Important Literature:
Ownbey, G. B. The genus *Argemone* for North America and the West Indies. Bull. Torr. Bot. Club 21:1–159; 1958.
Soreng, R. Status report on *Argemone pleiacantha* ssp. *pinnatisecta*. U.S. Fish and Wildlife Service; 1982.

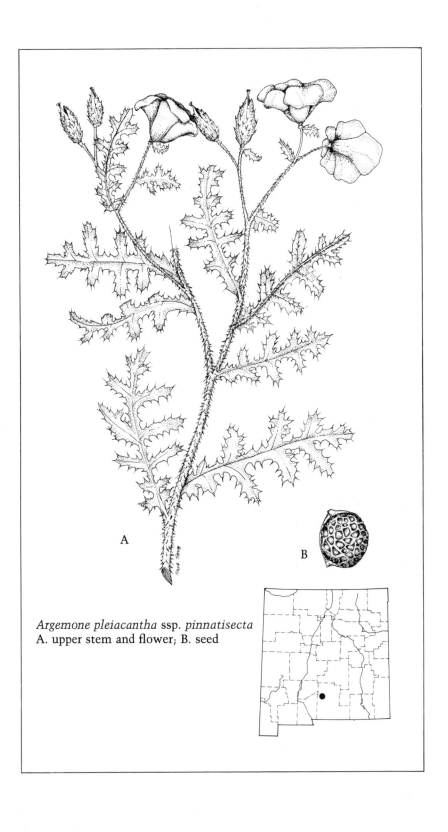

A

B

Argemone pleiacantha ssp. *pinnatisecta*
A. upper stem and flower; B. seed

Family: POACEAE (Gramineae)
Scientific Name: *Stipa curvifolia* Swall.
Common Name: Curlleaf needlegrass
Classification: Biologically threatened
Federal Action: Federal Register, 15 December 1980, removed from consideration for federal protection

Description: Perennial bunchgrass; stems to about 35 cm (14 in.) tall, with leaves clustered near the base; leaf blades rolled inward, becoming slightly curled with age; flower cluster compact, 7–8 cm (2.7–3.1 in.) long; outer pair of bracts of each spikelet about 10 mm (0.4 in.) long; seed body densely hairy, the awned tip 22–55 mm (0.75–1.0 in.) long, bent sharply about midway, sometimes with an obscure second bend closer to the tip, the lower half of the awn densely hairy. Flowers in April or May.
Known Distribution: Doña Ana and Eddy counties, New Mexico, western Texas and northern Chihuahua
Habitat: Limestone rims and steep slopes; 1,500–1,700 m (4,000–5,600 ft.)
Ownership: Bureau of Land Management, Department of Defense, Forest Service, private
Threats to Taxon: The primary threat to this taxon is overutilization as a forage species by livestock.
Similar Species: No other species of *Stipa* in this area has awns (seed tails) 2–3 cm (1 in.) long, bent once or merely curved.
Remarks: Recent exploration of limestone hills in Doña Ana County has turned up heretofore unknown populations.

Important Literature:
Hitchcock, A. S., and A. Chase. Manual of the grasses of the United States. USDA Misc. Pub. 200; 1950. (Reprint. New York: Dover, 2 vol.; 1971)
Spellenberg, R. Status report on *Stipa curvifolia*. U.S. Fish and Wildlife Service; 1981.

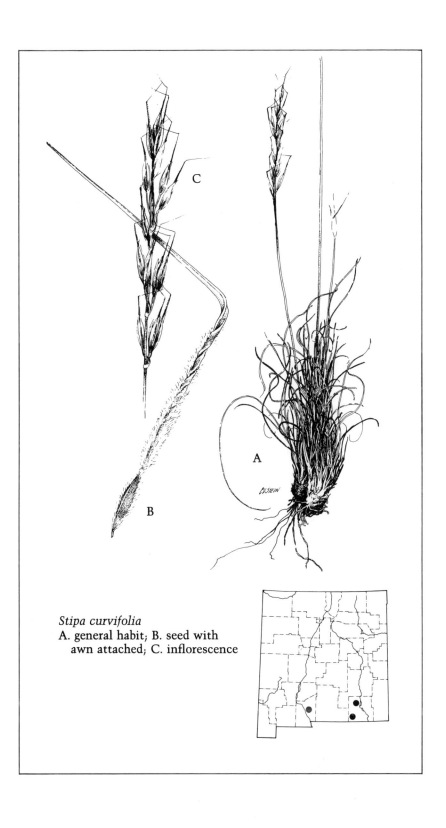

Stipa curvifolia
A. general habit; B. seed with
awn attached; C. inflorescence

Family: POLEMONIACEAE
Scientific Name: *Gilia formosa* Greene
Common Name: Beautiful gilia
Classification: Biologically threatened
Federal Action: None
Common Synonyms: None

Description: Perennial 7–30 cm (2.75–12 in.) tall, older plants woody at the base, glandular; stems numerous, branched; leaves entire 25 mm (1 in. long, sharp pointed; flowers pinkish purple, tubelike, about 22 mm (1 in.) long. Flowers April and May.
Known Distribution: San Juan County, New Mexico
Habitat: Sandstone outcrops at about 1,750 m (5,800 ft.)
Ownership: Bureau of Land Management
Threats to Taxon: None known
Similar Species: The perennial nature, woody base of older plants, entire leaves and pinkish purple flowers separate this from other *Gilias* in the area.
Remarks: This little-known species is known only from the type locality. It was named in 1907 and rediscovered in 1982.

Important Literature:
Greene, E. L. Das Pflanzenreich, vol. 27:119; 1907.

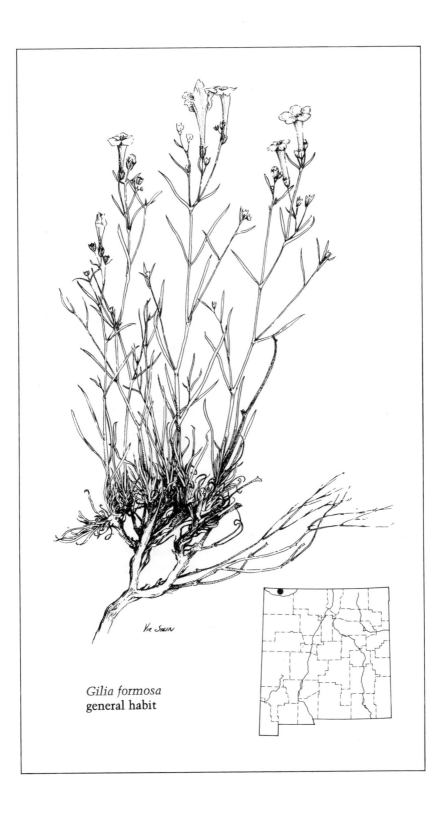

Vic Stein

Gilia formosa
general habit

Family: POLEMONIACEAE
Scientific Name: *Ipomopsis pinnatifida* (Cav.) Grant
Common Name: Bent-flowered gilia
Classification: Biologically threatened
Federal Action: None
Common Synonyms: *Gilia campylantha* Woot. & Standl.
Ipomopsis campylantha Martin & Hutchins

Description: Tufted perennial; stems slender, erect, to 30 cm (12 in.) tall, densely and finely hairy; leaves numerous, finely woolly, divided in a comblike manner into finely dissected segments with abruptly pointed bristlelike tips; flower cluster narrow, with flowers numerous and in small clusters; flower stalks short; calyx 3 mm (0.12 in.) long, slightly dry, thin, very finely hairy, the lobes as long as or longer than the flower tube, triangular-pointed; corolla white, sharply bent downward just above the calyx, the tube 8 mm (0.3 in.) long, the lobes oblong-elliptic, obtuse, about 4 mm (0.12 in.) long.
Known Distribution: Hidalgo County, New Mexico, and adjacent Mexico
Habitat: Middle elevations in mountainous terrain
Ownership: State of New Mexico, private
Threats to Taxon: None known
Similar Species: The short, downwardly bent white corolla distinguishes this from all other species in New Mexico.
Remarks: Virtually nothing is known regarding this (apparently) narrow endemic. It is clearly an *Ipomopsis* and should be placed in the genus. However, at present, the name *Gilia campylantha* has not yet been submerged under *I. pinnatifida*. Because this combination is presently being undertaken, we have opted to use *I. pinnatifida* in this work.

Important Literature:
Wooton, E. O., and P. C. Standley. Descriptions of new plants preliminary to a report upon the flora of New Mexico. Contr. U.S. Nat. Herb. 16:109–96; 1913.

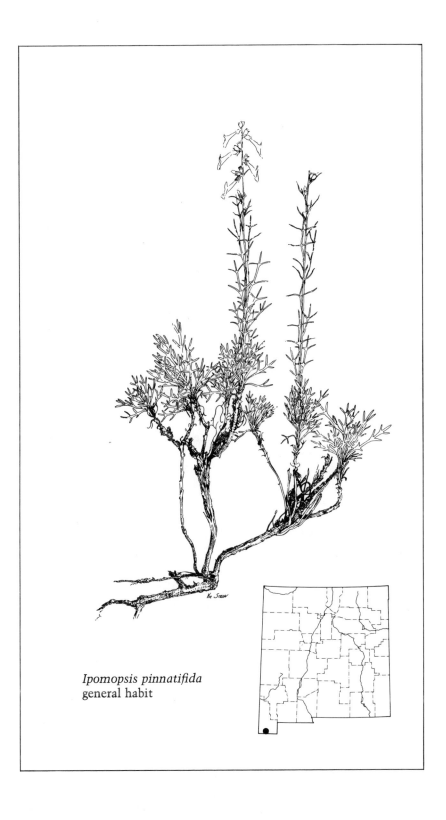

Ipomopsis pinnatifida
general habit

Family: POLEMONIACEAE
Scientific Name: *Phlox caryophylla* Wherry
Common Name: Pagosa phlox
Classification: State priority 1
Federal Action: Federal Register, 15 December 1980, candidate for federal protection
Common Synonyms: None

Description: Erect perennial from a somewhat woody base; stems to about 20 cm (8 in.) high, soft-hairy; leaves narrow, not exceeding 3 mm (0.12 in.) wide and 50 mm (2 in.) long; flowers in loose clusters, bright pink or purple, the flower parts united into a tube about 15 mm (0.6 in.) long, the petal lobes 6–10 mm (0.25–0.4 in.) long, 4–6 mm (0.16–0.25 in.) wide. Probably flowers from late May to July.
Known Distribution: Rio Arriba County, New Mexico, and adjacent Colorado
Habitat: Open slopes or in open woods in the mountains; 1,975–2,275 m (6,500–7,500 ft.)
Ownership: Forest Service
Threats to Taxon: None known
Similar Species: The most similar are *Phlox triovulata,* which has broader petals and *P. longifolia,* which has glandular pubescence on the inflorescence.
Remarks: The relationships between *P. caryophylla* and *P. longifolia* need clarification.

Important Literature:
Wherry, E. New phloxes from the Rocky Mountains and neighboring regions. Not. Nat. 146:1–11; 1944.
Wherry, E. The genus *Phlox.* Morris Arb. Monogr. 3:1–174; 1955.

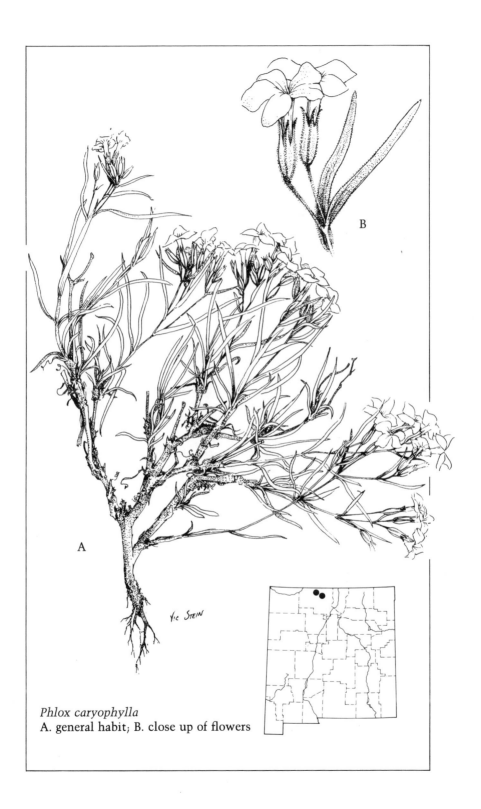

Phlox caryophylla
A. general habit; B. close up of flowers

Family: POLYGALACEAE
Scientific Name: *Polygala rimulicola* Steyer. var. *mescalerorum* Wendt and Todsen
Common Name: Mescalero milkwort
Classification: Biologically threatened
Federal Action: None
Common Synonyms: None

Description: Delicate, somewhat matted perennial from a woody base; stems numerous, glabrous, slender, mostly prostrate, branching, green, to 5 cm (2 in.) long; leaves slightly fleshy, elliptic-oval, 3 mm (0.12 in.) wide; one or two flowers at the end of the branches, rose-purple and white, about 5 mm (0.16 in.) long, the keel with a definite beak. Flowers from June to September.
Known Distribution: Doña Ana County, New Mexico
Habitat: Cracks of sandy, limestone cliffs; 1,600 m (5,100 ft.)
Ownership: Department of Defense
Threats to Taxon: None known
Similar Species: *Polygala rimulicola* var. *rimulicola*, which is easily distinguished by the absence of a prominent beak on the keel.
Remarks: At present, only about a hundred plants of this variety are known from two small cliff faces in the San Andres Mountains.

Important Literature:
Wendt, T., and T. K. Todsen. A new variety of *Polygala rimulicola* from Doña Ana County, New Mexico. Madroño 29(1):19–21; 1982.

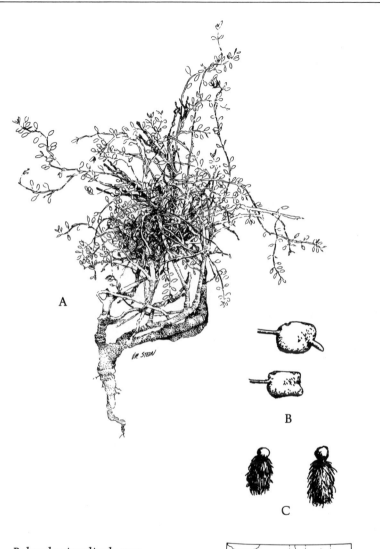

Polygala rimulicola var.
  mescalerorum
A. general habit; B. keel petal
  (var. mescalerorum—top,
  typical rimulicola—bottom);
C. seed (var. mescalerorum—
  right, typical rimulicola—left)

Family: POLYGALACEAE
Scientific Name: *Polygala rimulicola* Steyermark var. *rimulicola*
Common Name: Guadalupe milkwort
Classification: Biologically threatened
Federal Action: Federal Register, 15 December 1980, removed from consideration for federal protection
Common Synonyms: None

Description: Delicate perennial from a woody base; stems numerous, glabrous, slender, mostly prostrate, branching, up to 5 cm (2 in.) long; leaves green, elliptic-oval, 1.5–4.0 mm (0.06–0.16 in.) long; one or two flowers at the ends of branches, rose-purple to white, about 5 mm (0.16 in.) long, keel unbeaked or obscure. Flowers from June through September.
Known Distribution: Eddy County, New Mexico, and adjacent Texas
Habitat: Crevices of limestone boulders and cliffs; 1,550–2,400 m (5,000–8,000 ft.)
Ownership: Forest Service, National Park Service
Threats to Taxon: None known
Similar Species: *Polygala rimulicola* var. *mescalorum,* which is distinguished by its prominent beaked keel.
Remarks: This species appears to be rare throughout its range.

Important Literature:
Steyermark, J. A. Some new Spermatophytes from Texas. Ann. Missouri Bot. Gard. 19:289–395; 1932.

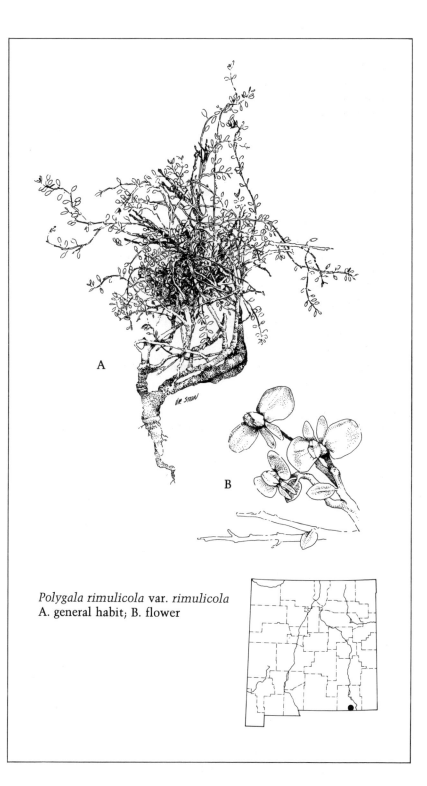

A

Ur Stein

B

Polygala rimulicola var. *rimulicola*
A. general habit; B. flower

Family: POLYGONACEAE
Scientific Name: *Eriogonum densum* Greene
Common Name: Woolly buckwheat
Classification: Biologically endangered
Federal Action: Federal Register, 15 December 1980, candidate for federal protection
Common Synonyms: None

Description: Annual; stems much branched, woolly to 15 cm (6 in.) tall; leaves clustered at the base of the stem, broadly oblong to nearly round, white woolly; flowers solitary or in small clusters in short-toothed, cup-shaped structures, about 1.5 mm (0.06 in.) long, the flower parts pinkish or whitish, usually fan-shaped, blunt-tipped; fruit three-angled. Flowers from June to October.
Known Distribution: Grant County, New Mexico
Habitat: Presumed to be dry slopes, at about 1,500 m (5,000 ft.)
Ownership: Bureau of Land Management, private
Threats to Taxon: None known
Similar Species: None
Remarks: *Eriogonum densum* may be a malformed *E. polycladon* produced by early browsing.

Important Literature:

Reveal, J. L. *Eriogonum* (Polygonaceae) of Arizona and New Mexico. Phytologia 34:409–84; 1976.

Spellenberg, R. Status report on *Eriogonum densum*. U.S. Fish and Wildlife Service; 1981.

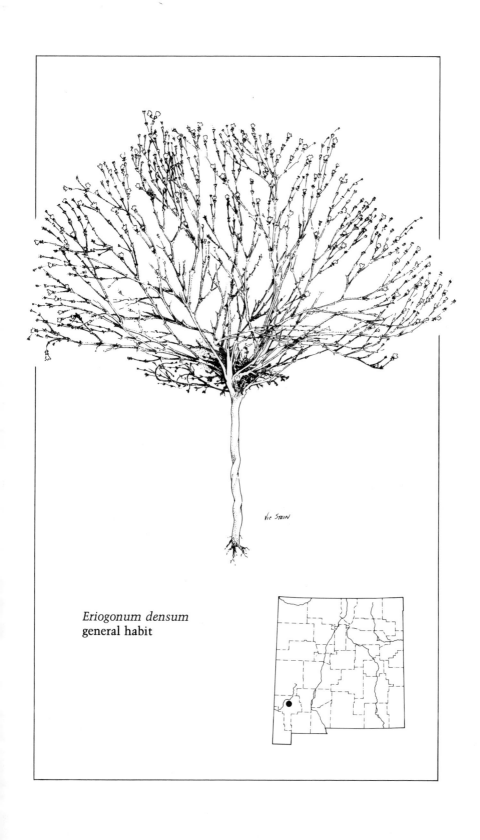

Eriogonum densum
general habit

Family: POLYGONACEAE
Scientific Name: *Eriogonum gypsophilum* Woot. & Standl.
Common Name: Gypsum wild buckwheat
Classification: Biologically endangered
Federal Action: Federal Register, 25 July 1980, federally threatened
Common Synonyms: None

Description: Tufted perennial; flower stalk 12–20 cm (5–8 in.) tall; leaves dark green, all basal, about a third as long as the flowering stalk, blades broad, shorter than their stalks; flowers arranged in tight groups, the clusters branched and usually broader than long; individual flowers tiny, yellow, about 2 mm (0.08 in.) long, with six petallike parts. Flowers in May and June.
Known Distribution: Eddy County, New Mexico
Habitat: Open, almost pure gypsum in grama grassland, at about 1,500 m (5,000 ft.)
Ownership: Bureau of Land Management, Bureau of Reclamation, private
Threats to Taxon: Gypsum mining and recreational development
Similar Species: In this area, other species of *Eriogonum* in the area with yellow flowers have woolly basal leaves or are annuals.
Remarks: This distinct species, consisting of but one population, has no known close relatives.

Important Literature:
Reveal, J. L. *Eriogonum* (Polygonaceae) of Arizona and New Mexico. Phytologia 34:409–84; 1976.
Wooton, E. O., and P. C. Standley. Description of new plants preliminary to a report upon a flora of New Mexico. Contr. U.S. Nat. Herb. 16:109–96 (original description); 1913.

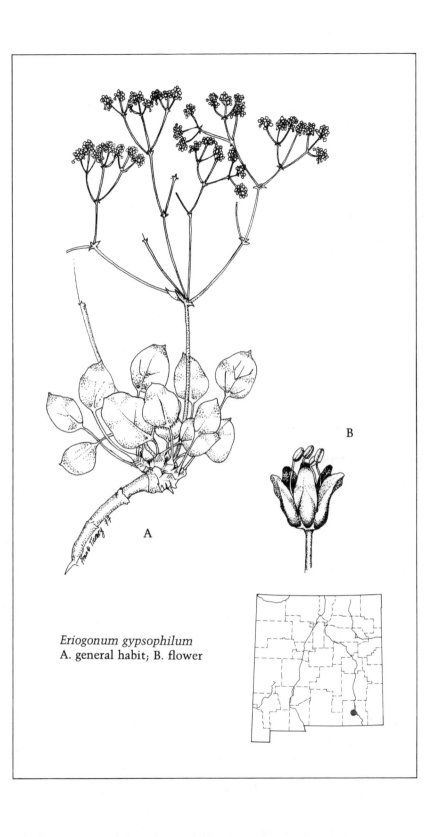

Eriogonum gypsophilum
A. general habit; B. flower

Family: POLYGONACEAE
Scientific Name: *Eriogonum jamesii* Benth. *in* DC. var. *wootonii* Reveal
Common Name: Wooton's buckwheat
Classification: State priority 1
Federal Action: None

Description: Tufted perennial forming mats to 50 cm (20 in.) across; leaves broadly elliptic, 3–15 cm (1.25–5.9 in.) long and 1.5–3.0 cm (0.6–1.2 in.) wide, the margin entire; flowering stems branched, 20–50 cm (7.9–20 in.) tall; bracts below flowers large, leaflike; flowers clustered, yellow; achenes three-angled, not winged. Flowers from June to September.
Known Distribution: Lincoln and Otero counties, New Mexico
Habitat: Roadcuts and small openings, primarily in mixed-conifer and spruce-fir forest; 1,800–3,500 m (6,000–11,500 ft.)
Ownership: Forest Service, Mescalero Apache Indian Reservation, private
Threats to Taxon: None known
Similar Species: No other clump-forming, perennial, yellow-flowered buckwheat occurs in this section of the state.
Remarks: This common endemic is one of a number of the rapidly evolving forms within the *Eriogonum jamesii* complex. While several have been named as distinct species or varieties, many are not yet different enough for taxonomic separation.

Important Literature:
Reveal, J. L. *Eriogonum* of Arizona and New Mexico. Phytologia 34:409–512; 1976.

Eriogonum jamesii var. *wootonii*
A. general habit; B. flowers
subtended by involucre

Family: POLYGONACEAE
Scientific Name: *Rumex tomentellus* Rechinger f.
Common Name: Mogollon dock
Classification: Biologically endangered
Federal Action: None
Common Synonyms: None

Description: Erect perennial at least 30 cm (12 in.) tall, with matted woolly hairs; basal leaves oblong with a heart-shaped base, tapering to the tip, 25–30 cm (9.8–11.8 in.) long, 7–11 cm (2.8–4.3 in.) wide, petiolate; the papery fruit covering less than 8 mm (0.3 in.) long; fruit a three-angled achene. Flowers in July.
Known Distribution: Catron County, New Mexico
Habitat: Wet ground and stream banks, at about 2,450 m (8,000 ft.)
Ownership: Forest Service, private
Threats to Taxon: Water development and recreation
Similar Species: No other tall *Rumex* in New Mexico has a covering of matted woolly hairs.
Remarks: Virtually nothing is known about this species. If taxonomically valid, it would be a good candidate for federal protection.

Important Literature:

Rechinger, K. H. Some new American species of *Rumex*. Leafl. West. Bot. 7:133–35; 1954.

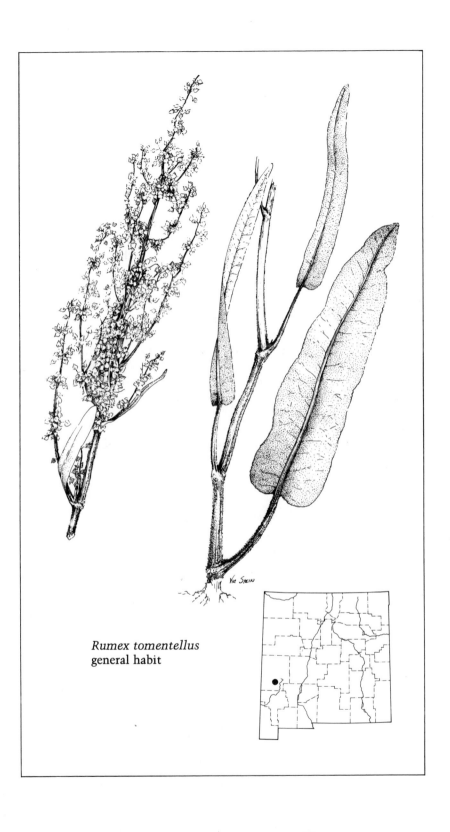

Rumex tomentellus
general habit

Family: PORTULACACEAE
Scientific Name: *Talinum humile* Greene
Common Name: Pinos Altos flame flower
Classification: Biologically threatened
Federal Action: None
Common Synonyms: None

Description: Tufted perennial; 5–8 cm (2–3 in.) tall, smooth, and hairless; succulent leaves cylindrical, 5.0–7.5 cm (2.0–2.9 in.) long, forming a basal cluster; flower stalks branched, not exceeding the leaves; 5–10 flowers in terminal clusters; sepals pointed; petals pale yellow, changing to orange in drying; seeds black, marked with circular lines. Probably flowers from July to September.
Known Distribution: Grant County, New Mexico
Habitat: Rocky, south-facing slopes; 1,825–2,450 m (6,000–8,000 ft.)
Ownership: Forest Service and possibly private
Threats to Taxon: None known
Similar Species: No other *Talinum* in New Mexico has yellow flowers in terminal clusters.
Remarks: The ecological relationships of this taxon are little known. It occurs in an area with extensive mining activity.

Important Literature:
Greene, E. L. New plants of New Mexico and Arizona. Bot. Gaz. 6:183–85; 1881.

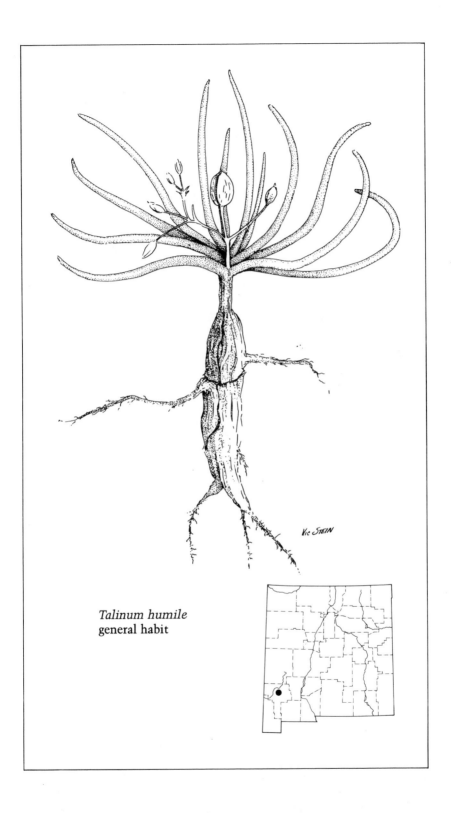

Vic STEIN

Talinum humile
general habit

Family: PORTULACACEAE
Scientific Name: *Talinum longipes* Woot. & Standl.
Common Name: Long-stemmed talinum
Classification: State priority 1
Federal Action: None
Common Synonyms: None

Description: Perennial herb; stems to 30 cm (12 in.) tall; leaves cylindrical, crowded toward the base, to 20 cm (8 in.) long, pointed at the tip; flowers 3–5 in an open terminal cluster, the flower stalks (pedicels) 3–6 mm (0.12–0.25 in.) long; sepals nearly round about 2 mm (0.08 in.) long; petals pink, 4–5 mm (0.2 in.) long; ten stamens; capsule nearly spherical 3–4 mm (0.16 in.) long. Probably flowers in July and August.
Known Distribution: Doña Ana County, New Mexico
Habitat: Dry hills at low elevations
Ownership: Bureau of Land Management, private
Threats to Taxon: None known
Similar Species: *Talinum calycinum*, which has 30 or more stamens
Remarks: This poorly understood species may be more extensive in Mexico.

Important Literature:
Wooton, E. O., and P. C. Standley. Descriptions of new plants preliminary to a report upon the flora of New Mexico. Contr. U.S. Nat. Herb. 16:109–96; 1913.

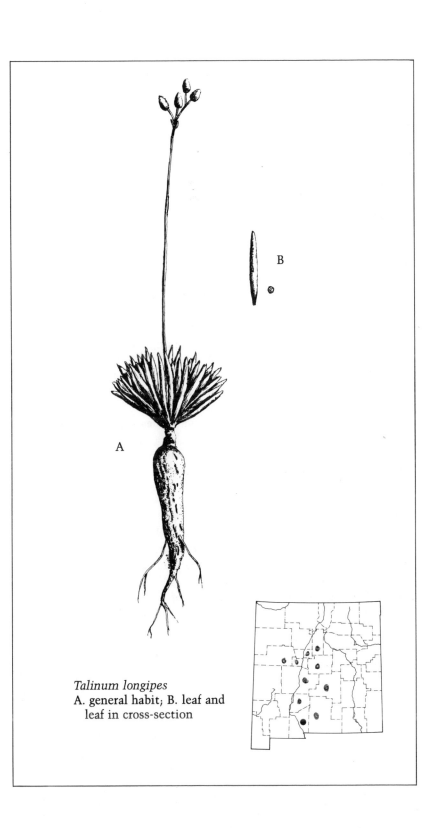

Talinum longipes
A. general habit; B. leaf and
leaf in cross-section

Family: RANUNCULACEAE
Scientific Name: *Aquilegia chaplinei* Standl.
Common Name: Chapline's columbine
Classification: Biologically threatened
Federal Action: Federal Register, 15 December 1980, candidate for federal protection
Common Synonyms: None

Description: Rhizomatous perennial; stems 20–50 cm (8–20 in.) tall; leaves two or three times divided into three parts, 5–12 cm (2.0–4.75 in.) long, slender; leaflets broadly wedge shaped to almost circular, deep green above, lighter beneath, lobed; flowers pale yellow; sepals lance shaped, 13–16 mm (0.5 in.) long, 4–6 mm (0.25 in.) wide; five petals, each with a free oblong portion 8–10 mm (0.4 in.) long, the base prolonged into a spur 3–4 cm (1.25–1.5 in.) long. Flowers from April to October.
Known Distribution: Eddy County, New Mexico, and adjacent Texas
Habitat: Permanently moist areas around springs and seeps, usually on the face of limestone bluffs; 1,400–1,675 m (4,700–5,500 ft.)
Ownership: Forest Service, National Park Service
Threats to Taxon: Water development threatens all populations, at least to some degree.
Similar Species: *Aquilegia chrysantha*, which has spurs longer than 4 cm (1.6 in.)
Remarks: The Sacramento Mountain populations of yellow-flowered columbines are somewhat intermediate between *A. chaplinei* and *A. chrysantha*.

Important Literature:

Correll, D. S., and M. C. Johnston. Manual of the vascular plants of Texas. Renner, Tex.: Texas Research Foundation; 1970.

Munz, P. A. *Aquilegia:* The cultivated and wild columbines. In L. H. Bailey, Gent. Herb. 7:1–150; 1946.

Payson, E. B. The North American species of *Aquilegia*. Contr. U.S. Nat. Herb. 20:133–57; 1918.

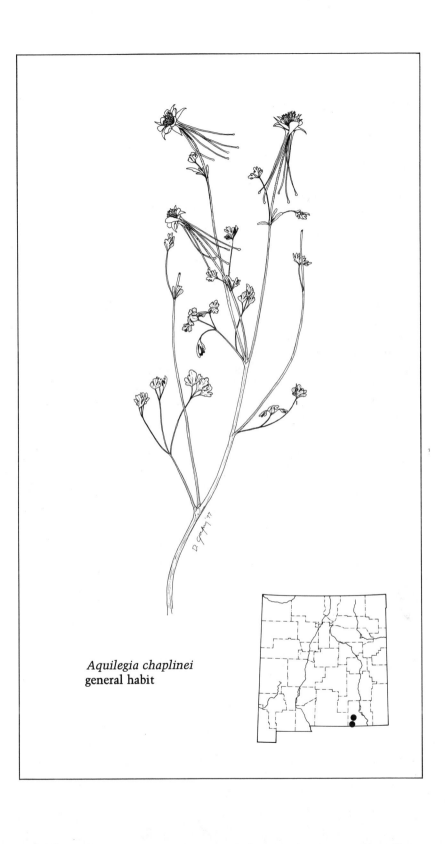

Aquilegia chaplinei
general habit

Family: RANUNCULACEAE
Scientific Name: *Delphinium alpestre* Rydb.
Common Name: Alpine larkspur
Classification: State priority 1
Federal Action: None
Common Synonyms: None

Description: Tufted perennial; stems slender, to about 15 cm (6 in.) long; leaves crowded toward the base, 2–3 cm (0.75–1.1 in.) long, palmately divided into five lobes; flower clusters short, few flowered; sepals dull bluish or tinged with brown, especially on the back, curved inward at the apex, about 11–15 (0.5 in.) long, the upper sepal with a spur about 7–9 mm (0.4 in.) long; the lower petals two-lobed. Flowers from July to September.
Known Distribution: Taos County, New Mexico, and adjacent Colorado
Habitat: Open montane meadows; 3,500–3,950 m (11,500–13,000 ft.)
Ownership: Forest Service
Threats to Taxon: None known
Similar Species: This is the only alpine larkspur in its area that does not grow taller than about 30 cm (1 ft.).
Remarks: This species is not often collected. Its remote habitat reduces its vulnerability to man-influenced disturbances.

Important Literature:
Ewan, J. A synopsis of the North American species of *Delphinium*. Univ. Colorado Stud. 2:55–244; 1945.

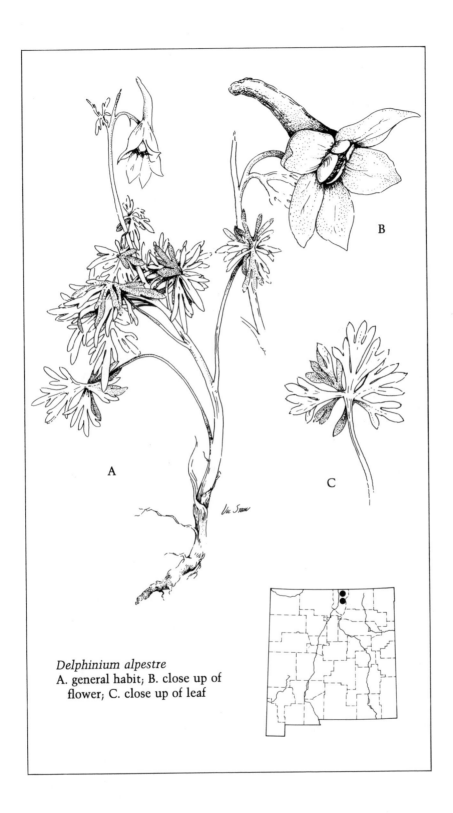

Delphinium alpestre
A. general habit; B. close up of
flower; C. close up of leaf

Family: ROSACEAE
Scientific Name: *Crataegus wootoniana* Eggl.
Common Name: Wooton's hawthorn
Classification: State priority 1
Federal Action: None
Common Synonyms: None

Description: Small tree or shrub to 3 m (10 ft.) tall; branches spiny, the spines purplish brown, 3–4 cm (1.5 in.) long; leaves egg shaped in outline, the margins with three or four broad lobes on each side, these finely toothed along the margin, becoming hairless with age; five petals, white, rounded, 6–8 mm (0.2–0.3 in.) wide; five to eight stamens; fruit brown to black, 7–8 mm (0.3 in.) in diameter. Flowers from April to June.
Known Distribution: Catron and Lincoln counties, New Mexico
Habitat: Along streams; 1,980–2,440 m (6,500–8,000 ft.)
Ownership: Forest Service and Mescalero Indian Reservation
Threats to Taxon: None known
Similar Species: *Crataegus erythrocarpa*, from which *C. wootoniana* differs by having finely toothed leaves instead of coarsely toothed ones (these teeth not gland tipped) and by having squared rather than wedge-shaped leaf bases
Remarks: Sufficient collections of this entity have not been made to allow a thorough analysis of its taxonomic status.

Important Literature:
Eggelston, W. W. *Crataegus* in New Mexico. Torreya 7:235–36; 1907.

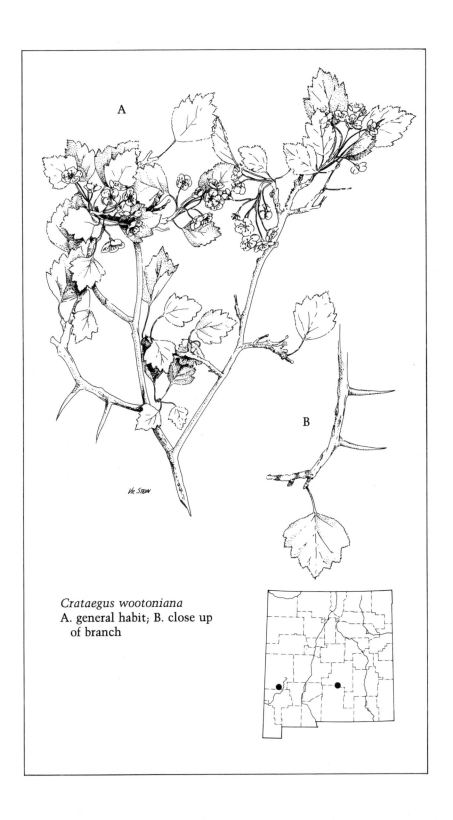

A

B

Vic Stow

Crataegus wootoniana
A. general habit; B. close up
of branch

Family: ROSACEAE
Scientific Name: *Potentilla sierrae-blancae* Woot. & Rydb.
Common Name: Sierra Blanca cinquefoil
Classification: Biologically threatened
Federal Action: Federal Register, 15 December 1980, candidate for federal protection
Common Synonyms: None

Description: Dwarf perennial seldom more than 8 cm (3.2 in.) tall, with numerous short, almost matted stems arising from a woody root crown; five leaflets, arising from one point, each divided terminally into three lobes, the largest leaflets about 20 mm (0.8 in.) long; flowering stems branching, usually bearing two leaves; flowers solitary at the end of each stem, with five yellow petals, each about 7 mm (0.3 in.) long; calyx strongly villous, about 4.5 mm (0.2 in.) long with papery, reddish margins at the tip of each sepal. Flowers in June and July.
Known Distribution: Lincoln and Otero counties, New Mexico
Habitat: Open windswept areas on thin soil or on rock outcrops; above 3,230 m (10,500 ft.)
Ownership: Forest Service, Mescalero Indian Reservation
Threats to Taxon: Recreational development in the Sacramento Mountains
Similar Species: None at this elevation
Remarks: This taxon is endemic to harsh, windswept, barren slopes in the higher elevations of the Sacramento Mountains. The major threat to this species is unregulated ski development and attendant recreational activity.

Important Literature:
Wooton, E. O., and P. C. Standley. Flora of New Mexico. Contr. U.S. Nat. Herb. 19:1–1,794; 1915.
Wooton, E. O., and P. A. Rydberg. Description of *Potentilla sierrae-blancae* from New Mexico. Mem. Dept. Bot. Columbia Univ. 2:57; 1898.

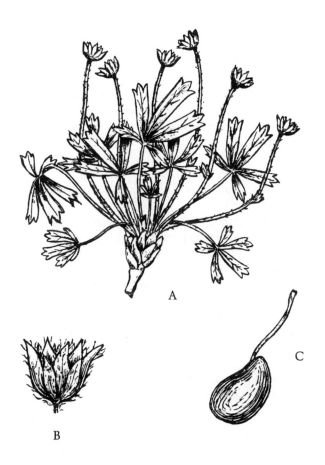

A

B

C

Potentilla sierrae-blancae
A. general habit; B. flower; C. seed

Family: ROSACEAE
Scientific Name: *Vauquelinia pauciflora* Standl.
Common Name: Few-flowered rosewood
Classification: Biologically threatened
Federal Action: Federal Register, 15 December 1980, candidate for federal protection
Common Synonyms: None

Description: Small tree with grayish bark, the young branches hairy; leaves 4–6 cm (1.5–2.25 in.) long, 6–11 mm (0.25–0.5 in.) wide, with parallel, evenly toothed, sides smooth above and below; sepals green; five petals, white, small; fruit woody, densely hairy. Probably flowers from May to July.
Known Distribution: Hidalgo County, and adjacent Arizona and Mexico
Habitat: Open, rocky limestone hills with little soil development; 1,250–1,830 m (4,100–6,000 ft.)
Ownership: Forest Service, State of New Mexico
Threats to Taxon: The Arizona populations are severely overgrazed. Novelty-wood collectors may pose a threat once locations become generally known.
Similar Species: *Vauquelinia californica* which has hairy leaf undersurfaces
Remarks: In New Mexico plants seem to be in sporadic distribution rather than in conspicuous populations, as in Arizona.

Important Literature:
Standley, P. C. New trees and shrubs from Mexico. Proc. Bio. Soc. Washington 31:1–1721; 1918.

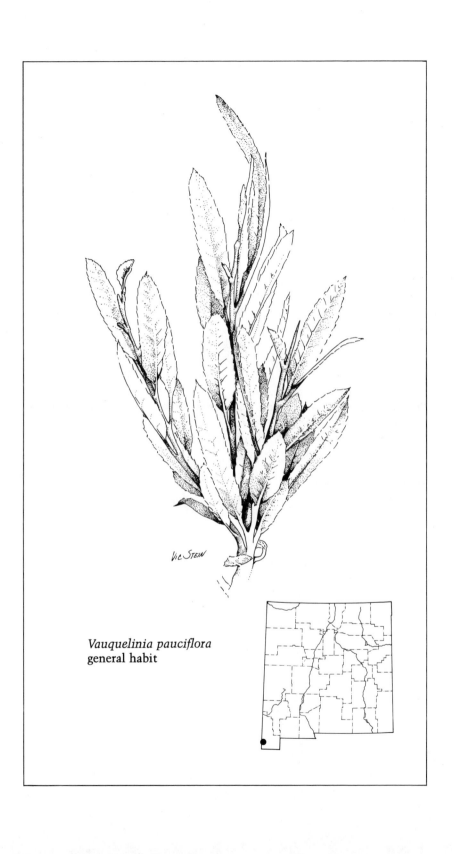

Vauquelinia pauciflora
general habit

Family: SAXIFRAGACEAE
Scientific Name: *Heuchera pulchella* Woot. & Standl.
Common Name: Sandia alumroot
Classification: State priority 1
Federal Action: None
Common Synonyms: None

Description: Perennial herb with leaves clustered near the base; stems 10–15 cm (4–6 in.) tall, covered with tiny glands; leaf blades 10–20 mm (0.4–0.75 in.) wide, toothed; the teeth bristle tipped, upper surface without hairs, the lower glandular; flowers crowded along one side of the stem; cuplike flower base about 4 mm (0.2 in.) long, densely glandular, bell shaped; sepals purplish pink; petals pink, very narrow; stamens as long as or longer than the sepals. Flowers from July to September.
Known Distribution: Bernalillo, Sandoval, San Miguel, Sierra, Socorro, and Torrance counties, New Mexico
Habitat: Moist rock faces cracks and ledges; 2,440–3,660 m (8,000–12,000 ft.)
Ownership: Fish and Wildlife Service, Forest Service
Threats to Taxon: None known
Similar Species: *Heuchera rubescens,* from which it is distinguished by having flowers crowded close together
Remarks: A rather narrowly distributed cliff-loving plant, endemic to the mountains of central New Mexico

Important Literature:
E. O. Wooton, and P. C. Standley. New Plants for New Mexico. Contr. U.S. Nat. Herb. 16:109–96; 1913.

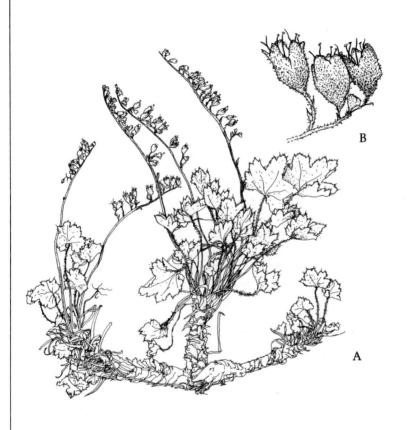

Heuchera pulchella
A. general habit; B. close up of flowers

Family: SAXIFRAGACEAE
Scientific Name: *Heuchera wootonii* Rydb.
Common Name: Wooton's alumroot
Classification: State priority 1
Federal Action: None
Common Synonyms: None

Description: Perennial herb with leaves clustered near the base; leaf petioles clothed with stiff hairs; leaves rounded, heart shaped at the base; flowers not crowded, greenish white; cuplike flower base 3–5 mm (0.2 in.) high, bell shaped; five petals, noticeably spoon shaped in outline, narrowing toward the base, exceeding the sepals; stamens much shorter than the sepals. Flowers from June to September.
Known Distribution: Catron and Lincoln counties, New Mexico
Habitat: Wooded mountain slopes and protected, usually north-facing, rock outcrops; 2,135–3,660 m (7,000–12,000 ft.)
Ownership: Forest Service, Mescalero Indian Reservation
Threats to Taxon: None known
Similar Species: *Heuchera wootonii* is differentiated in this genus of similar species by having petals longer than the sepals, stamens shorter than the sepals, and petioles with stiff hairs.
Remarks: *Heuchera wootonii* was described from the White Mountains. Collections from the Datil Mountains closely resemble this species.

Important Literature:
Rydberg, P. A. Descriptions of three new species of *Heuchera*. N. Am. Flora 22:110–13; 1905.

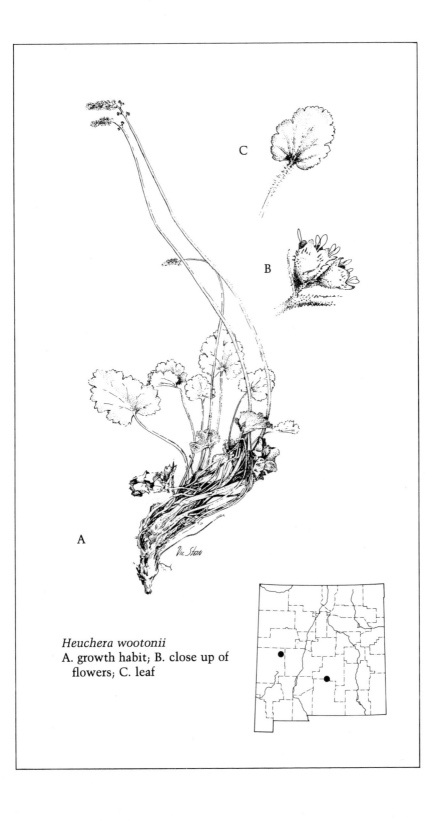

Heuchera wootonii
A. growth habit; B. close up of
flowers; C. leaf

Family: SCROPHULARIACEAE
Scientific Name: *Besseya oblongifolia* Penn.
Common Name: Sierra Blanca kittentails
Classification: State priority 1
Federal Action: None
Common Synonyms: None

Description: Perennial herb with flowering stalks to 30 cm (12 in.) high, densely hairy, usually with 12–16 small, bractlike leaves below the flower cluster; leaves oblong, mostly 7–11 cm (2.75–4.5 in.) long, 25–30 mm (1.0–1.1 in.) wide, rounded at the tip, with rounded teeth on the margins; petioles about 5–10 cm (2–4 in.) long, with longitudinal rows of soft hairs; flower clusters narrow, 5–10 cm (2–4 in.) long; flowers white, 5–6 mm (0.25 in.) long; pods hairy, 4–5 mm (0.12 in.) long. Flowers from June to September.
Known Distribution: Lincoln, Otero, and Taos counties, New Mexico
Habitat: Meadows; 3,350–3,600 m (11,000–12,000 ft.)
Ownership: Forest Service, Mescalero Indian Reservation
Threats to Taxon: None known
Similar Species: *Besseya plantaginea*, which has hairless capsules and sepals and leaves hairy at least beneath
Remarks: The plant is not easily seen amidst the grasses and other plants in its habitat.

Important Literature:
Pennell, F. W. A revision of *Syntheris* and *Besseya*. Proc. Acad. Philadelphia 85:83–93; 1933.

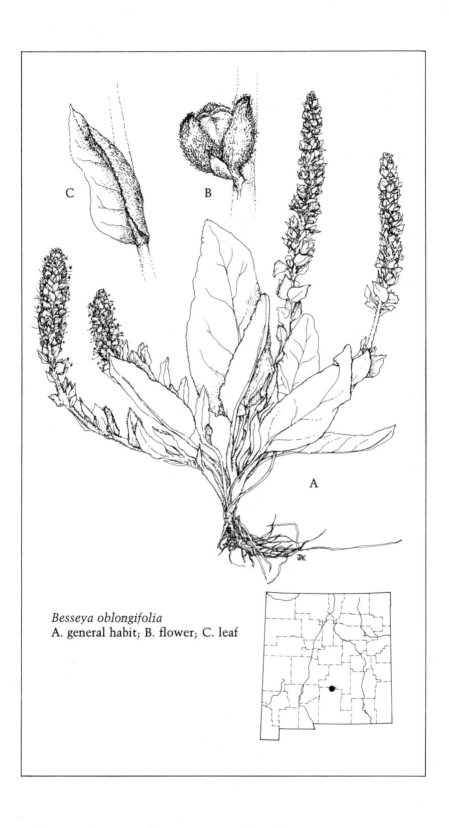

Besseya oblongifolia
A. general habit; B. flower; C. leaf

Family: SCROPHULARIACEAE
Scientific Name: *Castilleja organorum* Standl.
Common Name: Organ Mountain paintbrush
Classification: State priority 1
Federal Action: None
Common Synonyms: None

Description: Perennial branching herb with stem hairs stiffly spreading or bent downward; leaves narrow, devoid of teeth, rough to the touch; flower cluster short, few flowered, soft-hairy; floral bracts 15–20 mm (0.5–0.75 in.) long, unlobed, three-nerved; calyx hairy, yellowish green at the base, becoming bright red above the middle, split equally or both sides green, marked with red on the margins. Flowers June and July.
Known Distribution: Doña Ana, Grant, Sierra, and Socorro counties, New Mexico
Habitat: Montane slopes, usually open and rocky situations in canyons; 2,000–2,400 m (7,00–8,000 ft.)
Ownership: Bureau of Land Management, Department of Defense, Forest Service
Threats to Taxon: None known
Similar Species: *Castilleja austromontana* has long, stiff hairs beneath the leaves while *C. organorum* has short hairs beneath.
Remarks: *Castilleja organorum* appears to grade into *C. austromontana*.

Important Literature:

Olsen, M. A systematic study of the genus *Castilleja* in New Mexico. Albuquerque: Univ. of New Mexico; 1965. Ph.D. diss.

Standley, P. C. New southwestern *Castillejas*. Muhlenbergia 5:181–87; 1909.

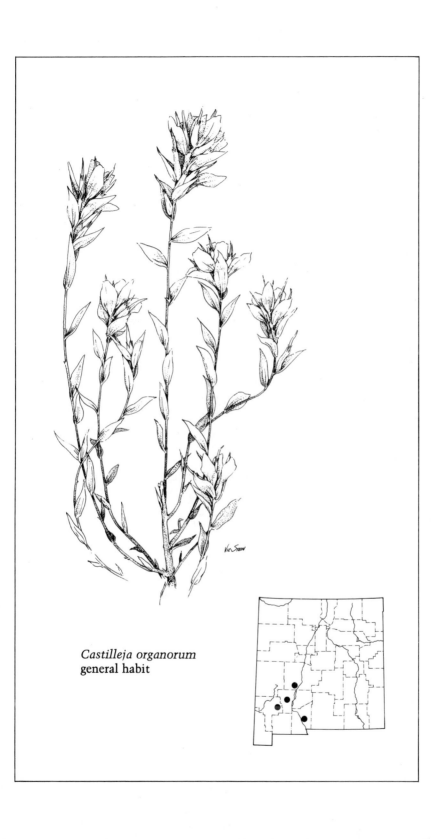

Castilleja organorum
general habit

Family: SCROPHULARIACEAE
Scientific Name: *Castilleja wootonii* Standl.
Common Name: Wooton's paintbrush
Classification: State priority 1
Federal Action: None
Common Synonyms: None

Description: Erect, usually branched perennial; leaves narrow, without teeth but sometimes with three very slender lobes, devoid of hairs except on margins and veins; flower cluster dense and elongated, soft-hairy; floral bracts shorter than the flowers, bright red at the tip and on the narrow lobes; calyx yellowish green, unequally split or divided, scarlet at the tip; flowers inconspicuous, greenish with red markings, the lower lip saclike. Flowers from July to September.
Known Distribution: Lincoln and Otero counties, New Mexico
Habitat: Dry montane slopes, in yellow pine or mixed conifer associations, mostly at about 2,275–3,650 m (7,500–12,000 ft.)
Ownership: Forest Service
Threats to Taxon: None known
Similar Species: The unequally split calyx, with hairless leaves, and hairless stems separates this species from others in its range.
Remarks: This species is fairly common, but of restricted distribution. Taxonomic relationships of this species require further investigation.

Important Literature:
Standley, P. C. Notes on the Flora of the Pecos River National Forest. Muhlenbergia 5:17–30; 1909.

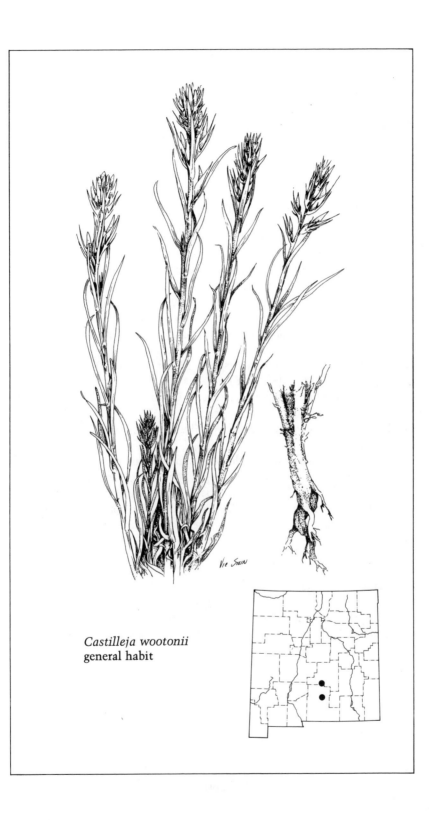

Castilleja wootonii
general habit

Family: SCROPHULARIACEAE
Scientific Name: *Penstemon alamosensis* Penn. and Nisbet
Common Name: Alamo beard tongue
Common Name: Biologically threatened
Federal Action: Federal Register, 15 December 1980, candidate for federal protection
Common Synonyms: None

Description: Green or grayish green perennial herbs with hairless stems and leaves; stems 30–100 mm (12–40 in.) tall, solitary or few; basal leaves elliptic or broadly lance shaped, the stem leaves much smaller, of 2–4 pairs, lance shaped; flowers in a long narrow inflorescence, often all turned to one side; the flowers borne in well-spaced clusters of 1–4 (usually 2) flowers each; corolla to 25 mm (1 in.) long, bright red, minutely glandular-pubescent outside, hairy, evenly funnel shaped; sterile stamen without hairs on tip. Flowers May and June.
Known Distribution: Doña Ana and Otero counties, New Mexico, and adjacent Texas
Habitat: Canyon bottoms, crevices, and pockets in rocky limestone hillsides; about 1,500 m (5,000 ft.)
Ownership: Bureau of Land Management, Department of Defense, Forest Service, private
Threats to Taxon: Overutilization by wildlife and livestock, and overcollection
Similar Species: Two other red-flowered penstemons grow in the same region. *Penstemon cardinalis* has a slight constriction at the mouth (outer end) of the corolla tube; the tube is broadest just behind the mouth. *Penstemon barbatus* has longer corollas, the upper lip extended forward like a visor, the lower sharply bent downward.
Remarks: A specialist is transferring this taxon to *P. havardii* in the near future.

Important Literature:

Nisbet, G. T., and R. C. Jackson. The genus *Penstemon* in New Mexico. Univ. Kansas Sci. Bull. 41(5):7–9–711; 1960.
Spellenberg, R. Status report on *Penstemon alamosensis*. U.S. Fish and Wildlife Service; 1981.

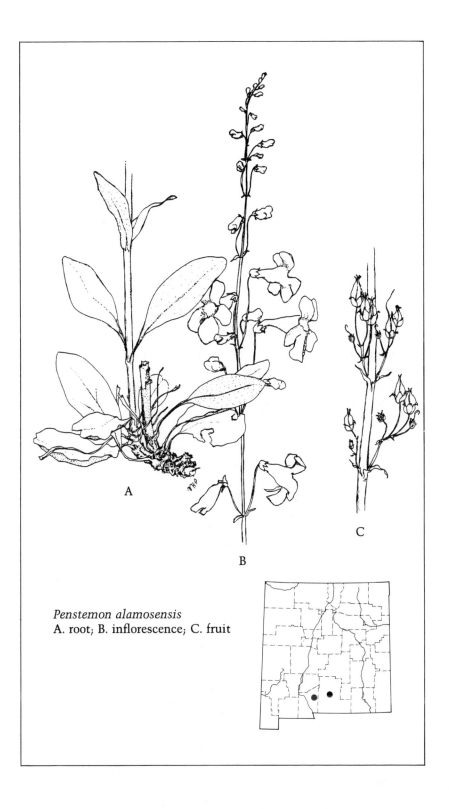

Penstemon alamosensis
A. root; B. inflorescence; C. fruit

Family: SCROPHULARIACEAE
Scientific Name: *Penstemon cardinalis* (Woot. & Standl.) ssp. *cardinalis*
Common Name: White Mountain beard tongue
Classification: State priority 1
Federal Action: None
Common Synonyms: *Penstemon crassulus* Woot.

Description: Perennial herb; stems to 70 cm (28 in.) tall, branching from the base; leaves opposite, slightly thickened, to 12 cm (4.75 in.) long, broadest above the middle; flowers mostly concentrated along one side of the stem; calyx about 3 mm (0.12 in.) long, the margins thinner than the middle; corolla red; 22–30 mm (0.9–1.25 in.) long, narrowed at the mouth, the lobes about 3 mm (0.12 in.) long, the lower lobes bearded with soft yellow hairs; sterile stamen bearded near the tip. Flowers in June and July.
Known Distribution: Lincoln and Otero counties, New Mexico
Habitat: Rocky slopes and canyon bottoms in association with ponderosa pine and Douglas fir; 2,100–2,700 m (7,000–8,800 ft.)
Ownership: Forest Service, Mescalero Indian Reservation, private
Threats to Taxon: None known
Similar Species: *Penstemon cardinalis* ssp. *regalis*, which has a slightly larger calyx and broader, thicker leaves
Remarks: This taxon occurs in small, widely scattered populations. The Sacramento Mountains separate the ranges of the two endemic populations of this species. The subspecies *regalis* is found in the Guadalupe Mountains well south of this taxon.

Important Literature:
Nisbet, G. T., and R. C. Jackson. The genus *Penstemon* in New Mexico. Univ. Kansas Sci. Bull. 41(5):706; 1960.
Wooton, E. P., and P. C. Standley. New plants from New Mexico. Contr. U.S. Nat. Herb. 16:109–96; 1913.

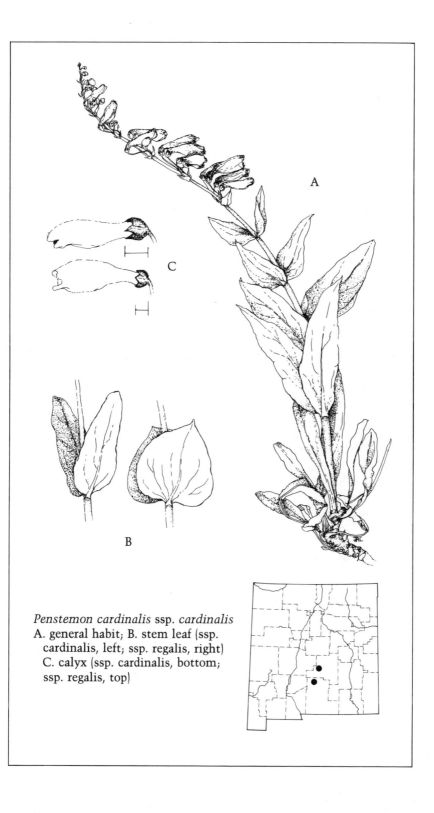

Penstemon cardinalis ssp. *cardinalis*
A. general habit; B. stem leaf (ssp.
  cardinalis, left; ssp. regalis, right)
C. calyx (ssp. cardinalis, bottom;
  ssp. regalis, top)

Family: SCROPHULARIACEAE

Scientific Name: *Penstemon cardinalis* (Woot. & Standl.) ssp. *regalis* (A. Nels.) Nisbet & Jackson

Common Name: Guadalupe beard tongue

Classification: State priority 1

Federal Action: None

Common Synonyms: *Penstemon regalis* A. Nelson

Description: Perennial herb; stems mostly 40–60 cm (16–24 in.) tall, branching from the base; leaves opposite, thick, to 6 cm (2.5 in.) long and 5 cm (2 in.) wide, heart shaped, often rather blunt at the tip, wider than in the typical subspecies; calyx 4–6 mm (0.25 in.) long; corolla 26–30 mm (1.0–1.25 in.) long, red, narrowed at the mouth, lobes about 3 mm (0.12 in.) long, the lower ones bearded with soft, yellow hairs. Flowers from May to July.

Known Distribution: Eddy and Otero counties, New Mexico, and adjacent Texas

Habitat: Rocky limestone canyon bottoms and steep slopes in the protection afforded by rock cracks and large boulders; 1,400–1,800 m (4,500–6,000 ft.)

Ownership: Forest Service, National Park Service

Threats to Taxon: None known

Similar Species: *Penstemon cardinalis* ssp. *cardinalis*, which has a shorter calyx. Other red *Penstemons* in the region do not have the mouth of the corolla cnstricted.

Remarks: Although restricted in range, this species is not uncommon within its habitat.

Important Literature:

Nisbet, G. T., and R. C. Jackson. The genus *Penstemon* in New Mexico. Univ. Kansas Sci. Bull. 41(5):691–759; 1960.

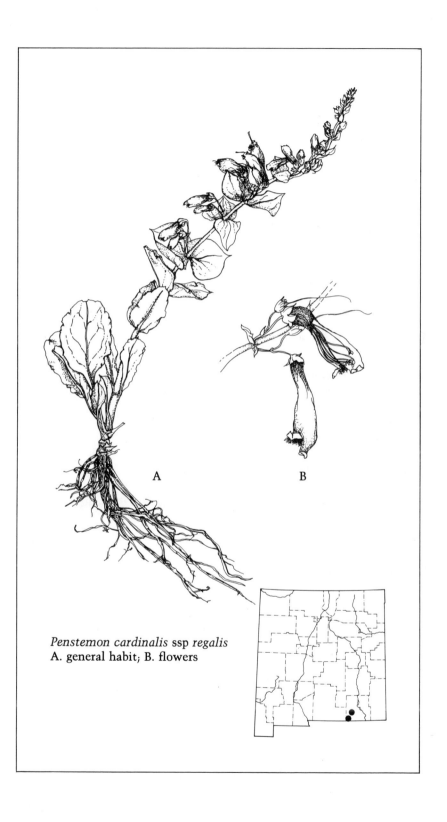

Penstemon cardinalis ssp *regalis*
A. general habit; B. flowers

Family: SCROPHULARIACEAE
Scientific Name: *Penstemon dasyphyllus* Gray
Common Name: Gila beard tongue
Classification: State priority 1
Federal Action: None
Common Synonyms: None

Description: Erect, densely hairy perennial to about 40 cm (16 in.) tall; leaves narrow, to about 6 cm (2.5 in.) long, usually not toothed on the margins; flowers clustered along one side of the stem; flowers blue or purplish, to about 30 mm (1.25 in.) long, tubular, the lower lobes of the flower longer than the upper ones, the sterile stamen without hairs. Flowers April to August.
Known Distribution: Hidalgo and Luna counties, New Mexico, and adjacent Arizona and Mexico
Habitat: Open, gravelly slopes and desert grassland; 1,225–1,675 m (4,000–5,500 ft.)
Ownership: Bureau of Land Management, private
Threats to Taxon: None known
Similar Species: None
Remarks: This poorly understood taxon may be primarily a Mexican species, its range in New Mexico peripheral.

Important Literature:
Nisbet, G., and R. Jackson. The genus *Penstemon* in New Mexico. Univ. Kansas Sci. Bull. 41(5):691–759; 1960.
Torrey, J. Botany of the boundary. In W. H. Emory, Report of the U.S. and Mexican Boundary Survey. House Exec. Doc. 135, 34th Cong., 1st session, vol. 2, part 1, 27–276; 1859.

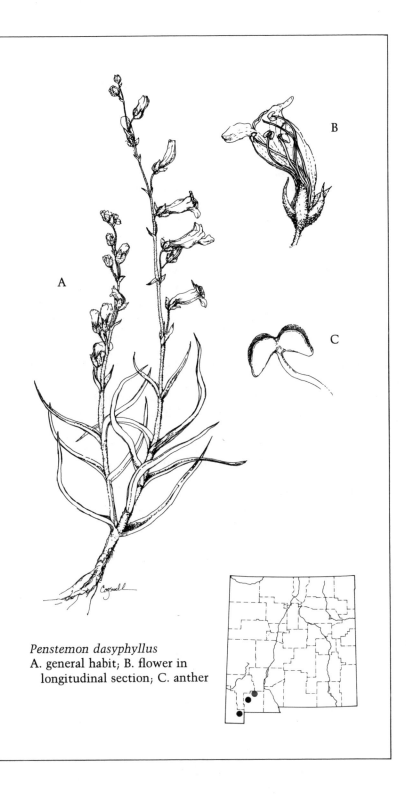

Penstemon dasyphyllus
A. general habit; B. flower in
longitudinal section; C. anther

Family: SCROPHULARIACEAE
Scientific Name: *Penstemon neomexicanus* Woot. & Standl.
Common Name: New Mexico penstemon
Classification: State priority 1
Federal Action: None
Common Synonyms: None

Description: Perennial; stems solitary or several, hairless and smooth, to 70 cm (28 in.) tall; basal leaves lance shaped to narrowly spoon shaped, these often absent on flowering plants; stem leaves lance shaped, occasionally linear, 6 to 18 mm (0.25–0.75 in.) wide; flowers on an elongate, multiflower stalk, with all of the flowers aligned on one side of the stalk; corolla (petals) blue, blue-purple or violet-blue, 25–36 mm (1.0–1.4 in.) long, the throat of the corolla tube expanded, 10–17 mm (0.4–0.7 in.) wide; the staminode (the fifth stamen which is easily identified by its lack of an anther) without hairs. Flowers from July to August.
Known Distribution: Lincoln and Otero counties, New Mexico
Habitat: Wooded slopes and glades in pine woodland; 2,180–2,800 m (7,000–9,000 ft.)
Ownership: Forest Service, Mescalero Indian Reservation, private
Threats to Taxon: None known
Similar Species: *Penstemon virgatus* is most similar, but is distinguished by its shorter corolla, 15–24 mm (0.6–1.0 in.) long, and the presence of minute hairs on the stem.
Remarks: This species is apparently endemic to the higher elevations of the Capitan and Sacramento mountains of New Mexico.

Important Literature:

Nisbet, G. T., and R. C. Jackson. The genus *Penstemon* in New Mexico. The Univ. Kansas Sci. Bull. 41:691–759; 1960.

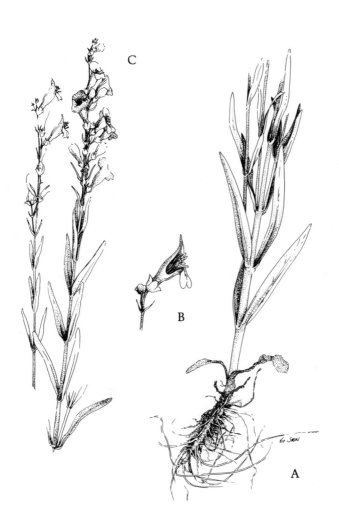

Penstemon neomexicanus
A. lower stem; B. flower in
   longitudinal section; C. upper
   stem and inflorescence

Family: SCROPHULARIACEAE
Scientific Name: *Scrophularia laevis* Woot. & Standl.
Common Name: Organ Mountain figwort
Classification: Biologically threatened
Federal Action: None
Common Synonyms: None

Description: Perennial herb; stems single, mostly unbranched, slender, bright green, to 120 cm (4 ft.) tall (but usually much shorter); leaf stalks usually about half as long as the broadly lance shaped, thin, bright green, glabrous leaf blades; flowers cluster at the top of the stem, usually short and sparse, with five or fewer pairs of branches; flowers tubular, dull greenish brown about 12 mm (0.5 in.) long. Flowers in July and August.
Known Distribution: Doña Ana County, New Mexico
Habitat: Shaded, moist canyons and slopes on quartz monzonite substrate; above 2,125 m (7,000 ft.)
Ownership: Bureau of Land Management, Department of Defense, State of New Mexico
Threats to Taxon: None known
Similar Species: The hairless stems and leaves and long petioles separate this plant from the other greenish brown scrophularias.
Remarks: *Scrophularia laevis* is known only from the Organ Mountains.

Important Literature:
Wooton, E. O., and P. C. Standley. New Plants from New Mexico. Contr. U.S. Nat. Herb. 16:109–96; 1913.

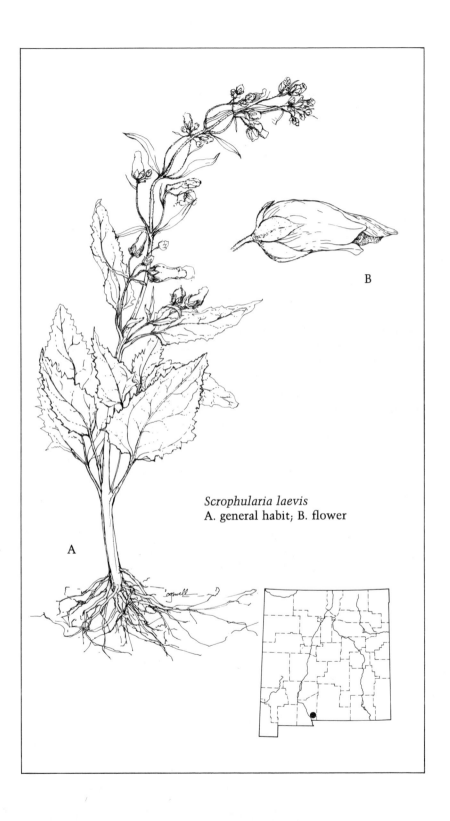

Scrophularia laevis
A. general habit; B. flower

A

B

Family: SCROPHULARIACEAE
Scientific Name: *Scrophularia macrantha* (Gray) Greene
Common Name: Mimbres figwort
Classification: Biologically threatened
Federal Action: Federal Register, 15 December 1980, candidate for federal protection
Common Synonyms: *Scrophularia coccinea* Gray, *Scrophularia neomexicana* Shaw

Description: Perennial herb to 1 m (3 ft.) tall; leaves opposite or whorled, somewhat triangular, toothed; corolla red, 15–20 mm (0.6–0.75 in.) long, two-lipped, four anther-bearing stamens; calyx five-parted. Flowers from July to September.
Known Distribution: Grant and Luna counties, New Mexico,
Habitat: Steep, rocky, usually north-facing slopes and occasionally canyon bottoms; 2,100–2,400 m (7,000–8,000 ft.)
Ownership: Bureau of Land Management, Forest Service, private
Threats to Taxon: Unregulated mining, road construction, and grazing are threats to this taxon.
Similar Species: The long red flowers readily distinguish this taxon from other southern New Mexico scrophularias.
Remarks: This plant occurs in several widely separated populations, yet is absent in similar habitat adjacent to these populations.

Important Literature:

Shaw, R. J. The biosystematics of *Scrophularia* in western North America. Aliso 5:147–48; 1962.

Spellenberg, R. Status report in *Scrophularia macrantha.* U.S. Fish and Wildlife Service; 1982.

Torrey, J. Botany of the boundary. In W. H. Emory, Report of the U.S. and Mexican Boundary Survey. House Exec. Doc. 135, 34th Cong., 1st session, vol. 2, part 1, 27–276; 1859.

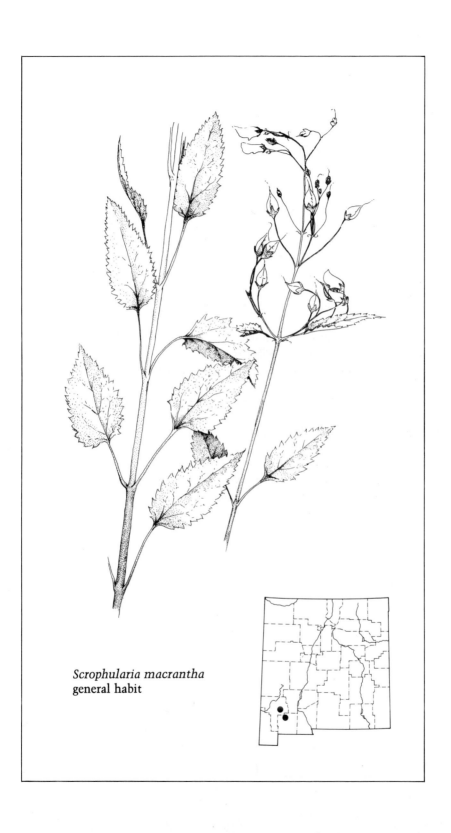

Scrophularia macrantha
general habit

Family: VALERIANACEAE
Scientific Name: *Valeriana texana* Steyerm.
Common Name: Texas tobacco root
Classification: State priority 1
Federal Action: Federal Register, 15 December 1980, candidate for federal protection
Common Synonyms: None

Description: Perennial herb to 30 cm (12 in.) tall, from stout conical tap roots; stems branching at or slightly below ground level; basal leaves numerous, entire, 4–16 cm (1.5–6.4 in.) long, broadest toward the ends, to 3 cm (1.25 in.) wide, without hairs; stem leaves similar but smaller; flowers many, in branched clusters, corolla whitish, 5.5 mm (0.25 in.) long. Flowers from April to July.
Known Distribution: Eddy and Otero counties, New Mexico, and adjacent Texas
Habitat: Shaded, moist limestone rock faces, occasionally in canyon bottoms; 1,800–2,500 m (6,000–8,000 ft.)
Ownership: Forest Service, National Park Service
Threats to Taxon: None known
Similar Species: The thick vertical roots separate this from other valerianas.
Remarks: This narrow endemic is common in its range.

Important Literature:
Steyermark, J. A. Some new Spermatophytes from Texas. Ann. Missouri Bot. Gard. 19:389–95; 1932.

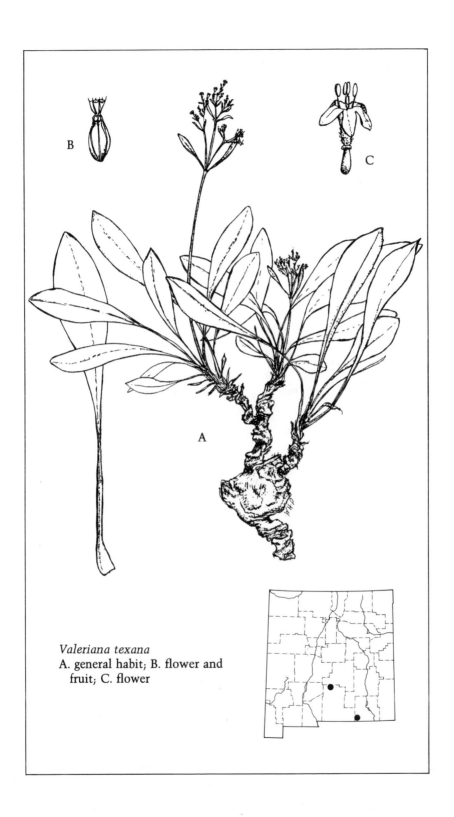

Valeriana texana
A. general habit; B. flower and
fruit; C. flower

GLOSSARY

Achene—a dry one-seeded fruit that does not split open, and whose outer coat is not attached to the enclosed seed

Acuminate—tapering into a long point

Acute—ending in a narrow angle

Alternate—referring to an orientation in which parts are attached singly, rather than in pairs

Annual—a plant completing its life-cycle in one season

Anther—the saclike portion of the stamen containing the pollen

Apical—at the tip or apex

Appressed—borne flat against a structure or surface

Areole—the portion of the cactus from which the spines develop

Aristate—bearing a stiff bristle point

Awn—a bristlelike appendage

Axil—the angle formed between two structures

Axillary—occurring in the angle a leaf makes with the stem

Banner—the upper petal in certain families of plants

Barbed—having reflexed or recurved points, like the barbs of a harpoon

Basal—referring to the base

Beak—a narrow projection like the beak of a bird, usually found on the fruit or flower parts

Bearded—having long hairs

Biennial—a plant completing development in two years

Bifid—referring to being split or cleft into two lobes

Bipinnate—twice pinnate

Blade—the expanded portion of a leaf

Bract—a modified leaf usually subtending a flower

Glossary

Bracteole—a small bract
Bristles—having stiff hairs
Bulb—an underground stem composed of fleshy scales
Calyx—the sepals of a flower as a unit, a collective term
Campanulate—bell shaped
Capillary—hairlike
Capitate—often referring to a dense headlike cluster
Capsule—a dry fruit, opening to release its seeds when ripe
Caudex—short, upright stem or rootstock
Cell—a cavity within the ovary of the flower
Central spine—usually conspicuous spines located in the center of a cluster of spines on a cactus, often somewhat different from the surrounding radial spines
Ciliate—having hairs or bristles at the margin of some structure
Cleft—split about halfway to the base
Clustered—arranged in a tight group
Compressed—flattened
Corolla—the petals of a flower taken as a unit, a collective term
Crest—a ridge on the surface of some structure
Disk—a large fleshy enlargement of the receptacle, e.g., the central portion of a sunflower, which bears the numerous disk flowers and eventually the ripened sunflower seeds
Disk flower—the flowers that make up the central portion of the flower head in many members of the sunflower family, e.g., the darker, small flowers in the eye of a sunflower
Dissected—divided into many segments
Divided—separated to the base or nearly so
Dolabriform—a type of hair attached in the middle rather than at the base, usually T-shaped
Elliptic—shaped like an ellipse
Entire—with an unbroken, smooth margin
Exerted—usually referring to some floral structure (e.g., stamens) extending out beyond the edge of the petals
Filament—the stalk of the anther
Filiform—threadlike
Fringed—having a conspicuous, often ragged edge
Fruit—a mature ovary
Funnelform—shaped like a funnel

Glabrate—having few hairs
Glabrous—without hairs
Gland—a structure capable of secretion
Glandular—bearing glands
Glandular-vicid—having a glandular, sticky surface
Globose—spherical
Glochid—a barbed hair or bristle usually associated with the cactus family
Herb—a nonwoody plant
Herbaceous—not woody
Involucre—a series of bracts subtending a group of flowers
Joints—in cactus, a part of the cactus that is capable of detachment, e.g., the pads of a prickly pear
Keel—a crease or ridge; in some families the lower boat-shaped petal
Lanceolate—lance shaped, broader below the middle
Leaflet—a division of a compound leaf
Linear—slender, having parallel sides, usually 8–10 times longer than wide
Lobe—the segment of an organ resulting from a partial division
Nodes—the place of leaf attachment
Oblanceolate—inverted lance shape
Oblong—elongate, with the sides relatively parallel
Obovate—inversely ovate
Obtuse—blunt at the apex, the angle wide
Odd-pinnate—pinnately compound with a terminal leaflet
Oil blister—a translucent blisterlike structure on the surface of leaves or stems
Opposite—with organs in pairs
Orbicular—circular in outline
Oval—broadly elliptic
Ovary—the part of the flower containing the ovules, which will develop into the fruit
Palmate—with separate parts diverging from a common point, something like the fingers arising from the hand
Panicle—a compound inflorescence composed of several flowers, each with an individual stalk
Pappus—modified sepals at the top of the achene found in the sunflower family

279

Glossary

Pedicel—the stalk of a single flower

Peduncle—the stalk of a cluster of flowers

Perennial—a plant living more than two years

Petal—a single unit of the corolla, usually the showy part of a flower

Petiole—the stalk of a leaf

Phyllary—one of several bracts constituting the involucre

Pinnate—a leaf that is divided into smaller leaflets, these usually arranged in two rows along a central axis

Pinnatifid—cleft or divided in a pinnate manner

Pistil—the female reproductive parts of a flower

Pod—a dry fruit which opens when ripe

Raceme—an unbranched flower cluster, usually on an elongate stalk, with each flower attached to the main axis by its own stalk

Radial spine—on cactus, the spines along the edge of a spine cluster

Ray flower—usually the showy flowers along the edge of the flower head in members of the sunflower family, e.g., the yellow part of a sunflower

Reclining—lying down

Recurved—curved downward or backward

Reflexed—bent sharply backward or downward

Resin dotted—dotted with small drops of resin

Rhizome—a horizontal underground stem

Ribs—the prominent veins of a leaf, in some cactus the elongate projections bearing the spine clusters, e.g., the ribs of a saguaro cactus

Rotate—wheel-shaped

Scale—a thin, membraceous modified leaf

Scabrous—rough to the touch

Seed—a mature ovule

Sepal—a unit of the calyx, usually just below the petals of the flower

Serrate—with teeth inclined forward

Sessile—not stalked, e.g., leaves without stalks

Sheath—a tubular covering often, but not always, surrounding the stem

Spatulate—narrow at the base and broader at the apex, shaped like a spatula

Spherical—globular

Spreading—extending outward

Spur—a hollow projection from the calyx or corolla

Stamen—the male structure of the flower

Staminate—bearing stamens

Stigma—area of the pistil receptive to pollen

Stipule—a leaf appendage, if present, at the attachment point of the leaf to the stem

Succulent—juicy, fleshy

Style—the stalklike connection between the stigma and the ovary

Taproot—the primary root, usually longer than the other roots

Tendril—a leaf modified into a twining, holdfast structure

Throat—the point where the tube of a tubular flower expands outward to the limb or edges of the flower

Transversely—across, at right angles to the longitudinal axis

Tube—the lower, usually cylindrical part of a united calyx or corolla

Tuber—a thickened, fleshy, underground stem, e.g., potato

Tubercle—on cactus, the nipplelike projections that bear the spine clusters

Turbinate—top-shaped

Twice compound—referring to the primary leaf stalk bearing secondary leaf stalks, each with leaflets

Umbel—a flower cluster where all of the pedicels of the flowers originate from one point

United—having parts joined together

Villous—a surface covered by soft, elongate hairs

Vining—having a twining growth form

ABBREVIATIONS OF THE AUTHORS' NAMES

L. C. Anderson   Loran Crittenden Anderson, 1936– , professor of botany, Kansas, student of the Compositae

Barneby   Rupert C. Barneby, 1911– , author of monograph on the genus *Astragalus* and *Dalea*, student of the Leguminosae, New York Botanical Garden

L. Benson   Lyman Benson, 1909– , professor of botany, author, student of the Cactaceae

Benth.   George Benthman, 1800–84, outstanding English botanist, author of numerous floras, president of the Linnaen Society

Berger   Alwin Berger, 1871–1931, student of the Cactaceae, curator of the Botanical Gardens at La Mortola, Italy

Bigel.   Jacob Bigelow, 1787–1879, author of several floras, professor of botany in Boston

Blake   Sidney Fay Blake, 1892–1959, student of the Compositae, author of *The*

Abbreviations of authors

	Geographical Guide to the Floras of the World
Boedeker	Frederick Boedeker, 1933– , student of the Cactaceae, Germany
Boiss.	Pierre Edmond Boissier, 1810–55, Swiss by birth, one of the outstanding botanists of the nineteenth century
Brand	August Brand, 1863–1930, student of the Polemoniacene and Boraginaceae
Britt.	Nathaniel Lord Britton, 1859–1934, director of the New York Botanical Garden, and author of several floras
Brown	S. W. Brown, 1918– , professor of genetics, California
Bush	Benjamin Franklin Bush, 1858–1937, amateur botanist, Missouri
Castetter, Pierce, and Schwerin	E. F. Castetter, Prince Pierce, Carl Schwerin, students of the Cactaceae, New Mexico
Cav.	Antonio Jose Cavanilles, 1745–1804, Spanish botanist, director of the Botanical Gardens at Madrid
Clover	Elzadau Clover, student of the Cactaceae
Cockll.	Theodore Dru Alison Cockrell, 1866–1948, plant explorer of the southwestern United States
Correll	Donovan Stewart Correll, 1908– ,

author of several floras, student of
Solanaceae

Coult.

John Merle Coulter, 1851–1928, founder
of the *Botanical Gazette*, professor of
botany at Chicago, author of several
floras

Coult. & Rose

J. M. Coulter; Joseph Nelson Rose, 1862–
1928, student of the Cactaceae

Cronq.

Arthur John Cronquist, 1919– , curator
of the New York Botanical Gardens,
author of several floras, student of the
Compositae

DC.

Augustin Pyramus de Candollee, 1778–
1841, Swiss botanist, first in an
illustrious line of Systematists

Epling

Carl Clawson Epling, 1894– , professor
of botany in California, student of the
Labitae

Engelm.

George Engelmann, 1809–84, eminent
botanist, physician, student of the
North American flora

Eggl.

William Webster Eggleston, 1863–1935,
botanist, student of poisonous and drug
plants

Greene

Edward Lee Greene, 1843–1915, first
professor of botany at the University of
California, Berkeley, famous
southwestern plant collector

Gray

Asa Gray, 1810–88, professor of botany,

Abbreviations of authors

	author of numerous floras and textbooks on botany, eminent botanist of the nineteenth century
Heimerl	Anton Heimerl, 1857–1942, professor of botany in Vienna
Heiser	Charles Bixler Heiser, 1920– , professor of botany, student of the Compositae
Hester	J. Pinckney Hester, contemporary California writer on succulents
Hitchc. & Maguire	Charles Leo Hitchcock, 1902– , professor of botany, Washington; Basset Maguire, 1904– , curator of the New York Botanical Gardens
Holz.	John Michael Holzinger, 1853–1929, German-born American bryologist
Hook.	Sir John Dalton Hooker, 1816–1911, British botanist and explorer, director of Kew Gardens
Irving	Robert Stewart Irving, 1942– , botanist, University of Montana, student of the Labitae
Isley	Duane Isley, 1918– , professor of botany, student of the Leguminosae
Jackson	Raven C. Jackson, 1928– , student of the Compositae
James	Edwin James, 1797–1861, surgeon-naturalist, first botanical collector in Colorado

286

I. M. Johnst.	Irving Murray Johnston, 1898–1960, professor of botany, Harvard University, explorer and author
Jotter	T. Jotter, contemporary student of the Cactaceae
O. Ktze	Carl Ernst Otto, 1843–1921, nineteenth-century botanist
Lint	Harold L. Lint, 1916– , California State Polytech College
W. T. Marshall	William Taylor Marshall, 1886–1957, student of the Cactaceae
Martin	William C. Martin, professor of botany, University of New Mexico, author of *The Flora of New Mexico*, 1981
Math., Const., & Theobald	Mildred Ester Mathias, 1906– ; Lincoln Constance, 1909– ; students of the Umbelliferae
Macbr.	James Francis Macbride, 1892– , Gray Herbarium, student of western American flora
A. Nels.	Aven Nelson, 1859–1952, professor of botany at the University of Wyoming
Nesom	Guy Nesom, student of the genus *Erigeron*
Nisbet	Gladys T. Nisbet, 1895– , Arizona botanist
Orcutt	Charles Russell Orcutt, 1864–1929, San Diego collector

Osterh.	George Everett Osterhout, 1858–1937, Colorado amateur botanist
Ownbey	Gerald Ownbey, 1916– , student of the Papaveraceae
Penn.	Francis Whittier Pennell, 1886–1952, curator of botany, Academy of Natural Science, Philadelphia
Pays.	Edwin Blake Payson, 1893–1927, professor of botany, Wyoming
Porter	Thomas Conrad Porter, 1822–1901, professor of botany, Pennsylvania, student of Colorado flora
Poselger	Heinrich Poselger, died 1883, Germany, student of the Cactaceae
Powell	Albert Michael Powell, 1937– , Sul Ross State University, student of the Compositae
Reveal	James Lauritz Reveal, 1941– , student of the genus *Eriogonum*
Robins.	Benjamin Lincoln Robinson, 1864–1935, curator of the Gray Herbarium, student of the Compositae
Roll.	Reed Clark Rollins, 1911– , director of the Gray Herbarium, student of the Cruciferae
Roth	Albrecht Wilhelm Roth, 1757–1834, German botanist

Rose   Joseph Nelson Rose, 1862–1928, U.S.
                        National Herbarium, student of the
                        Cactaceae

Rydb.   Per Axel Rydberg, 1860–1931, curator of
                        the New York Botanical Garden, author
                        of *The Flora of Colorado*

Schum.   Karl Moritz Schumann, 1851–1904,
                        German botanist

Shaw   George Russell Shaw, 1849–1937,
                        student of the genus *Pinus*

Sheld.   Edmund Perry Sheldon, 1869–?,
                        botanist of Oregon

Shinners   Lloyd Herbert Shinners, 1918– ,
                        Canadian-born botanist, student of the
                        flora of central Texas

Soreng   Rob Soreng, 1952– , contemporary
                        New Mexico botanist at New Mexico
                        State University

Spellenberg   Richard Spellenberg, 1940– ,
                        contemporary New Mexico botanist,
                        professor of botany at New Mexico State
                        University

Steyerm.   Julian Alfred Steyermark, 1909– ,
                        curator Chicago Field Museum, student
                        of South American flora

Swall.   Mason Richard Swallen, 1903– ,
                        curator of U.S. National Herbarium,
                        student of the Gramineae

Abbreviations of authors

Theobald & Tseng	William Theobald, 1936– ; Charles T. Tseng, contemporary students of the Umbelliferae
Todsen	Thomas Todsen, contemporary New Mexico botanist
Torr.	John Torrey, 1796–1873, professor of chemistry and botany, physician, outstanding botanist of the nineteenth century
Toumey	James William Toumey, 1864–1932, professor of forestry at Yale University
Turner	B. L. Turner, 1940– , contemporary Texas botanist, professor of botany at Austin State University
E. E. Wats.	Elba Emanuel Watson, 1871–1936 high school teacher in biology, amateur botanist
Wats.	Sereno Watson, 1826–92, curator of the Gray Herbarium, student of western American plants
Welsh	Standley Welsh, contemporary Utah botanist, professor of botany at BYU
Wendl.	Hermann Wendland, 1823–1903, director of the Botanical Garden at Hannover, England
Weniger	Del Weniger, contemporary student of the Cactaceae
Wherry	Edgar Theodore Wherry, 1885– ,

professor of botany, University of
Pennsylvania

Wiggins   Ira Loren Wiggins, 1899–   , professor of
                            botany at Stanford University

L. O. Williams   Louis Otho Williams, 1908–   , American
                            botanist

Wooton   Elmer Otis Wooton, 1865–1945, student
                            of New Mexico flora, author of *The Flora
                            of New Mexico* (1915), and *The Trees
                            and Shrubs of Mexico*

Woot. & Standl.   E. O. Wooton; Paul Carpenter Standley,
                            1884–1963, student of New Mexico flora,
                            curator of the U.S. National Herbarium

D. Zimmerman   Dale Zimmerman, student of the
                            Cactaceae in New Mexico